D0857742

MEDIEVAL SCOTLAND

A. D. M. BARRELL

PUBLISHED BY THE PRESS SYNDICATE OF THE UNIVERSITY OF CAMBRIDGE
The Pitt Building, Trumpington Street, Cambridge, United Kingdom

CAMBRIDGE UNIVERSITY PRESS
The Edinburgh Building, Cambridge CB2 2RU, UK http://www.cup.cam.ac.uk
40 West 20th Street, New York, NY 10011–4211, USA http://www.cup.org
10 Stamford Road, Oakleigh, Melbourne 3166, Australia
Ruiz de Alarcón 13, 28014 Madrid, Spain

First published 2000

Printed in the United Kingdom at the University Press, Cambridge

Typeface Monotype Bembo 11/12.5 pt *System* QuarkXPress™ [SE]

A catalogue record for this book is available from the British Library

Library of Congress Cataloguing in Publication data

Barrell, A. D. M. (Andrew D. M.)
Medieval Scotland / A.D.M. Barrell.
p. cm. – (Cambridge medieval textbooks)
Includes bibliographical references and index.
ISBN 0 521 58443 4 – ISBN 0 521 58602 x (pbk)
1. Scotland – History – 1057–1603. 2. Scotland – History – To 1057. I. Title. II. Series.
DA775.B37 2000
941.1 – dc21 99-086098

ISBN 0 521 58443 4 hardback
ISBN 0 521 58602 x paperback

CONTENTS

FIGURES

PREFACE

Writers of textbooks are faced with many challenges, not least that of deciding which aspects of their topic should be included and which left on the sidelines. In the case of a volume on medieval Scotland which aims to cover several centuries, it is inevitable that large areas of scholarly activity will be bypassed in an attempt to retain the length of the book within reasonable bounds. My approach to the subject has been a traditional one, and I have concentrated on political and ecclesiastical history rather than on the economy and society, although I have endeavoured to retain an awareness of the effect of social and economic changes on the people of Scotland. Despite the paucity of Scottish sources, scholars have increasingly found it possible to investigate the lives of those below the political elite, and have thereby immeasurably enriched our view of medieval life, but it was impossible to do their work full justice in this volume. Other areas, including relations with Scandinavia, Germany and the Low Countries, the development of Scots law, and the flowering of Scottish literature, have also been given less attention than they deserve. Political history, however, provides one of the most accessible approaches to the past and to the lessons that we can learn from it. If we are to discover the origins and nature of Scottish identity, we must strive to understand the development of the institutions of the state, the relations between the crown and the nobility, the distinctive features of ecclesiastical life in Scotland, and the significance of the Wars of Independence.

My debt to the work of other scholars will be apparent throughout the book. Their challenging new interpretations and exploration of fresh areas of Scottish history have led academics, students and the general public to question old orthodoxies and view the past with a different perspective. I hope that I have not misconstrued their arguments too grievously, and that this volume will stimulate further debate about the history of Scotland and the country's place in the wider world. In a book of this nature it is inappropriate to footnote the discussion in full, although I have given references for some specific points, and have used the bibliography to list those works which I have found especially valuable.

I have been fortunate to be able to develop courses in medieval Scottish history at The Queen's University of Belfast, and have learnt much from the challenging questions and thoughtful insights provided by my students over several years. I am greatly indebted to the university for granting me a semester's study leave to enable me to complete this book. My research on papal relations with Scotland has continued during the preparation of this volume and has informed the chapters on the church, and I am most grateful to the staff of the Department of Scottish History at the University of Glasgow, especially Professor James Kirk, for their hospitality on my visits to consult the Ross Fund collection of microfilms from the Vatican. Finally, I offer my thanks to William Davies and his colleagues at Cambridge University Press for their care and attention during the publishing process.

ABBREVIATIONS

APS	*The Acts of the Parliaments of Scotland*, ed. T. Thomson and C. Innes, 12 vols. (Edinburgh, 1814–75)
ASR	*Anglo-Scottish Relations, 1174–1328*, ed. E. L. G. Stones, 2nd edn (Oxford, 1970)
Barrow Essays	*Medieval Scotland: Crown, Lordship and Community. Essays Presented to G. W. S. Barrow*, ed. A. Grant and K. J. Stringer (Edinburgh, 1993)
BIHR	*Bulletin of the Institute of Historical Research*
Chron. Bower	Walter Bower, *Scotichronicon*, ed. D. E. R. Watt and others, 9 vols. (Aberdeen and Edinburgh, 1987–98)
Chron. Holyrood	*A Scottish Chronicle known as the Chronicle of Holyrood*, ed. M. O. Anderson with some additional notes by A. O. Anderson (Scottish History Society, 1938)
Chron. Stephen	*Chronicles of the Reigns of Stephen, Henry II, and Richard I*, ed. R. Howlett, 4 vols. (Rolls Series, 1884–9)
CPL	*Calendar of Entries in the Papal Registers Relating to Great Britain and Ireland: Papal Letters*, ed. W. H. Bliss and others (London

	and Dublin, 1893–)
Dryb. Lib.	*Liber S. Marie de Dryburgh* (Bannatyne Club, 1847)
EHR	*English Historical Review*
ES	*Early Sources of Scottish History, A.D. 500 to 1286*, ed. and trans. A. O. Anderson, 2 vols. (Edinburgh, 1922)
Howden, *Chronica*	*Chronica Rogeri de Hovedene*, ed. W. Stubbs, 4 vols. (Rolls Series, 1868–71)
Howden, *Gesta*	*Gesta Regis Henrici Secundi Benedicti Abbatis*, ed. W. Stubbs, 2 vols. (Rolls Series, 1867)
IR	*Innes Review*
Paris, *Chron. Maj.*	Matthew Paris, *Chronica Majora*, ed. H. R. Luard, 7 vols. (Rolls Series, 1872–83)
RMS	*Registrum Magni Sigilli Regum Scotorum*, ed. J. M. Thomson and others, 11 vols. (Edinburgh, 1882–1914)
RRS, i	*Regesta Regum Scottorum: The Acts of Malcolm IV, King of Scots, 1153–1165*, ed. G. W. S. Barrow (Edinburgh, 1960)
RRS, ii	*Regesta Regum Scottorum: The Acts of William I, King of Scots, 1165–1214*, ed. G. W. S. Barrow with the collaboration of W. W. Scott (Edinburgh, 1971)
RRS, v	*Regesta Regum Scottorum: The Acts of Robert I, King of Scots, 1306–1329*, ed. A. A. M. Duncan (Edinburgh, 1988)
RRS, vi	*Regesta Regum Scottorum: The Acts of David II, King of Scots, 1329–1371*, ed. B. Webster (Edinburgh, 1982)
SHR	*Scottish Historical Review*
TRHS	*Transactions of the Royal Historical Society*
Vet. Mon.	*Vetera Monumenta Hibernorum et Scotorum Historiam Illustrantia*, ed. A. Theiner (Rome, 1864)

Map 1 Earldoms and major lordships in medieval Scotland

Map 2 Ecclesiastical centres

Map 3 Scotland, showing some of the more significant places mentioned in the text

I

EARLY MEDIEVAL SCOTLAND

An observer of the political configuration of the island of Britain in the sixteenth century would be aware of the existence of two well-defined and long-established kingdoms. The peoples of England and Scotland were often suspicious of one another, sometimes even at war, but both realms could boast a sequence of monarchs stretching back far into the mists of time. From such a vantage point, the development of the two kingdoms might seem an inevitable consequence of historical processes centuries earlier, but in fact there was nothing inevitable about it, especially in the case of Scotland. Rather, the creation of the medieval realm was a remarkable achievement in view of the political, cultural and geographical factors which conspired against it. Other Celtic lands, most notably Wales and Ireland, never achieved unity under a single line of rulers as Scotland did, nor did circumstances ever exist there in which warring tribes and dynasties could be assimilated into a single political entity, even though the ethnic and linguistic diversity of Ireland and Wales was less marked than in Scotland. The Scottish achievement was all the greater for being realised in a land of which large parts are mountainous and suffer very heavy rainfall, rendering them inconducive to settled patterns of agriculture and incapable of sustaining a large population. Land communications between different regions of Scotland were seriously impaired by the existence of extensive areas of barren upland and long firths and sea-lochs, while the relative ease of seaborne travel tended to encourage contact with outsiders rather than fellow-inhabitants of another part of Scotland. One of the principal themes of this book is an exploration of how these problems were overcome, what impact cultural and physical barriers continued to have on the course of Scottish history, and the extent to which an identifiable Scottish nation was born in the later Middle Ages.

The people known as the Scots originated in Ireland. Some had presumably already crossed the North Channel by the time that Fergus Mor mac Erc, king of Dalriada, moved his power base from the coastal region of what is now County Antrim to Argyll sometime around 500. The old Irish territories of Dalriada continued to be ruled from Scotland until the middle of the seventh century, but the future of the Scots was to lie in the geographical area to which their name was ultimately to be given. Their cultural dominance from the middle of the ninth century onwards must not, however, conceal the fact that Dalriada was but one of the territorial and political divisions of early Scotland, and rarely the most important or most powerful. Indeed, the word 'Scotland' is somewhat inappropriate when used in connection with the early medieval period, for writers of that time normally use the word 'Scots' to refer generally to the inhabitants of Ireland, and by extension to Irish colonists elsewhere. Even the Latin *Scotia*, often taken in a twelfth- and thirteenth-century context as referring to the whole area north of the marshy isthmus between the long firths of Forth and Clyde, was capable of a more restricted meaning, not necessarily including the territory of the old kingdom of Dalriada where the Scots had originally settled. Although in this volume the word 'Scotland' is used in its familiar modern sense, it was not until the thirteenth century that the whole area ruled by the king of Scots came to be called 'Scotland', while the idea that the Scots were a distinct race rather than being a people of Irish origin was first fully articulated only during the crisis of the Wars of Independence.

When the kingdom of Dalriada was establishing itself on the western seaboard in the early years of the sixth century, most of the landmass north of the Forth and Clyde, and probably Orkney and parts of the Hebrides too, were occupied by the Picts. Few peoples in the early Middle Ages have engendered more controversy than the Picts, and hardly any aspect of their society can be established on an indisputable basis. Their principal material remains consist of a fine series of stones with distinctive, if now largely impenetrable, symbols incised or sculptured in relief on them. We also have several lists of their kings with indications of how long each reigned, although in their present form they date from a later period. The deeds, and more especially the deaths, of many of these kings are recorded in Irish annals, which enables historians to place what is essentially a bare list of names into a chronological context. However, although the Picts appear usually to have been territorially and militarily superior to their neighbours, their culture and political organisation effectively disappeared after the sudden overthrow of the native rulers by Kenneth MacAlpin, king of Scots, in around 843.

Later sources suggest that Pictland was divided into seven provinces. It would be convenient if these could be made to correspond to the historical earldoms, which were clearly of ancient origin, but the connections have never been fully and satisfactorily established. From the evidence of other Dark Age societies, it would be reasonable to suppose that the rulers of the Pictish provinces were semi-independent potentates or perhaps tribal chiefs, albeit owing some allegiance to a high king; by this theory the names in the regnal lists would broadly constitute a series of over-kings with the addition in some versions of rival claimants to that dignity. There is, however, no evidence that the Picts had firm political divisions of this sort. Although the Roman writer Ammianus Marcellinus and the Northumbrian monk and historian Bede draw an apparent distinction between the northern and southern Picts, all the Pictish kings mentioned in foreign sources also appear in the regnal lists, and so arguably the rulers of individual provinces, later sometimes called *mormaers* or great stewards, were, as that title implies, merely royal officials with little effective independence of action.

The geographical realities of Scotland must, however, have militated against a united Pictish kingdom. The Mounth, the great eastward extension of the Highland massif which almost reaches the coast near Stonehaven, was a formidable obstacle, and even as late as the early thirteenth century royal control over the areas to the north of it was fitful. It is surely possible that in practice a distinction between the northern and southern Picts, perhaps even between individual provinces, would have been meaningful in political terms, although powerful rulers might be able to dominate on both sides of the Mounth simultaneously. Even if it is, on balance, unlikely that separate lines of kings emerged, the experience of contemporary Dalriada would suggest that rival dynasties, each claiming descent from a common ancestor, could easily have developed in Pictland, and our sources are so exiguous that it is very dangerous to assume that semi-independent rulers did not hold sway in some areas, as they certainly did in the north and west of Scotland in later centuries. Even if a *mormaer* was theoretically a royal agent, he was surely the effective lord of his province under all but the most powerful kings.

One of the striking features of the Pictish king-lists is that, at least until the ninth century, no king was the son of a previous king of the Picts. Bede states that succession was matrilineal, at least when the identity of the next ruler was in doubt; in other words the claim to the throne was passed through females rather than males, although it is noteworthy that the names of very few Pictish women have come down to us. Some elaborate genealogical diagrams have been constructed to show how this unusual system might have worked, but other scholars have challenged the whole concept of matrilineal succession, noting that in most early medieval societies it was unusual for a king to be succeeded immediately by his son because the latter tended to lack the experience and personal following necessary to become an effective warlord in a predominantly martial society. The controversy need not concern us here, except that matriliny may explain how some Pictish kings appear to have come from ruling dynasties elsewhere in the Celtic world; the principle of matrilineal succession may, therefore, have had the effect of encouraging contact between different peoples, thereby perhaps facilitating the later consolidation of different ethnic groups into a single kingdom.

The union of the kingships of the Picts and Scots by Kenneth MacAlpin has traditionally been regarded as the beginning of the Scottish realm, and there has been a tendency (by no means always followed) to give regnal numbers to the kings from Kenneth onwards. The convention that Kenneth's reign marked a fresh beginning is a very old one, for the king-lists clearly regard him as having been the first of a new regime, even though he was probably not the first king of Dalriada to exercise lordship over the Picts. The previous three centuries had seen many fluctuations in the respective fortunes of Pictland and Dalriada, and of the dynasties within the Dalriadan ruling house, and although the great mountainous spine of Druim Alban served as a physical barrier between western and eastern Scotland there can be no doubt that the Picts and Scots came into contact on many occasions through both marriage and battle. What made Kenneth MacAlpin different is, therefore, unclear, except that he founded what was to be a permanent patrilineal dynasty, which with the benefit of hindsight may have seemed significant to the compilers of the king-lists. Several years elapsed before Kenneth subdued his remaining Pictish rivals, but the changed political configuration brought about by his achievement was to prove permanent.

From the last decade of the eighth century Britain and Ireland came under assault from Scandinavian raiders, and it is possible that this provided the circumstances for Kenneth's takeover of Pictland. Opinions differ as to the intentions of the Vikings and over whether their raiding was more violent than that of other contemporary bands of warriors, but there can be no doubt that the Norse invaders caused severe material destruction, particularly to the island monasteries of western Scotland which were both temptingly wealthy and peculiarly exposed to attack from a seafaring foe. Equally it is certain that many Scandinavians settled in the British Isles and indulged in the peaceful activities of agriculture and trade. Shetland, Orkney and the north-east corner of the Scottish mainland were colonised by Norwegians in considerable numbers, as is seen by the disappearance of all but a handful of non-Norse place names; settlement in these areas was understandable because the climatic and agricultural conditions were similar to those in Norway itself, Orkney and Caithness being particularly fertile. Norwegians also settled on the western seaboard, probably to a much lesser extent, although place-name evidence does not conclusively reveal whether the Gaelic language survived the initial onslaught of Viking incomers or made a comeback in the Hebrides only later.

The arrival of the Vikings put pressure on both the Scots of Dalriada and the Picts, especially those north of the Mounth. The appearance of Norwegians on the western seaboard may have encouraged the Scots to move eastwards, which would explain why Norse settlers seem to have established themselves on the west coast so easily. The Picts may have collapsed under the joint threat, especially if (as seems likely) the Dalriadan dynasty known as the Cenél Loairn attacked northern Pictland at the same time as the Cenél nGabráin under Kenneth invaded the more southerly regions. Irish annals report that in 839 a fierce battle was fought between the Norse and the Picts (or at least those south of the Mounth), and this may have weakened the Pictish establishment to such an extent that it could be eclipsed by the Scots within a few years. However, later tales of how treachery assisted Kenneth's destruction of the Pictish nobility tell us little about what happened to the Picts as a whole. It is surely likely that many survived, albeit now under different rulers; it was not until around 900 that the notion of a Pictish realm disappears from contemporary sources to be replaced by the Gaelic name of Alba.[1] The kingdom of the Picts did not become Scottish overnight.

The southern part of the later Scottish realm had not, except fleetingly, been under the close control of either the Picts or the Dalriadan Scots. The British kingdom of Strathclyde or Cumbria was still in existence in the ninth century, stretching southwards from the northern end of Loch Lomond; from the middle of the tenth century it probably included the English Lake District, but earlier kings ruled over a much smaller, though fluctuating, area.[2] In language and political organisation its closest parallels were in Wales, and it was essentially a relic of the once more extensive territories of the ancient Britons, who had been forced westwards by the Anglo-Saxon invaders. Of the Anglo-Saxon kingdoms, the most northerly was Northumbria, stretching from the Humber to the Forth, although at times it was divided between Deira (roughly Yorkshire) and Bernicia. Northumbrian expansion northwards was checked by the Picts at Dunnichen in Angus in 685, but in the eighth century the Angles attained at least a measure of supremacy in Galloway, the extreme south-western corner of the Scottish mainland.

The early history of Galloway remains obscure, despite a very important series of archaeological excavations at Whithorn, an ancient ecclesiastical site traditionally associated with St Ninian.

[1] D. Broun, 'Defining Scotland and the Scots before the Wars of Independence', in D. Broun, R. J. Finlay and M. Lynch, eds., *Image and Identity: The Making and Re-making of Scotland Through the Ages* (Edinburgh, 1998), 7.

[2] A. Macquarrie, 'The kings of Strathclyde, *c.* 400–1018', in *Barrow Essays*, 18–19.

Anglian control of the area may date from the third quarter of the seventh century, when Northumbria was still extending its sphere of influence, although it has been suggested that the great crosses at Bewcastle in Cumberland and Ruthwell in Dumfriesshire, erected perhaps around 700, were primarily symbols of propaganda which demonstrate Northumbrian aspirations rather than real power.[3] An Anglian bishopric was established at Whithorn around 730, and a number of eighth-century bishops are known, although religious life at the site can be traced back to about 500 and possibly even earlier. Place names indicate an enclave of Anglian settlement around Whithorn, but it must have come under threat from Norse raiders and also possibly from Irish adventurers, to say nothing of the local native inhabitants. There was a serious fire at Whithorn in about 845, and although limited contact with Northumbria continued for a few years, it was greatly diminished even before York fell to the Danes in 866.

Strathclyde also came under Norse attack. In 870 the great rock-fortress of Dumbarton fell after a four-month siege, a very unusual event in Dark Age Britain. Aggressive actions by the Vikings in southern Scotland may have been aimed at securing a route between Ireland and eastern England via the waterways of Clyde and Forth, a more obvious line of communication to a seafaring people than might seem likely today. Norse successes posed a threat to the descendants of Kenneth MacAlpin, but also provided opportunities for southward expansion at the expense of the emasculated kingdoms of Strathclyde and Northumbria. Although both Constantine I in 876 and Idulb in 962 met their deaths in battles against the Vikings, and many raids are noted in near-contemporary sources, the way was now open for the Scottish kings to enlarge their territory and they may have entered into alliances with the Scandinavian rulers of York and Dublin in order to further this ambition.

Expansion southwards was both easier and potentially more lucrative for the kings of the MacAlpin dynasty than consolidation of the old Pictish and Scottish kingdoms. Norse settlers were now well established in the north and west, and it is likely that the rival Cenél Loairn was dominant in Moray. It was normally the rulers of Moray, sometimes termed kings by contemporaries, who made

[3] A. P. Smyth, *Warlords and Holy Men: Scotland AD 80–1000* (Edinburgh, 1989), 26.

alliances with other northern powers such as the earls of Orkney, while the MacAlpin kings turned their eyes towards Northumbria. Kenneth I is said to have invaded the lands south of the Forth on no fewer than six occasions, burning Dunbar and seizing Melrose, and many of his successors were to follow this policy of aggrandisement, terrorising neighbouring peoples and rewarding their own followers with the spoils of victory, although the sources do hint also at more constructive activities on the part of the kings, such as lawmaking and the establishment of ecclesiastical institutions. Nonetheless, the Scottish kings took advantage of the fact that the most powerful remaining English kingdom was that of Wessex, which was both distant and, moreover, separated from northern Northumbria by the Danes' possession of York. Although the precise chronology is impossible to ascertain, the influence of the Scots in Lothian was probably well established by the middle of the tenth century, when Edinburgh was abandoned to them, although later reverses such as the failure of Malcolm II to take Durham in 1006 may have served to revive the fortunes of the English aristocracy in the area. The need to establish relations with the house of Wessex, whose authority was steadily spreading northwards, led to both military confrontation and political agreements which left the Scottish king in effective control of the area north of the Tweed in return for an acknowledgement of the Anglo-Saxon monarch's superior power. The disintegration of Northumbria under Scandinavian pressure had, therefore, enabled both the rulers of Wessex and the descendants of Kenneth MacAlpin to fill a political vacuum, and the scene was set for the twelfth-century struggles over the location of the border with England.

The fate of Strathclyde is much disputed. The fall of Dumbarton must have weakened the British kingdom as a viable political unit, and the expulsion of Eochaid son of Rhun in 889 has been regarded as marking the end of the line of native British kings. Rhun had married a daughter of Kenneth MacAlpin, and it has been argued that from around 900 Strathclyde was bestowed on the heir to the Scottish kingdom as a means of recognising his claim and thereby (at least in theory) avoiding bloodshed between rival lines of the royal dynasty.[4] This theory is, however, based on very tenuous and

[4] Ibid., 216–18, 220–1.

much later evidence, and in any case it is not clear why the Scottish kings would have wanted to preserve Strathclyde as a separate realm, even for the purpose of its forming an appanage for their chosen successor, when other British kingdoms had disappeared on being absorbed into a larger political unit. It seems rather that an obscure line of native rulers, probably now based at the ancient centre of Govan rather than Dumbarton, continued until Owain the Bald died around 1018. Even thereafter Strathclyde was perhaps not totally subservient to the Scottish kings, for in the early twelfth century the future David I, invested as ruler of southern Scotland during his elder brother Alexander's lifetime, seems still to have regarded Govan as a threat.

All these early kingdoms had at some point come under the influence of Christianity, for Dark Age Scotland had received religious instruction from a number of different sources. In the fifth or sixth century St Ninian evangelised the people of parts of what is now southern Scotland. St Columba's monastery on Iona, founded in or shortly after 563, was to become the fulcrum of a community of religious houses across northern Britain; he and other Irish missionaries visited and probably converted the Picts, while St Aidan brought the Christian faith from Iona to the people of Northumbria. In the 680s the Northumbrian church established an episcopal see among the Picts at Abercorn. Although the bishop had to withdraw after the Anglian defeat at the battle of Dunnichen, the Pictish king Nechton sent to Northumbria around 710 for detailed guidance about the controversy over the date of Easter, and his espousal of Roman customs probably led to a church among the Picts which owed more to Anglian organisation than to Columban traditions; certainly Nechton saw fit to expel the Iona clergy from eastern Scotland. Other holy men, such as St Kentigern, the traditional founder of Glasgow, St Maelrubha of Applecross and St Donnan of Eigg all played their part in bringing Christianity to the peoples of the future kingdom of Scotland. Religious beliefs and practices had, therefore, been imported from a variety of places, and the traffic was by no means all one way.

The vibrancy of the Christian church in eighth-century Scotland is not in doubt, but the cultural milieu which produced the Lindisfarne Gospels and the Book of Kells was greatly harmed by the beginning of Viking raids on the British Isles in the 790s.

Whatever the ultimate inspiration was for the Scandinavians' voyages to the west, there can be no doubt that many religious settlements suffered as a result. Iona had already been attacked at least three times when in 825 Abbot Blathmac was martyred for refusing to divulge the whereabouts of Columba's shrine. Some of Columba's relics were later transferred to Dunkeld by Kenneth MacAlpin, a move which reflects his own new-found authority over the Picts and perhaps marks a further stage of cross-fertilisation between different Christian traditions, but which also demonstrates the vulnerability of Iona. Norse settlement severed the lines of communication which had helped to bind together the different strands of Celtic Christianity, and it is difficult to assess either the spirituality or the organisation of the church in the very obscure period which followed.

There is, however, no doubt that the institutions of the church continued in existence, since many religious communities which are attested in the twelfth century were clearly very ancient. Some of the most prominent consisted of groups of Culdees or *célidé*, who owed their origin to an eighth-century Irish monastic reform movement, although there were also churches of secular priests which are broadly comparable to Anglo-Saxon minsters. There was an albeit hazy tradition of some sort of episcopal organisation, especially in the former Pictish kingdom, as well as sequences of abbots. Many communities doubtless fell under the influence of individual kin-groups, whose members used the endowment for their own ends, but this does not necessarily imply that they performed no pastoral function. We know nothing of how churchmen were perceived by their flocks, but worshippers surely cared much less than fervent reformers about matters such as irregular ordination. The strength of these ancient communities can be gauged by noting how long they survived and how much their presence influenced the twelfth-century ecclesiastical reforms which will be discussed in a later chapter.

The eleventh-century kingdom of the Scots was a somewhat uneasy amalgam of several different peoples, languages and cultures. It had been drawn together by a combination of circumstances and was to prove remarkably resilient as a political entity, despite its internal diversity. However, problems of geography made land communications difficult and gave some of its people a maritime outlook which brought them into contact with Ireland, the Scandinavian lands and other parts of the Irish Sea and North Sea worlds. A virtually independent line of rulers in Moray continued to be a thorn in the side of the Scottish monarchs and, despite the Dalriadic origins of the dynasty, royal influence west of Druim Alban and in Galloway, to say nothing of the Western Isles, was virtually non-existent. On the other hand, the line of Kenneth MacAlpin, albeit in different branches, was well established as the ruling house in at least the southern part of the former Pictland, and there had been substantial territorial gains south of the Forth, including fertile areas in the Tweed valley and the coastal strip of Lothian. The kingdom of Scotland familiar to later ages was beginning to emerge from the early medieval mists.

2

FEUDAL SCOTLAND

Shakespeare's Scottish play has given some of the characters of eleventh-century Scotland a celebrity which they would not otherwise have been accorded. Like many other dramatic reconstructions of the past, however, Shakespeare's portrayal of MacBeth leaves much to be desired when viewed from the standpoint of sober history. Shakespeare, of course, relied on the sources of information available to him, and they were unsympathetic towards a ruler who, although of royal lineage, had usurped the throne when Duncan I was killed at Pitgaveny near Elgin in 1040, but yet had not succeeded in establishing a ruling dynasty. Because subsequent Scottish kings were all descended from Duncan, it is not surprising that MacBeth's reign came to be seen as an unfortunate interlude, a regrettable reversion towards barbarism in what was otherwise an age of progress.

In fact MacBeth was a successful ruler.[1] By contemporary standards the length of his reign was highly respectable, and Scotland was sufficiently peaceful for him to be confident enough to leave it in 1050 to make a pilgrimage to Rome. A Latin poem describes his reign as a fertile period, which suggests favourable weather but also points to an absence of the civil strife which always brings hardship in a rural society. There is no hint in contemporary sources that he

[1] See E. J. Cowan, 'The historical MacBeth', in W. D. H. Sellar, ed., *Moray: Province and People* (Edinburgh, 1993), 117–41.

was a tyrant, and it is inconceivable that he would have reigned for so long if he had been. His branch of the Dalriadan royal house, the Cenél Loairn, had dominated Moray for two centuries, and MacBeth appears as an intruder only because, unusually, he was able to exercise authority south of the Mounth at the expense of the descendants of Kenneth MacAlpin. That a northern potentate could temporarily usurp the position of the established dynasty was due to a number of factors. MacBeth's marriage to Gruoch, granddaughter of Kenneth III, enabled him to combine his own claim to the throne, strengthened by the fact that his mother was probably Malcolm II's sister, with that of his wife, while the succession of Duncan I, grandson of Malcolm II through the latter's daughter, may have disturbed not only the Moray kindred but also others who feared that the establishment of the principle of primogeniture would permanently exclude their families from the throne. Little is known of Duncan's reign, but his failure to take Durham in 1040 must have caused his rivals to question whether he had the military prowess requisite in a Scottish king and encouraged them in their opposition; it is possible that his fatal expedition north of the Mounth was in part an attempt to reassert his authority. Circumstances thus combined in MacBeth's favour, but he was still surrounded by enemies, both in the earldom of Orkney and in English Northumbria, to say nothing of the representatives of the line of Malcolm II. In 1045 Crinan, abbot of Dunkeld and Duncan's father, was killed in battle, and Earl Siward of Northumbria may have launched an unsuccessful invasion of Scotland. Nine years later a great battle was fought between the Scots and English, with Siward now supporting Duncan's son Malcolm; this time MacBeth was on the losing side, although it was not until 1057 that he was killed at Lumphanan in Aberdeenshire. He was briefly succeeded by his stepson Lulach, whose inadequacy as a ruler enabled Malcolm III to recover his heritage, but Moray remained a problem for the Scottish monarchs until well into the thirteenth century.

It is tempting to see the accession of Malcolm III as heralding a new era. His descendants are sometimes referred to as the 'House of Canmore' after the by-name traditionally bestowed on Malcolm III, and their success in consolidating royal power in Scotland and introducing social, administrative and ecclesiastical changes has made it convenient for historians to look to their common ancestor as the instigator of a new age. By his second marriage to Margaret, granddaughter of the English king Edmund Ironside but exposed to continental influences during her family's exile in Hungary, Malcolm can be portrayed as having begun the process whereby Scotland was drawn from Celtic introspection into the international family of European states. An apparent reaction after his death in 1093, when his English adherents were driven out of Scotland by his conservative brother Donald Bán, can be seen as proving Malcolm's credentials as an outward-looking reformer. By this interpretation, Donald's usurpation was merely a last desperate attempt by the old order to resist the inevitable advance of new ideas.

There is good reason to suppose that religious reforms, and in due course changes in the structure of society, would have reached Scotland whatever the attitude of her kings, such was the cultural unity of the ancient Northumbria. But Malcolm Canmore's role in these developments must be critically reassessed. The importance of his marriage to the saintly Margaret must not be overemphasised. While she was undoubtedly pious, her subsequent reputation largely rests on the work of her chaplain and biographer, the monk Turgot, who almost certainly credits her with much greater influence over her husband than is credible in a male-dominated, martial society. His sons by Margaret bore names which were novel in the Scottish ruling house, but Malcolm was, and remained, a warlord. He emulated his predecessors by launching several devastating raids into English Northumbria, aware that royal authority in eleventh-century Scotland largely depended on the king's ability to reward his followers with military success in the form of booty. The influence of his wife doubtless brought Englishmen into Malcolm's court, but their expulsion in 1093 should not be seen in racial terms, for Donald inevitably sought to displace those of Malcolm's adherents who wished the late king to be succeeded by one of his sons rather than his brother. Although primogeniture came to prevail in Scotland for the next two centuries, the concept was still unusual in 1093, when kingdoms throughout Europe still required adult rulers of proven worth in war. Donald failed in his attempt to retain the throne, being defeated by Malcolm's son from his first marriage, Duncan II, in 1094, and then, after his temporary restoration, by Edgar, son of Malcolm and Margaret, in 1097. Donald's rivals were supported by the Norman kings of England, and this link proved crucial in the introduction of administrative and social changes in twelfth-century Scotland, but in the immediate context of the 1090s too much significance should not be accorded to this. For them, as for Donald and his elder brother Malcolm in 1040, it was a question of seeking allies, or at least sanctuary, where they could be found; even MacBeth used Norman mercenaries in 1054. We must not view the late eleventh century from the standpoint of our knowledge of what was to happen in David I's reign, for Malcolm Canmore's policies were in most respects traditional. Court poets during the reigns of future kings had every incentive to praise Malcolm and his pious wife and to stress Margaret's beneficent influence on her sons, and the emphasis placed on the supposed contrast between Malcolm on the one hand and MacBeth and Donald Bán on the other was useful propaganda for as long as there were rival claimants to the throne capable of winning support in northern Scotland.

The development of Scotland from a traditional Celtic society to a kingdom which could take its place among the states of western Europe is the principal theme of Scottish history in the twelfth and thirteenth centuries. Some of the changes came in the ecclesiastical sphere, others were marked by territorial consolidation within Scotland and by more closely defined relationships with the rulers of England. These issues will be analysed in subsequent chapters. It is necessary first to examine the development of feudal practices in Scotland, the impact of the arrival of settlers from England and France, and the administrative and institutional changes which were introduced broadly contemporaneously. The key figure in these developments was David I, youngest son of Malcolm and Margaret, who became king in 1124.

Feudalism is a problematic concept. In popular usage it is often equated with backwardness, brutality and the domination of one class over another. Even in historical works the term often appears with an underlying assumption that its meaning is both clear and familiar. Some, by contrast, argue that the word should not be used at all, but it remains an appropriate means of describing a particular form of social organisation which was found widely throughout western Europe and came increasingly into prominence in Scotland in the twelfth century.

Feudalism was essentially a system of personal relationships. At the upper levels of society these normally took the form of a grant of land by a superior lord, often the king, to someone termed a vassal, who did homage and swore fealty to the lord, in effect promising to 'be his man' and to be faithful to him, and undertook to perform specified services which were normally (though not always) of a military nature, such as service in war and the performance of garrison duty in castles. In Scotland many of the recipients were trained knights who had already served in a noble household, and the land is commonly termed a knight's feu or fief. As well as giving the vassal title to land, often on an hereditary basis, the lord promised to protect him. The arrangement was usually marked by the issue of a charter, and because many such documents have survived we can study feudalism much more fully than the landholding structures which preceded it.

Many of those who obtained land from the king in turn granted some of it to others, a process known as subinfeudation, although the holder of the feu remained answerable to his lord for the whole of it. The structure thus resembled a pyramid, with the king at the apex, although it was not uncommon for an individual to hold some land directly from the crown and other estates from one of the king's vassals. In entering into reciprocal arrangements, the lord surrendered some of his authority and undertook to meet certain responsibilities, but in return he received specified services as well as the right to relief (a payment made when the holding passed to the vassal's heir) and wardship (the control of heirs who were under age when they succeeded). Although strictly the lord had not alienated the land itself, but merely granted the use of it, the vassal enjoyed security of tenure, and could forfeit his lands only if he failed to meet his obligations or broke his oath of fealty. Feudalism therefore conferred advantages on both parties.

In Scotland the arrival of feudal practices was closely connected with the influx of foreign settlers. Many of the immigrants were of French origin, and were recruited either directly from France, especially from Normandy, Flanders and Brittany, or from families which had settled in England in the wake of William the Conqueror's triumph in and after 1066. They were already accustomed to the institutions of feudalism, and were instrumental in encouraging the use of feudal patterns of landholding in Scotland, but this does not explain why they sought lands in Scotland in the first place.

It is generally accepted that the eleventh and twelfth centuries witnessed a period of population pressure. In the upper echelons of society, many younger sons had little prospect of obtaining estates at home commensurate with their status, and were thus encouraged to seek their fortune elsewhere. This helps to explain the enthusiasm for crusading and the establishment of Latin principalities in the Holy Land, and it also accounts for the remarkable migration of Normans to Sicily, England and ultimately Scotland. In this respect Scotland, like the kingdom of Jerusalem, was a land of opportunity, offering the chance of extensive estates and the political and economic power which went with them. Encouragement from the Scottish kings was, however, of critical importance. The sons of Malcolm and Margaret had become familiar with the Norman rulers of England, and drew upon Norman military might to secure their throne. After he received the earldom of Huntingdon around Christmas 1113 the future David I became a major English magnate, and he continued to have a close personal relationship with Henry I, who had married his sister. It is hardly surprising that David became steeped in the culture of the Anglo-Norman court, and it was from England that he derived most of his ideas on governmental reform, his belief in the value of feudalism as a means of ordering aristocratic society, and many of the settlers themselves.

It is understandable that the lands of the earldom of Huntingdon provided a ready source of potential settlers, many of them well known to David I and possessing the knightly skills which were essential for the military feudalism which he wished to introduce to Scotland. The importance of Huntingdon must not be overstated, for some of David's closest associates, such as Robert de Brus (more familiar as Bruce), Hugh de Moreville, Ranulf de Soules and Robert Avenel, were probably recruited directly from Normandy, where Henry I may have granted David a modest estate, and perhaps owed their lands in the English Midlands to their prior connection with the Scottish king rather than the other way round.[2] But while a

[2] G. W. S. Barrow, *The Anglo-Norman Era in Scottish History* (Oxford, 1980), 99.

substantial number of immigrants to Scotland had no direct connection with Huntingdon, the earldom was still an important recruiting ground in David I's reign, becoming less significant only when political vicissitudes interrupted his descendants' possession of their English estates and the personal connections that would have accompanied it.

One of the most important sources of settlers was Yorkshire. There are a number of reasons for this, one of which is the cultural and historical connection provided by the old kingdom of Northumbria, which had stretched from the Humber to the Forth. Lothian, as the Scottish portion of this extensive area, was therefore particularly attractive to the leading English families of Yorkshire, many of whom retained their social status in the wake of the Norman Conquest more successfully than their counterparts further south. But Frenchmen too moved into Scotland from Yorkshire, some of them following Robert Bruce into the great lordship of Annandale which David I had bestowed upon him. It is significant that many Flemings settled in south-west Scotland, probably recruited from the Bruce estates in Cleveland, which had earlier attracted Flemish immigrants.[3]

French settlement in Scotland added another element to the already complex racial mixture, although the net result of immigration was probably to anglicise Lowland Scotland and to accentuate the contrast with the Gaelic-speaking north and west, rather than to imbue it with a culture that was definably French. This was because of the English adherents who moved north with their lords or on their own initiative, and the increased contact between Scotland and England through the development of a baronage which had interests in both realms. The attitude of successive kings demonstrates how Scotland was drawn into a wider, predominantly Frankish, aristocratic world. David I's years at the court of Henry I made him familiar with that world, but his grandsons were even keener to absorb chivalric culture. Malcolm IV, who succeeded David in 1153, had an almost plaintive wish to be knighted, while his brother William was an enthusiastic participant in tournaments and was renowned among contemporary chroniclers for his partiality to Frenchmen; it has been written that 'no king of Scots did more than William to Normanise his country'.[4] In order to play a fitting

[3] Ibid., 48, 106–17.

[4] G. W. S. Barrow, *Scotland and Its Neighbours in the Middle Ages* (London, 1992), 72.

part in the world of chivalry, the Scottish kings had to have a knightly following commensurate with their regal status, and this partly explains the continued encouragement of immigrants in the second half of the twelfth century. There was little bullion in circulation in Scotland, so the obvious means of reward was land, hence the feudalisation of Clydesdale under Malcolm IV and of Gowrie, Angus and Mearns under his younger brother. Settlement was a deliberate royal policy.

However, unlike England in the aftermath of the battle of Hastings, Scotland was not a conquered country. Despite their newfangled ideas, the twelfth-century kings of Scots succeeded to the throne because they were direct descendants of earlier rulers, and they had to marry feudalism with the older forms of landholding and social structure which still prevailed throughout the realm. There could not be a major expropriation of native lords or widespread displacement of the peasantry; even in Lothian, which was probably the most heavily feudalised region, the native Northumbrian aristocracy was by no means eliminated. Although the population of Scotland in the twelfth century was only a few hundred thousand, it was widely spread throughout those parts of the land which could sustain agriculture. Scotland was not virgin territory, and both kings and settlers therefore had to tread warily. The evidence for bishops of native stock and the numerous examples of royal officials and attendants with Gaelic names in David I's reign, doubtless inherited from the court of his predecessors, demonstrate a realisation on the king's part that successful governance depended on the assimilation of new ideas into old structures, and this was surely true of landholding as well.

The impact of Anglo-Norman immigration on the peasantry is almost impossible to assess. Landholding gave the new lords power over their tenants, but it is doubtful whether the replacement of one lord by another created major upheavals at the level of local society, at least in the short term. It is unclear to what extent a manorial system on the classic English model was feasible in Scotland, where pastoral farming was proportionately more significant; some tillers of the soil were undoubtedly bound tightly to their lords, and could be sold or given away in the manner of chattels, but we do not know whether the creation of knights' feus in itself altered the status of such individuals. Although some specialist workers, such as cooks and scribes, came to Scotland in the households of immigrants, it is unlikely that the twelfth century saw peasant immigration into Scotland on more than a very limited scale.

The extent to which the new feudatories displaced the native lords depends on the source of the land which was granted to them. If the king used his demesne estates, namely those that were exploited in his own interest, or other lands which were temporarily in his possession, then effectively he was rewarding settlers from his own resources. If, however, he chose to bestow lands which were under the control of others, then he faced the prospect of serious opposition. Although some highly favoured supporters, such as Bruce, received vast tracts of land – Annandale was held for the service of ten knights – most of the settlers were granted fairly small estates, many of them consisting of merely one or two villages.

It is reasonable to assume that many of the newly created feus coincided with earlier secular divisions, and this raises the issue of shires and thanages. Early medieval kings were not sedentary. They had estates in different parts of their realm and travelled between them, spending some time at each administering justice and demonstrating lordship in the personal manner which was necessary at that period. Their subjects within these estates were required to render goods or services to the king and his extensive household under the supervision of a local official. In eastern Scotland these administrative and socioeconomic units were usually called shires, and the principal royal officer was called a thane, although in some places he bore the title of sheriff. It should be noted that these terms had a rather different meaning in England, and that sheriffs in this context must not be confused with the more powerful officers of the same name who emerged in the twelfth century, even though the latter performed broadly similar functions.

The thane's primary task was to administer a specific unit of demesne on behalf of his overlord. Within it he had responsibilities for supervising justice, collecting revenues and leading the inhabitants in war, but his role was essentially managerial; although his position was often hereditary, he was not a proprietor. In theory a shire controlled by a thane could be granted as a knight's feu to a new settler, who could (if he so wished) leave the existing social structure essentially untouched and simply replace the previous lord as the local figurehead and chief beneficiary of the shire's produce.

The use of royal demesne in this way would have enabled the Scottish kings to grant land to incomers on a feudal basis without running the risk of displacing existing proprietors, and Barrow has argued forcefully that this was exactly what happened, especially in southern Scotland, where David I surrounded the royal castle of Edinburgh with a ring of close friends and adherents, bound to perform military service and fill administrative offices in return for their land.[5]

The problem with this theory is that the crown relied on its demesnes for much of its revenue. Twelfth-century kings received renders from their demesne tenants, usually in kind, and these would cease if the land was granted away. Other Scottish lords, faced with a similar situation, appear to have been markedly reluctant to reward their followers from the demesne, and to have drawn a distinction between their traditional hereditary lands and those which had come into their possession more recently. The lords of Galloway, for example, maintained control of their patrimonial lands in the extensive uplands of northern Galloway, but were much more ready to create feudal holdings in Desnes Ioan, the area east of the river Urr which had probably come into their possession only in the 1160s. A similar policy was adopted by the earls of Strathearn, who likewise granted only peripheral lands to settlers and kept a firm hold of the upland parts of their territory, especially around Loch Earn.[6]

There is some evidence that the crown too preferred to grant lands which had fallen into its hands relatively recently. In Moray, for instance, feudal settlement began in the wake of the defeat and death of Earl Angus in 1130. The earldom remained dormant from David I's reign until 1312, and it is reasonable to conjecture that the new settlers in Moray, such as the Fleming Freskin, were rewarded from the estates previously controlled by Angus rather than out of whatever royal demesne there may have been in that province. Further south, the earldoms of Gowrie and Mearns were both vacant in the twelfth century, although they do seem to have existed as political units at an earlier period. Here too the king had lands at his disposal which had come into the crown's possession fairly

[5] Ibid., 56–7.

[6] R. D. Oram, 'A family business? Colonisation and settlement in twelfth- and thirteenth-century Galloway', *SHR*, 72 (1993), 142–4.

recently and could either be bestowed on his supporters or retained as royal demesne; some of the area became a hunting reserve. Rather than reviving the earldoms, therefore, David I and, more particularly, his successors chose to partition the former earls' estates into knights' feus. Even in Angus, where there was a succession of native earls, there are indications of a similar process. The first recorded earl of Angus, Gillebrigte, appears at the end of David I's reign, and later evidence suggests that the earldom was poorly endowed and that there was much royal demesne in the area. It may be that Angus too had been in royal hands and that only part of the ancient lands were bestowed on Gillebrigte, the remainder being either kept by the crown or granted to feudatories.[7] The lands of the earldom of Fife in the twelfth century were also less extensive than might have been anticipated. Their personal names suggest that the earls of Fife were closely linked with the royal house, probably as descendants of King Dub, who ruled in the 960s, hence the name MacDuff which is peculiarly associated with this family.[8] In any event, it can be conjectured that Fife was in crown hands in the late tenth, if not the eleventh century, and that some lands there were retained by the king and later granted to knights.

The survival of thanes north of the Forth also argues against widespread alienation of royal demesne. Although grants of estates on feudal terms and the development of a system of sheriffdoms in the twelfth and thirteenth centuries created different types of link between the crown and the localities, thereby reducing the importance of the thane as an agent of royal administration, many thanages (as they came to be called) survived. Some, namely Clackmannan, Kinross and for a time Auchterarder, even became sheriffdoms, and many appear to have remained under royal control until the reign of Robert I, when a new policy caused many of them to be alienated. This change in practice is probably a reflection of the diminished administrative significance of thanages by the early fourteenth century, and the fact that the tendency for offices to become hereditary had, over time, reduced the number of thanes as a result of families dying out in the male line. The existence of thanages without a thane to preside over them indicates that they had become something of an anomaly, but their survival into Robert I's reign suggests

[7] A. A. M. Duncan, *Scotland: The Making of the Kingdom* (Edinburgh, 1975), 165.
[8] J. Bannerman, 'MacDuff of Fife', in *Barrow Essays*, 20–38.

that the twelfth-century kings were reluctant to alienate ancient demesne. On the contrary, they saw thanages as areas from which the crown's authority could offset that of powerful local magnates, and as such they played an important role in the consolidation of royal power.[9]

The theory that the king preferred to grant lands which had formerly pertained to native earls helps also to explain the geographical distribution of feudal settlement. Anglo-Norman colonisation was especially dense in Fife, Gowrie, Angus, Mearns and the lowland parts of Moray, the very areas where earlier comital demesnes appear to have fallen into the hands of the crown. South of the Forth, especially in Lothian, knights' feus were numerous and must mostly have been created (as elsewhere) from lands in royal possession. However, although the Scottish kings had controlled Lothian for over a century before David I's time, it may still have been regarded as recently acquired land, as the lords of Galloway viewed Desnes Ioan. Royal policy south of the Forth was not, therefore, necessarily identical to that pursued in the ancient heartland of the kingdom.

Although David I and his grandsons took advantage of earldoms which had fallen into their hands through genealogical accident or forfeiture, the remaining native earls retained considerable territorial, political and military power. Here there is a marked contrast with England, where conquest had allowed the Normans to create a new governing class. In Scotland there was much greater continuity, and in particular the earls still controlled the mustering and recruitment of the 'common army', which existed long before feudalism arrived and remained an essential component of the military capability of the Scottish state into the early modern period. Heavily armed knights and castles, though important features of military feudalism, were in themselves insufficient to defend the realm, still less to enable the king to go on the offensive, and their arrival in Scotland should be seen as representing the introduction of new specialisms to complement existing military capabilities. The obligation to serve in the common army was rarely waived by the crown, and at least in the twelfth century the earl frequently led the men of his province. At the battle of the Standard in 1138 the men of Lothian followed Cospatric, to whose father and namesake

[9] A. Grant, 'Thanes and thanages, from the eleventh to the fourteenth centuries', ibid., 39–81.

Malcolm III had given estates in south-east Scotland which came to form the somewhat anomalous earldom of Dunbar or March. When Cospatric was killed his troops took flight. Even in David I's reign, and in the context of Lothian, the earl's military importance is clear to see.

Some native earls embraced feudalism, for the same reasons as Anglo-Norman immigrants were attracted by it. By seeking a royal charter they could secure their lands for themselves and their heirs and in turn could create knights' feus to bestow upon supporters in return for military or other specialised services. For instance, in around 1136 Duncan, earl of Fife, obtained a charter to his earldom from David I, and proceeded to extend his landholding by royal favour. He and his kinsmen also took advantage of the opportunities in Moray, especially after the defeat of a rebellion there in 1187, and have been described as 'internal colonists'. Although Fife was regarded as the premier earldom of Scotland, this did not prevent its holders from taking advantage of feudal conventions, by which they both increased their own power and retained their place in society alongside Anglo-Norman incomers.[10] The earls of Fife were, however, probably not typical. They were unusually closely linked with the royal house by personal loyalty and marriage ties, and probably also by blood. It would be rash to assume that other native earls embraced feudalism with comparable enthusiasm, and although by the thirteenth century they had been brought into a strictly feudal relationship with the crown, and sometimes held land by knight service, it is doubtful whether they had entered into similar military obligations in respect of the earldoms themselves. Many of them sought to preserve a degree of independence, which might be reflected in marriage alliances with other native lords or even with magnates outside the realm; the lords of Galloway and the chieftains of the western seaboard certainly retained their freedom of action by such means.

Feudalism in Scotland was largely a lowland phenomenon. Although some knights' feus were established on the fringes of the highland zone, for example in the glens of Perthshire and (especially in the thirteenth century) in Easter Ross and Sutherland, much of the north and west remained a tribal society. Even if individual

[10] Barrow, *Anglo-Norman Era*, 85–7.

chieftains entered into feudal relationships with the crown, we must be cautious about assuming that patterns of landholding changed significantly in areas where ties of kinship remained of paramount importance. Surviving charters from Argyll and other parts of western Scotland are couched in feudal terminology, but this is inevitable when such was the very essence of this type of document, and a different type of military service was sometimes sought by the crown from the chiefs of the western seaboard. Robert I, whose authority in the west was arguably greater than that of any other medieval Scottish monarch, usually demanded a fixed number of birlings (galleys) of a specified capacity rather than knight service. In one sense this shows the flexibility of feudal arrangements, but it also demonstrates the very different lifestyle of western as opposed to eastern Scotland.

The military aspects of feudal tenure encouraged kings from David I onwards to use trusted followers to defend the often ill-defined frontier between the heartland of the realm and the peripheral areas which scarcely acknowledged royal authority. We have seen how the lands of dormant earldoms were granted to feudatories, and from a military standpoint this was especially important in Moray and further north. Freskin, for instance, received large estates from David I and Malcolm IV, while William the Lion's grant of the lordship of Garioch in Aberdeenshire to his brother David secured lines of communication to the north which were essential if the king was to launch military expeditions to Moray and Ross. In south-west Scotland also large lordships were bestowed on settlers, some of whom founded families (most notably Bruce and Stewart) which were to play a central role in subsequent Scottish history.

Strathclyde was, of course, a British kingdom. Its inhabitants spoke a version of Celtic most akin to Welsh, and its administrative divisions were similar to the cantrefs and commotes of medieval Wales. These territorial units were dictated by topography and were usually larger than the shires and thanages of eastern Scotland, which partly explains why a few favoured settlers received such extensive holdings. Military considerations were, however, even more significant. South-west Scotland, especially Annandale, Nithsdale and Ayrshire, contained an unusually large number of mottes, the normally artificial mounds topped by a timber fortification which were a characteristic feature of Norman expansion. Castles could be status symbols, but their original purpose was military, and the proliferation of them in the south-west suggests that this area was both dangerous and difficult to control. The powerful settlers who moved to the region clearly needed to provide for their own protection, but may also have been used by the crown forcibly to impose Anglo-Norman values, and thereby royal authority, on peripheral areas. Although some mottes, notably the Moreville stronghold at Borgue, were in Galloway proper, few have been discovered in the interior of the largely independent lordship, suggesting that the policy was one of containment and coastal settlement rather than of outright conquest by military might.

The king naturally seized any opportunity to increase his authority in the south-west. When Ralph son of Dunegal, lord of Nithsdale, died sometime after 1165 William the Lion was able to redistribute his lands to new families or on new terms to existing holders, a process which gave the crown closer control over the fortress and river-crossing at Dumfries, where a royal burgh and major administrative centre were established. But penetration to the west was not always easy, as is seen by the fact that William's brother David had only temporary possession of the earldom of Lennox, the upland area around Loch Lomond.[11] The king had presumably envisaged that David would establish an outpost of royal power; his failure to do so emphasises the continuing strength of the native lords of the old kingdom of Strathclyde.

When King Edgar died in 1107, he bequeathed much of southern Scotland to his younger brother David. David experienced some opposition from the new king Alexander I, but succeeded in securing his inheritance around 1113 with the assistance of forces supplied by Henry I. His area of influence included Strathclyde, and it is in this context that the grant of Annandale to Robert Bruce should be seen. The surviving charter was probably issued soon after David I succeeded to the throne in 1124, but Bruce may have been given lands in Annandale somewhat earlier, probably in order to act as a bulwark against potential incursions from Galloway.[12] There is other evidence that David was imposing his reforming ideas on

[11] *RRS*, ii, 257; there is no indication in the document itself that the grant of Lennox was intended to be temporary as implied in the editor's note.

[12] J. A. Green, 'David I and Henry I', *SHR*, 75 (1996), 12.

Strathclyde at this time. The establishment of an episcopal see at Glasgow probably dates from the second decade of the twelfth century, perhaps as a deliberate act on David's part to diminish the importance of the ancient church at Govan. It has been shown that Govan also had a court hill, suggestive of Norse influence, and was probably the administrative and ceremonial centre of the kingdom of Strathclyde up to the eleventh century. Leaving aside the controversy as to whether Strathclyde had an independent existence after the death of Owain the Bald, it seems that David deliberately turned his back on the past and based the ecclesiastical government of the huge diocese on a new centre.[13] In this context, it is surely conceivable that he established Bruce in Annandale before his accession to the throne, thereby using feudal lordship not only as a military expedient but also as a means of increasing the authority of the House of Canmore in an area which was still largely outside royal control. Edgar's bequest to David is in itself an indication that the area south of the Forth, especially the south-west, required more direct lordship than a king based in the old Pictish heartlands was able to provide.

The question of when feudalism reached Scotland is a controversial one. There is no doubt that numerous knights' feus were established during the reign of David I and that the process continued apace under his grandsons Malcolm IV and William the Lion. Evidence for feudalism before 1124 is slender. Malcolm III's foreign followers, wherever they originated and however numerous they may have been, were almost certainly household servants, and it is improbable that they were rewarded with lands under feudal tenure. Edgar and Alexander I, who both benefited from the support of the Norman kings of England, were surely aware of feudal conventions, and indeed acknowledged themselves to be vassals of William Rufus and Henry I. Whether they introduced settlers to southern Scotland and made grants of land to them in return for military service, as their brother David was to do, remains unclear. Much of what we know about Edgar concerns his activities in Lothian, most notably his devotion to St Cuthbert. He may have encouraged, or at least not actively discouraged, further English settlement north of the Tweed, but there is no evidence that he risked native hostility

[13] S. T. Driscoll, 'Church archaeology in Glasgow and the kingdom of Strathclyde', *IR*, 49 (1998), 95–114.

by introducing Frenchmen to Scotland beyond the Forth. Alexander I's kingdom had a more northerly focus, inevitably so in view of Edgar's bequest to David. It has been argued that Alexander, instead of relying on mercenaries for military support, built castles, for example at the strategically vital crossing of the Forth at Stirling, and created knights' feus in Scotland,[14] but we would expect to see the first signs of feudalism in the south and it is more cogent to regard David as the principal force behind the revolution in landholding.

Feudalism arrived in Scotland as a finished product. This is shown by the existence of feus which were held for a fraction of the service of a knight. Sometimes these came about because not enough land was available to endow a vassal with sufficient resources to support a knight, but in these cases a promise was usually made that the shortfall would be supplied at a later date. On other occasions it seems to have been envisaged that vassals would share their obligation to their superior lord, although sometimes this came about because of partition between heiresses. Lauderdale, for example, was probably originally held for the service of six knights, and Cunningham for two, because in 1296 Helen la Zouche, who held a sixth of the former Moreville lands, was said to owe one knight's service for her portion of Lauderdale and to hold her share of Irvine in Cunningham for the service of a third of a knight. In view of the fact that there was no equivalent in Scotland to the English levy of scutage, a payment in lieu of military service which may have encouraged an artificial fractionalisation of feudal obligations, there may be some territorial logic in the wide variety of fractions found in Scottish documents. However, the increasing cost of knighthood from the late twelfth century onwards must also have been a factor, and military obligations were frequently commuted into money payments or other service, or used as the basis for the rendering of aids to the king, practices which may have stimulated, and been stimulated by, the creation of units of various sizes. In any event, the system is sufficiently sophisticated to demonstrate that the ruling classes which participated in it were fully familiar with its conventions.[15]

It is important to assess the extent to which Scottish landholders also had interests outside the realm, for such interests might on

[14] G. W. S. Barrow, *Kingship and Unity: Scotland 1000–1306* (Edinburgh, 1989), 32.

[15] Barrow, *Anglo-Norman Era*, 131–5.

occasion influence their behaviour in Scotland. Barrow has argued that Scotland was a land of opportunity for younger sons with little prospect of advancement at home, and that Scottish kings discouraged their vassals from possessing estates in England or France since they did not want their leading subjects to be absentees; moreover, their military function, arguably the chief reason behind their recruitment, could not be adequately performed unless they both resided in Scotland and regarded service to its king as the predominant call on their loyalty. The importance of this last point is demonstrated by the letters written by thirteenth-century kings to excuse their subjects' service in respect of their English lands, as when in 1282 Alexander III asked Edward I to waive his demand for the earl of Buchan to join an expedition to Wales since the earl had been sent by the Scottish king to the far north of his realm.[16] The example of the Stewarts can be used to illustrate how younger members of a family often took greater risks than their elder siblings and might ultimately obtain greater rewards. The family originated in Brittany, where Alan son of Flaald served the bishops of Dol. His eldest son and his descendants inherited the family's modest estates; the second son took over many of the lands which Alan had obtained in England and was the progenitor of the great family which ultimately became earls of Arundel; but the youngest son, Walter, became David I's household steward, received a substantial lordship around Renfrew and lands in the Ayr valley and Tweeddale, and founded a family which in due course became the ruling dynasty of Scotland.[17]

While there can be little doubt that younger sons were often the most readily disposed to move to distant regions to seek their fortune, there is no neat pattern whereby families divided their landed possessions on the basis of boundaries between states. Holding land from more than one lord was not uncommon in feudal society, and problems arose only when his superiors' conflicting interests forced a vassal to choose between them. In the twelfth and thirteenth centuries there were lengthy periods of peace between the kings of England and Scotland, and some individuals

[16] *Foedera, Conventiones, Literae et Cuiuscunque Generis Acta Publica*, ed. T. Rymer (4 vols. in 7 parts, London, 1816–69), i, 610–11.

[17] This argument is given in full in Barrow, *Anglo-Norman Era*, ch. 1.

had major interests on both sides of the political border, even though distant estates could be hard to manage effectively. Division of lands could be a useful expedient in a time of crisis, but it was by no means an invariable rule, nor was Scotland attractive only to younger sons. When Robert Bruce received Annandale from David I, he was already lord of Brix in Normandy and Cleveland in Yorkshire and was the senior member of his family. His loyalty was put to the test when David launched a major expedition into England in 1138, and he formally severed his bond of fealty to the Scottish king, but his younger son Robert continued to adhere to David and duly succeeded his father in Annandale on the latter's death in 1142. In this case political considerations and an understandable desire to preserve the family estates led to a division of lands in the second generation, but the stability offered by the Scottish king contrasted sharply with the civil strife in England in Stephen's reign; even if David's actions caused the Bruces some consternation, others like Walter son of Alan may have been encouraged to strengthen their links with him.

The Moreville family also benefited from David I's largesse. Hugh de Moreville, constable of Scotland, was granted Lauderdale and Cunningham, and also held the lordship of Appleby in Westmorland. From 1135 to 1157 the Morevilles' main interests were in the dominions of the king of Scots, for during those years the whole of Cumbria was firmly under Scottish control, but when it reverted to English rule their estates straddled the political frontier. When William de Moreville died in 1196 his heir was his sister, who had married Roland, lord of Galloway. The family lands were therefore subsumed in the even more extensive territories of Roland, but he and his son Alan moved in the same social orbit as the Morevilles and likewise had extensive cross-border interests. By contrast, the Balliols, who in the second half of the thirteenth century fell heir to the lordship of Galloway and briefly held the throne of Scotland itself, were a family whose holdings had previously been predominantly in England, although in the 1140s Bernard de Balliol had accepted the political realities of David I's power in the northern counties. Such examples could be multiplied. Families with vested interests in more than one country were not uncommon, and although the desire not to break faith with one's lord could cause crises of conscience and impel families to split their holdings as a precaution, it was only the advent of a period of sustained Anglo-Scottish warfare in 1296 which finally caused the disintegration of collections of estates which had been accumulated, often through marriage rather than by direct royal grant, on both sides of the border. Even then it was several decades before some families relinquished their hopes of recovering lost lands.

The fact that many of the closest counsellors of the Scottish kings also had interests in England had a number of consequences. Because in the twelfth and thirteenth centuries estates could so readily be acquired on both sides of the border, the precise location of the political frontier was less significant, and therefore less contentious, than it might otherwise have been. Also, the dual loyalty which many magnates held inclined them towards upholding the peace between Scotland and England, as is seen for instance when war threatened in 1244. Within Scotland too, Anglo-Norman settlement probably had a harmonising effect, in that it brought different regions of Scotland into a relatively standardised pattern of landholding and thereby served to undermine the fierce particularisms which could be engendered by the ancient earldoms. Furthermore, because many of the settlers, at least initially, had close links with the crown and owed their lands to royal favour, they were more likely to be in attendance at court than the native earls and so acted as more effective conduits whereby the king's authority could be transmitted to the provinces. In that sense the establishment of feudal lordships increased the influence of the crown, but it also benefited the recipients of such lordships. By the late thirteenth century, for instance, the Stewarts not only held Renfrew and parts of Ayrshire, but also controlled Bute and much of Kintyre; from being a bastion of Anglo-Norman influence against the chieftains of the west coast they had become Highland chiefs themselves, with a fleet of galleys and many Gaelic-speaking dependants. The Comyns too had built up considerable political and territorial power, especially in northern Scotland, where branches of the family had obtained the earldoms of Buchan and briefly Menteith by marriage, as well as the great upland lordship of Badenoch by gift of Alexander II. Although these families remained loyal to the crown, their local and national influence emphasises the fact that effective royal power in Scotland throughout the Middle Ages depended on constructive relations between the king and his magnates rather than on bureaucratic centralisation.

Alongside the arrival of immigrants and the introduction of feudalism were a number of administrative and judicial developments. These are sometimes seen almost as consequences of feudalisation, as though they could not have existed independently. While it is undoubtedly true that many of David I's ideas on the nature of government, like his espousal of feudalism and his desire to reform the church, were derived from his experiences at Henry I's court, earlier kings must have possessed administrative machinery, even if it has left little trace in the sources, and it is likely that David built on these foundations. Moreover, David and his successors did not create an administrative edifice on the scale of Norman England; the Scottish kings did not need one because, unencumbered by continental territories, they tended to be resident in their realm.

We have seen how the crown possessed widely distributed areas of demesne governed by thanes. As well as renders from these districts, which were paid overwhelmingly in kind in what was still a virtually moneyless economy, the king had the right to certain levies, most notably cain and conveth. Cain was tribute due to a lord by virtue of his mere lordship, and was normally rendered every two or three years, although annual levies are not unknown. Conveth was the annual obligation to offer hospitality to one's lord and as a royal revenue was paid in respect of estates which were, or anciently had been, in the hands of the king. These ancient dues, which are found throughout the Celtic world and to some extent elsewhere, continued to be important, although cain became a less lucrative source of income by the thirteenth century because those who held land by military service were exempt from it, and so the area liable for cain was reduced as feudalisation became more widespread. In northern England cornage, which was similar to cain in that it was often paid every three years, was also normally not paid by military tenants, at least in the later twelfth century, so Scotland was not unique in this respect. William of Malmesbury asserts that David I exempted knights and barons from cain if they were prepared to accept a civilised, namely Anglo-Norman, way of life,[18] and the cancellation of this native due was surely used as an incentive to settle in Scotland, the crown presumably hoping to recoup any losses through feudal incidents such as relief and wardship.

From the twelfth century onwards the king also levied duties on ships carrying merchandise,[19] and so had an incentive to encourage trade. It is generally believed that there was an increase in the volume of trade throughout Europe at this period, and Scotland played a part, albeit a limited one, in this expansion. The introduction of coinage by David I was an important development, and until 1367 Scottish coins, as a matter of policy, were of the same weight and fineness as English ones. However, in the twelfth century transactions in cash must have remained unusual in most of Scotland, at least outside the burghs. A burgh was a privileged trading community, established by the king, though sometimes in the interest of a lay or ecclesiastical magnate, and considerable numbers were set up in the twelfth and thirteenth centuries, especially on the east coast. Some centres such as Perth and Stirling, situated at points where navigable rivers could be forded, were probably well established by the early twelfth century; others, like Inverness and Ayr, were created partly as a means of encouraging loyal subjects to settle in areas where royal authority was tenuous. David I's interest in burghs was doubtless fostered by his desire to realise at least some of his revenues in cash; he could exploit trade by establishing boundaries within which all goods for sale had to be presented to the burgh market, and then levying tolls on the produce. The establishment of a monopoly benefited the king as well as the merchants, for the collection of royal revenues was significantly eased by concentrating trade in a few specified centres. Nor were the king's emoluments restricted to trade, for in his burghs he also received rents from burgage tofts and tenements, the revenue from mills, and the profits of justice. It was only in the later Middle Ages, when many burghs were granted at feu-ferm for a fixed sum, that the king's direct interest in his towns diminished.

[18] William of Malmesbury, *De Gestis Regum Anglorum*, ed. W. Stubbs (2 vols., Rolls Series, 1887–9), ii, 477.

[19] *RRS*, i, 54; A. Stevenson, 'Trade with the south, 1070–1513', in M. Lynch, M. Spearman and G. Stell, eds., *The Scottish Medieval Town* (Edinburgh, 1988), 180–2.

Many early burghs developed in the shadow of royal castles, and often formed the administrative centres of sheriffdoms, through which the Scottish kings from the twelfth century onwards endeavoured to govern their realm. The sheriff was the principal local royal officer, with responsibility for raising military forces, collecting crown revenues, conducting inquests and assizes, and administering justice. His role in the twelfth century was closely modelled on that of his English equivalent, but the Scottish sheriff retained more of his original authority than his counterpart south of the border. This was partly because it was only at the end of the Middle Ages that Scotland developed a system of centralised courts, the establishment of which in England had served to diminish the sheriff's judicial role. For the same reason, the office of justiciar, which was also brought to Scotland in the twelfth century, continued to exist in its original form there much longer than in England. By the end of William the Lion's reign there is a degree of evidence for three justiciars, for Scotia (the area north of the Forth), Lothian and Galloway respectively, and sometimes deputies are attested. The justiciars made a circuit of the sheriffdoms which was known as an ayre, and theoretically visited each twice a year, hearing serious cases which were beyond the competence of the sheriffs and baronial courts, but their duties ranged much more widely than the judicial sphere and in many respects they acted as the crown's principal administrative officers. Most of the early references relate to Lothian, which may be a trick of the sources, although it could reflect the existence there of legal procedures familiar in England, such as the use of local juries of presentment to report crimes. Justiciars enjoyed higher status and wider powers than sheriffs, thanes and the native legal experts, termed *judices* in Latin documents, who existed in Scotland as elsewhere in the Celtic world. The office was thus normally held by a major magnate or at least by a baron of the first rank who could exercise authority effectively in a fundamentally conservative society; the Comyns, for instance, dominated the justiciarship of Scotia in the thirteenth century, a member of the family holding it for around two-thirds of the time. The first recorded justiciar of Galloway was Roland son of Uhtred, who may have been given judicial powers in the south-west in the hope that he would act as a royal agent as well as being lord of Galloway, although sometimes the justiciarship was granted to a powerful magnate in the simple realisation that he effectively controlled the area, and the level of Roland's subservience to the crown must be questioned; it is noteworthy that the next record of a justiciar in Galloway comes only in 1258, after the lordship had ceased to exist as a political entity. King William did, however, take a personal interest in law enforcement and the execution of justice, and perhaps as early as 1166 some offences, including homicide, rape and arson, had been reserved as 'pleas of the crown', to be impleaded before royal justiciars.

The establishment of sheriffs and justiciars in the twelfth century served to eclipse, though not to destroy, earlier administrative arrangements. Sheriffdoms were normally larger than the existing shires and thanages, but the boundaries of early sheriffdoms were usually natural and sometimes can be shown to be ancient, corresponding closely to older territorial divisions, and although some of the obligations enforced by sheriffs, such as castle-guard, may have been novel, many of the rents and services owed by the king's subjects were traditional and customary. It is perhaps appropriate, therefore, to see sheriffdoms as evolving from the existing shires rather than constituting a totally new development; at Berwick, Haddington, Linlithgow and Stirling, for instance, the old shire became the nucleus of a much larger administrative unit.[20] Moreover, the establishment of sheriffdoms was a very long process, and the arrangements remained fluid: in the early thirteenth century, for example, new sheriffdoms were created in Moray, presumably in the hope of establishing closer royal control over a still turbulent area. It was probably not until after Alexander II took control of Galloway in the mid-1230s that sheriffdoms were introduced there; John Balliol's attempt to appoint sheriffs on the western seaboard was thwarted by the Wars of Independence; even in the sixteenth century large areas of the north and west were effectively beyond the reach of royal officials. The significance of sheriffs, especially in the twelfth century, should not be overstated. Some who are designated as sheriffs in contemporary sources, such as Cospatric son of Uhtred of Roxburgh and Maeldomhnaich of Scone, were in fact managers of existing shires or thanages, many of which may have originated in Pictish times, and as we have seen it

[20] G. W. S. Barrow, *The Kingdom of the Scots: Government, Church and Society from the Eleventh to the Fourteenth Century* (London, 1973), 38.

was not until the fourteenth century that the crown dismantled this old system. In the field of justice, the native system of *judices* and mairs was not deliberately displaced but rather assimilated into the administrative structures of the new sheriffdoms: the *judex* became the dempster of the courts, and mairs performed executive duties by making arrests, serving summonses and carrying out judgements.[21] Again, continuity is the key feature.

The Norman Conquest of England had precipitated the establishment of a harsh and much hated forest law, under which large tracts of countryside were reserved for the hunting of game. Agricultural activity and wood-cutting in the forest were strictly controlled, and breaches of the regulations were severely punished. Forests on this model were also established in Scotland, probably from the 1130s onwards, but, perhaps surprisingly in view of the strong links which Scottish kings and barons had with England, the conditions were much less severe than south of the border. All royal forests in Scotland were created on estates in the king's hands, and their administration was much less rigorous than in England. In the twelfth and thirteenth centuries the offices of sheriff and forester were often combined, suggesting that the sheriff took responsibility for royal forests as for other crown demesne, although his necessarily part-time interest in the forest was presumably offset by the appointment of deputies. In due course many forests were reduced in extent so as to concentrate on the better hunting districts; this implies that the king's officials had found it impossible to uphold his rights effectively over larger areas, but it may also be connected with the growth in population and the consequent need to exploit the forests for agricultural purposes where appropriate. The reservation of large swathes of land for the sport of the king and his leading subjects could be directly at odds with economic imperatives, and there is evidence that in the thirteenth century the owners of forests, however reluctantly, came to recognise this.[22]

Many Scottish offices were hereditary, or at least became so. Walter son of Alan was the king's steward, hence the name of the family he founded. Under David I other household offices appear,

[21] H. L. MacQueen, 'Scots law under Alexander III', in N. H. Reid, ed., *Scotland in the Reign of Alexander III, 1249–1286* (Edinburgh, 1990), 82.

[22] See generally J. M. Gilbert, *Hunting and Hunting Reserves in Medieval Scotland* (Edinburgh, 1979).

such as the constable, butler and marischals. These were important posts, albeit soon to become largely honorific and ceremonial. More significant in terms of administrative development were the chamberlain, who was responsible for royal finances, and the chancellor, who was usually a senior cleric. In William the Lion's reign we can detect an increase in efficiency, with chamberlains' and sheriffs' accounts, greater professionalism in the royal chapel, and evidence from the 1190s that copies of documents were now being preserved. While the bureaucracy of the medieval Scottish state was never as extensive as that in England, the subsequent destruction of many of the records of central government should not cause us to diminish the modest, but nonetheless real, achievements of the clerks around the kings of the Canmore dynasty.

The success of Malcolm Canmore's sons, especially David I, in consolidating royal authority in Scotland was crucial to the survival of the dynasty. Rival claimants to the throne remained active, however, until well into the thirteenth century, and David was therefore determined to ensure the succession of his direct descendants. Before 1144, probably in the 1130s, his son Henry was formally designated as his successor and closely associated with David's acts as ruler, a practice followed in Capetian France but unusual in England, and after Henry's premature death in 1152 the earl of Fife took David's grandson Malcolm on a circuit of the kingdom in order to secure support for him. While Henry would have succeeded as an active and respected adult, Malcolm was only a child, and his acceptance as king has sometimes been seen as reflecting the maturity of Scottish politics, for the principle of primogeniture, though increasingly used for feudal holdings, still did not necessarily apply to kingdoms. In England, John succeeded to the throne in 1199 against the claims of Arthur of Brittany, who was the son of his elder brother, and there was no certainty that John himself would be succeeded by his son. The contemporary Scottish king William the Lion may have feared that his brother David might succeed instead of his son Alexander. David did homage to his young nephew only in 1205, although the other magnates had sworn fealty to him four years earlier,[23] and William's mysterious agreement with King John in 1212 may also

[23] *ES*, ii, 354, 365.

have had the purpose of ensuring the still youthful Alexander's untroubled succession. It is, therefore, unsurprising that David I went to such lengths to support the claim to the throne of his son and ultimately of his grandson, but Malcolm still faced opposition from native magnates for much of his twelve-year reign. It is scarcely remarkable that Malcolm was an ardent advocate of feudal settlement in Clydesdale, an area through which the troublesome chieftains of western Scotland could gain access to the heartland of his realm.

The succession of the seven-year-old Alexander III in 1249 was uncontested, although acceptance of the principle of primogeniture was easy in the absence of a viable alternative. The accession of a king who was so young meant that the work of government devolved on leading nobles and officials, and the minority of Alexander III was politically turbulent. Henry III of England also became involved in Scotland, nominally acting in the interests of his daughter, who married Alexander in 1251, and so it has suited some historians to draw a distinction between an 'English' party and a 'native' or 'patriotic' one. While it cannot seriously be questioned that the minority saw much squabbling between individuals and groups who were vying for political power and the opportunities for patronage which it presented, it is far too simplistic to define this scramble for position in emotive, nationalistic terms. It is more cogent to examine the period in terms of those who supported or opposed the Comyns, the most powerful family of thirteenth-century Scotland. Their chief opponent, Alan Durward, was prepared to invoke English assistance to further his political ambitions, but it seems to have been his supporters, rather than the Comyns, who opposed the levy of papal taxes in Scotland for Henry III's ill-starred attempt to conquer Sicily, and who petitioned the pope for permission to have Alexander III anointed. Both sides realised that the support, or at least the benevolent neutrality, of Henry III was essential for stability in Scotland during the minority, but amid the faction-fighting the machinery of government continued to function.

Alexander's adult reign has often been portrayed as a golden age, a period of further territorial consolidation and economic development during which the king was able to quell the discord which had arisen during the minority and impose his authority on fractious nobles, an interlude of internal and external peace which thereafter was to be shattered by the aggression of Edward I of England and the crisis of the Wars of Independence. Alexander's unexpected death in a fall from his horse in March 1286, leaving no direct male heir, could readily be seen as one of those rare events which radically change the course of history, and it is easy to understand how the myth soon developed of a prosperous reign cruelly cut short.

In reality Alexander III's reign was much less spectacular. There was certainly further consolidation of royal authority, the Western Isles were ceded by the Norwegian crown in 1266, and there is some evidence that the chieftains of the western seaboard were brought increasingly into the social and political structure of the Scottish realm, but none of these developments marked a major innovation in royal policy. Relations with England were generally smooth, and many of the internal threats to the Scottish crown, particularly in the north and Galloway, had disappeared. There is, therefore, some truth in the view that Alexander III's reign was an age of peace. Material prosperity is much more difficult to gauge, and while it is undeniable that conditions in Alexander's time were more favourable to commerce than they became after 1296, when much of Scotland suffered from the effects of military activity, the later thirteenth century was not without its economic problems. Historians of England are divided as to whether the sustained increase in population had brought about a situation by 1300 in which many were living at subsistence level, and Scotland has virtually no economic data on which to base an assessment, but poor harvests created real hardship. Bad weather in the summer of 1256 led to famine the following year, and the fifteenth-century chronicler Walter Bower mentions frequent food shortages and draws attention to 'sterility of the land'. Although Alexander III imposed duties on the export of wool and hides, which suggests considerable overseas trade in those commodities, the only specific evidence of material prosperity comes in a description of the wealth of Berwick in the mid-1260s. In economic terms Berwick was Scotland's principal burgh, well placed for cross-border commerce and for the arguably more important trade with the countries across the North Sea. It is unlikely that Berwick was typical of the country as a whole, and indeed the very fact that a chronicler draws specific attention to its opulence may indicate that it was unusual.[24]

[24] N. H. Reid, 'Alexander III: the historiography of a myth', in Reid, ed., *Scotland in the Reign of Alexander III*, 210 n.63.

Alexander III's success in quelling discord must also not be overstated. During the minority noble families had inevitably attempted to exploit the situation to their own advantage, and there was no sudden change when Alexander began to rule in his own right in 1260 other than that the magnates once again had to operate under the aegis of an adult monarch. Like his father, he ruled the north and south-west of his realm in close co-operation with his leading subjects such as the Murrays (descendants of the Fleming Freskin), the Stewarts and the Comyns; these men both displayed loyalty to the crown and had the authority locally to act as effective royal agents. Of the two families which contested the throne after Alexander's death, the Balliols appear in the king's circle only occasionally, while the Bruces concentrated largely on English affairs, at least until Robert (father of the future king) married the heiress to the earldom of Carrick around 1271. Internal stability and external peace contributed to good crown–magnate relations, and Alexander III continued to put his trust in well-established noble families.

Even if Alexander III's importance is downplayed, however, the Scotland of his day was very different from the country over which Malcolm Canmore had ruled. Malcolm had inherited a remote Celtic realm, albeit one which had acquired more than a foothold in English-speaking Lothian and could boast a line of kings who had been acknowledged, if sometimes grudgingly, as overlords of a considerable territory. By 1286 Scotland had seen an influx of immigrants of French origin, and had witnessed their absorption into Scottish society in a way that allowed continental ideas and social structures to become firmly established without displacing the older aristocracy, especially in the north. The introduction of feudalism had encouraged, and been encouraged by, Anglo-Norman settlement, and in its wake came castles and a more specialised knightly elite, but Scotland's defence in times of crisis still depended on the common army summoned by the earls and sheriffs. The twelfth-century kings had brought coinage to a hitherto moneyless realm, had encouraged commerce by establishing burghs, had developed the network of shires and thanages into the larger units of sheriffdoms, and had enhanced the institutions of royal justice. Alexander II and Alexander III had built on these foundations, defeated internal threats, and enjoyed generally peaceful relations with England. But the scale of the transformation must be kept in proportion. Much of Scotland was still Gaelic-speaking; kinship ties, especially (though not exclusively) in the Highlands, remained more important than feudal ones; large areas of the realm were still beyond the reach of royal sheriffs; outside the major burghs much trade was still localised and cash transactions a recent innovation; provincial loyalties remained strong. Much had been achieved, but Alexander III's death put it in jeopardy. The difficult years after 1286 were to test Scotland's credentials as a state and the Scots' identity as a people.

3

THE TRANSFORMATION OF THE SCOTTISH CHURCH

The late eleventh and twelfth centuries witnessed one of those periods of spiritual revival and renewal which have characterised the Christian era. Great churches were built to magnify the glory of God, and religious houses were founded in considerable numbers throughout Europe, many of them espousing new monastic rules which aimed to return their communities to a purer, more ascetic form of life and worship. The church also became more self-confident: successive popes and reforming bishops strove to reduce the influence of secular powers in ecclesiastical appointments and the control exercised by laymen over church property, and the papacy became an important player in its own right in the political controversies of the period. There was also a degree of reorganisation in the church's administrative structures, with dioceses being created and the parochial system becoming more widely and firmly established.

Scotland was not immune from these developments. The twelfth century saw the re-emergence of a diocesan structure throughout the realm and the establishment of several major monasteries, and through the efforts of reforming churchmen and their royal or lay patrons attempts were made to bring the practices of the Scottish church into line with the rest of western Christendom under the supervision of an increasingly active papacy. Even if two Scottish prelates who attended the Third Lateran Council in 1179 cut unimpressive figures,[1] there can be no doubt that by this date Scotland was very much part of the universal church. Much of the credit for the reforms has traditionally been given to David I or to his mother Margaret, who was canonised in around 1249 and thereby provided the Canmore dynasty with the political advantage of having a saint in the family. It is certainly true that Margaret was responsible for introducing to Scotland some of the ideas which were beginning to develop on the Continent, and David I and his Anglo-Norman followers undoubtedly took the lead in bringing representatives of the new monastic orders to the realm, but the reforms were probably less fundamental and widespread than has sometimes been supposed.

The history of the church in early medieval Scotland remains shrouded in mystery. It has left few material remains and little in the way of documentary evidence, in sharp contrast to the reformed church of the twelfth century and later. Because of Scotland's isolation, particularly when the Vikings occupied the northern and western coasts and controlled York, it was inevitable that the practices of the Scottish church would differ from those seen elsewhere. Some of these practices may well have horrified Queen Margaret, but deviations from the canonical norm did not in themselves mean that the native clergy were not performing an important role in the spiritual welfare of their people. There is even some evidence that Margaret supported certain traditional communities such as Loch Leven and Laurencekirk, although her supposed involvement with Iona must be questioned. Nor did the arrival of Margaret mark a turning-point in Scottish relations with the papacy. In 1050 MacBeth visited Rome and, we are told, scattered money like seed to the poor, while at around the same time Earl Thorfinn the Mighty of Orkney made a similar journey, during which he probably arranged for the establishment of a bishopric at Birsay which also exercised jurisdiction in Caithness. The archbishop of York had earlier sent a missionary bishop to Orkney, so the alleged isolation of the eleventh-century Scottish church was clearly not total. We therefore need to penetrate the

[1] *ES*, ii, 300.

fog of obscurity and misrepresentation in later and often hostile sources in order to assess the vitality of the Celtic church and the extent to which it was reformed in the twelfth century.

It is no longer believed that the diocesan structure of late medieval Scotland was created by David I, although it was in his reign that it took shape across the realm as a whole. With the possible exception of Caithness, the sees were based on existing foundations, although in many cases the sequence of bishops had been long interrupted, if there had indeed ever been a meaningful sequence at all. The bishops of the Celtic church were usually lower in status than the abbots of the great monasteries, and they did not preside over geographically definable dioceses akin to those which appear in Scotland from the twelfth century onwards. Although bishops are sometimes found in early sources with territorial designations, this does not mean that the place in question was established as an episcopal seat in the sense understood by David I and his contemporaries.

The ancient origin of some of the dioceses which emerged in the twelfth century is, however, betrayed by geographical and jurisdictional peculiarities which show that the reformers were unable to start with a clean sheet. Some dioceses, for instance Moray and Ross, were based on the provinces of the same name, and the close correlation between province and diocese is demonstrated by the fact that the bishops were given a provincial designation rather than being identified by the name of their cathedral city; in the case of Moray, indeed, it was only after several moves that the administrative and liturgical centre of the diocese came to be placed at Elgin. The large diocese of Glasgow was roughly coterminous with the old kingdom of Strathclyde, and shared its aspirations for territory in north-western England, at least until the creation of the English see of Carlisle in 1133. But the situation in eastern Scotland is much more complex, and there the bishoprics were based on a number of ancient religious centres. The diocese of St Andrews stretched from just south of Aberdeen to the English border, but contained within its geographical bounds those parishes which formed the diocese of Brechin and also scattered churches which pertained to Dunkeld and Dunblane. The diocese of Dunkeld was also huge until the see of Argyll was carved out of it towards the end of the twelfth century, and its outliers such as the island of Inchcolm in the Firth of Forth and two churches in Berwickshire were probably lands over which the now secularised abbey had enjoyed jurisdiction. Similar circumstances help to explain the geographical peculiarities of the small dioceses of Brechin and Dunblane, although it should be noted that comparable ancient centres such as Meigle, Abernethy and St Vigeans did not develop into episcopal sees. It is insufficient to suggest that the latter were hopelessly decayed by the twelfth century, because the possessions of St Vigeans were still sufficiently homogeneous to be granted to the abbey of Arbroath, which was founded only in 1178,[2] and Abernethy slowly evolved into a secular college. The bishops of Dunblane were often designated 'of Strathearn', and the earls of Strathearn were patrons of the see, so the diocese can be regarded as being of the territorial type, which helps to explain how it survived great poverty, a move to Dunblane from the older centre of Muthill, and the possibility (unrealised in the event) of a later translation to the abbey of Inchaffray. Why a bishopric developed at Brechin and not at other apparently similar places, however, remains something of a puzzle, although the twelfth-century diocesan restructuring may reflect a traditional fourfold division of southern Pictland;[3] if this is so, then it suggests a faithfulness to a very ancient system of political and ecclesiastical organisation. What the arrangements in eastern Scotland undoubtedly show is that the lands and privileges enjoyed by these venerable churches could not easily be set aside; the proprietary rights which they had built up in an undocumented period were upheld, even at the cost of creating a tangle of jurisdictions and great disparities between the wealth of individual dioceses. That surely points to the continuing vitality of such institutions, however secularised they may have become.

The recreation of a diocesan system was important to David I and his successors, not only because it brought Scotland into line with the rest of western Christendom, but because bishops could be valuable royal agents in distant parts of the realm. The role of the crown in the appointment of bishops is often overstated, especially after cathedral chapters had developed a sense of corporate purpose and pressed their canonical rights of election. In the twelfth and

[2] A. Macquarrie, 'Early Christian religious houses in Scotland: foundation and function', in J. Blair and R. Sharpe, eds., *Pastoral Care Before the Parish* (Leicester, 1992), 125.

[3] J. Bannerman, 'The Scottish takeover of Pictland and the relics of Columba', *IR*, 48 (1997), 32n.

thirteenth centuries, however, many bishops were effectively promoted by the crown or at least in accordance with the king's wishes, and some were even appointed in the royal court: for instance, both Jocelin of Glasgow in 1174 and Roger of St Andrews in 1189 were elected at Perth. Disputes nonetheless arose, and could be bitter and prolonged: one at St Andrews lasted from 1178 to 1188, and led to the temporary excommunication of the king by papal mandate. On other occasions the crown approached the pope for assistance, as in 1239 when Gregory IX refused to sanction the proposed translation of Bishop Geoffrey of Dunkeld to St Andrews, thereby allowing the election of David de Bernham, who was probably more acceptable to the king. Ecclesiastical strictures did not prevent the king from ensuring that many of his own candidates were appointed to bishoprics and thus able to spread royal influence throughout the realm, although royal involvement was probably most frequent in the wealthier and politically more important sees.

In the twelfth century the archbishop of York claimed jurisdiction over the Scottish bishops, asserting that his metropolitan province stretched throughout northern Britain. The kings of Scots, especially David I, endeavoured to circumvent the threat of clerical subjection to an authority outside the realm by persuading the pope to create a Scottish province with its own archbishop, presumably at St Andrews, which was seen as the premier see in Scotland. Such a request was in accord with that made by other small countries in the twelfth century. In the kingdom of Norway, for example, the see of Nidaros or Trondheim became metropolitan in 1153, with authority over the bishops of Orkney and those of Sodor or the Isles, a reflection of the fact that the Northern and Western Isles still pertained to the Norwegian crown. But the Scottish request was continually refused, perhaps because the popes were loath to antagonise the powerful kings of England, but also because, characteristically, the medieval papacy was reluctant definitively to set aside what might prove to be York's legitimate claims to jurisdiction. Until the 1160s successive popes formally upheld York's position, but the Scottish bishops managed to evade recognising the archbishop's authority, and so crucially he was unable to cite a specific occasion when any of the Scottish bishops, with the exception of those of Whithorn, had sworn unconditional allegiance. In the Middle Ages precedent was crucial, and in this case none could be found. When William the Lion was captured in 1174, he was forced by Henry II of England to accept, inter alia, that the Scottish church should show due obedience to its English counterpart, but an argument between the two English archbishops at a council at Northampton in January 1176 allowed the Scots to slip away without admitting their subjection. Later in the same year Pope Alexander III, angry that a secular prince should presume to determine matters which properly were the concern of the church, issued a bull, *Super anxietatibus*, which granted the Scottish bishops independence from York until the archbishop should prove his case. Some years later, possibly as early as 1189, the bull *Cum universi* declared that the Scottish church was to be a 'special daughter' of the papacy and that no foreigner could be a legate in Scotland unless he had been sent specially by the pope. It thus secured independence from York's metropolitan jurisdiction and thwarted the archbishop's attempts to intervene in Scotland in his capacity as papal legate in his province. The bull built upon earlier exemptions granted from 1175 onwards to Jocelin, bishop of Glasgow, the prelate who was most under threat from York because his diocese had once stretched into what was now northern England and because a series of eleventh-century suffragan bishops appointed by York were regarded there as bishops of Glasgow, even though their influence had probably been confined to the area south of the twelfth-century border.[4] Whithorn, however, was excluded from *Cum universi*, presumably because its bishops had sworn obedience to their English metropolitan and Bishop Christian had refused to attend a legatine council for the Scottish church in Edinburgh in 1177 on the grounds that his diocese was part of the province of York. It is likely that the archbishop of York had been the inspiration behind the re-establishment of a bishopric at Whithorn around 1128;[5] certainly he had secure grounds for claiming that it was part of his province, as it remained until the middle of the fourteenth century. The subsequent relationship between the other Scottish bishops and the pope was unusual, if not quite unique, and it prevailed until St Andrews was raised to the status of an archbishopric in 1472.

[4] N. F. Shead, 'The origins of the medieval diocese of Glasgow', *SHR*, 48 (1969), 220–5.

[5] R. D. Oram, 'In obedience and reverence: Whithorn and York, *c.* 1128–*c.* 1250', *IR*, 42 (1991), 89–90.

Because there was no archbishop to confirm the elections of bishops and consecrate them, *Cum universi* effectively made the pope the metropolitan of Scotland. In the thirteenth century, however, bishops rarely had to travel to the papal curia for confirmation. It was much more normal for the pope to commission a panel of Scottish prelates to examine the election and consecrate their new colleague, holding a fresh election in the event of any irregularity. This system was much less cumbersome and expensive than its later medieval equivalent of papal appointment to all bishoprics, and it seems to have worked efficiently, for it was fundamentally sensible to entrust the examination of episcopal elections to fellow-bishops in the locality.

The development of a diocesan structure had significant consequences for the organisation of the Scottish church. Within each diocese, archdeaconries and rural deaneries were established, providing further tiers of administrative and judicial control. The archdeacon was responsible for local ecclesiastical courts, and although he could exploit his office or use it merely as a source of income, archidiaconal jurisdiction was a significant means of upholding spiritual discipline. Most Scottish dioceses had only one archdeacon, although the larger ones such as Glasgow and St Andrews had two. Rural deans, usually referred to as deans of Christianity in Scottish sources, operated at a more local level. Most dioceses had several rural deaneries by the early thirteenth century, although the names attached to them do not appear consistently in the sources, and it is possible that their boundaries fluctuated. The dean of Christianity was responsible for convoking local synods, and acted as the representative of the clergy under his jurisdiction. The same period also saw the appearance of Officials, men who represented the bishop in his capacity as judge over those cases which were appealed to him from subordinate courts or fell to him directly on account of their serious nature.

The establishment and expansion of cathedral chapters was also a feature of the period. Cathedrals were major corporations in their own right, with widespread business interests and an elaborate liturgy, and the chapter had a role in electing a new bishop. In England several major cathedrals, including Canterbury, Winchester and Durham, had a monastic chapter; in other words a religious house controlled the cathedral church, often bitterly clashing with the bishop over matters of jurisdiction and exemption. In Scotland only two cathedrals were in the hands of the regulars, the Augustinians at St Andrews and the Premonstratensians at Whithorn. The remainder had secular chapters, although these were slow to develop in the more distant sees such as Argyll and Sodor, where a combination of poverty and conservatism inhibited the growth of the cathedral as an institution. Most Scottish secular cathedrals were closely modelled on their English counterparts, and some took their statutes directly from England; Glasgow, for example, used the constitution of Salisbury. The chapter usually consisted of four major dignitaries, namely the dean, chanter, chancellor and treasurer, who sometimes had designated deputies called subdean, subchanter and so forth, and a variable number of simple canons; archdeacons were normally also members of the chapter. Members derived income both from common funds, which were generally divided among those who were resident at the cathedral for a specified length of time each year, and from individual prebends. A prebend was a source of income attached to a particular canonry, usually consisting of the revenues of an annexed parish church, but sometimes a specified sum of money or other endowment, and the number of prebends in each cathedral increased over time. In Glasgow, for example, there were probably eight prebends at the end of the twelfth century, but twenty-three by 1401 and thirty-two by the Reformation, of which four were held by the dignitaries and two by the archdeacons.[6] Prebends varied in value, but they carried no pastoral responsibilities and so were, in contemporary language, sinecures. They could be held by clerks who were absent from the cathedral on a virtually permanent basis, and so were keenly sought by those churchmen with duties elsewhere, for example in royal service, for whom they provided a useful source of income. In the course of time, prebendaries were obliged to pay for a substitute in choir (a vicar-choral) and, if the prebend was based on a parochial living, a permanent vicar in that church, but the remaining revenues were theirs to keep. The dignitaries had administrative and liturgical functions within the cathedral, the chanter for instance regulating the music and the treasurer looking after the ornaments and finances, but even they were frequently absent for lengthy periods.

[6] I. B. Cowan, *The Medieval Church in Scotland*, ed. J. Kirk (Edinburgh, 1995), 84–6.

One of the more enduring legacies of the twelfth-century reform of the Scottish church was the foundation of monasteries, some of whose buildings survive to this day, albeit in a ruinous state, to provide a tangible link with the medieval world. In a period when the regular life was widely regarded as the highest of ideals, it was inevitable that those influenced by continental developments and unimpressed by the native monastic communities would seek to establish religious houses in Scotland. Utilising her links with the church of Canterbury, Queen Margaret founded a Benedictine priory at Dunfermline in Fife, but it was the new, reformed orders such as the Cistercians which made the greatest impact in Scotland in the twelfth century. The Cistercians' ideal of simplicity and self-sufficiency appealed both to potential recruits and to donors, and the order rapidly spread throughout Europe. Other French orders also made an impression in Scotland, especially the Tironensians, who were introduced to Selkirk in 1113 by the future David I and later moved to Kelso, the earliest establishment anywhere in Britain of one of the new orders. Communities of the reformed orders were normally founded from a mother-house, which retained a certain supervisory role. Several Scottish monasteries were offshoots of English houses, such as Melrose and Dundrennan, both founded from Rievaulx in Yorkshire, but orders like the Tironensians and Valliscaulians came to Scotland directly from France rather than via England. Moreover, the religious orders were international institutions, and their establishment in Scotland helped to bind the realm more closely to the other powers of Latin Christendom. Political borders were no handicap to monastic expansion, and many Scottish houses were granted lands in England by their benefactors, while Melrose had a daughter-house at Holm Cultram in Cumberland.

Although their broad estates gave monasteries a significant role in Scottish society as landowners and agricultural improvers, the spiritual impact of monasticism must not be overemphasised. While the foundation of religious houses was a significant feature of the twelfth- and thirteenth-century reform of the Scottish church, many orders eschewed pastoral work and other contact with the sinful world. The early Cistercians even refused to accept grants of churches and the teinds (the equivalent of English tithes) which went with them. This asceticism and zeal for isolation soon diminished, but monks and regular canons must be regarded as examples of an ideal religious life rather than as active evangelists of an ignorant and misguided people. Nor were monasteries founded evenly throughout Scotland. Most were in the south and east of the country, many in places where upland pastures provided resources for the sheep-farming which later made many houses extremely wealthy. Although the Galwegian lords, especially Fergus, were prominent in founding religious houses in their territory, most Scottish monasteries owed their origin and the bulk of their funding to the crown or Anglo-Norman immigrants or at least to those who had been strongly influenced by developments in England or France. Members of the family of Somerled, the 'king of the Isles' who died in 1164, founded the abbey of Saddell and priory of Ardchattan in Argyll, and were generous benefactors of the Cluniac house of Paisley, but the western seaboard remained largely devoid of religious houses in the later Middle Ages, and those which did exist were usually impoverished. Somerled himself, indeed, may well have been hostile to the new orders, for there is evidence that in 1164 he was endeavouring to revitalise the community of Iona on conservative lines, and his descendants continued to promote the interests of that ancient site as the premier monastic establishment in their sphere of influence.[7] The area which had seen the greatest flowering of the Columban church was thus the least affected by the new orders which came to Scotland in the twelfth century.

We must ask why so many prominent figures chose to found or endow religious houses. David I was so generous that he was later dubbed 'ane sair sanct for the Croune', and his example was followed by his successors and many of his greatest subjects, who bestowed lands, churches and rights on their favoured monasteries. In a single conveyance, Earl David of Huntingdon granted to his foundation at Lindores all the churches in Scotland which were in his patronage, along with two in England, together with certain lands, rights and the 'second tenth' from his revenues in the lordship of Garioch in Aberdeenshire. Was this simple munificence, or should we look for an ulterior motive? After all, in other contexts the same donors were jealous of their possessions and privileges, and

[7] R. A. McDonald, *The Kingdom of the Isles: Scotland's Western Seaboard, c. 1100–c. 1336* (East Linton, 1997), 205–6.

did not lightly surrender them, so it must be presumed that they expected some return on their investment. It is possible that some apparent donations were in fact outright sales of land couched in pious terminology, but there is no firm evidence for this in Scotland, and spiritual considerations are likely to have had a greater influence on the minds of benefactors. They felt that the lifestyle and ascetic zeal of the religious orders made them especially good intermediaries between mankind and God; in other words, the prayers of monks and canons-regular were deemed to be more efficacious than those of the secular clergy. The regulars could be expected, or even required, to pray for the souls of their benefactors and thus speed them through the pains of purgatory to the blessedness of heaven, and in the context of late medieval spirituality such benefits were worth paying a heavy price for. It is, therefore, unsurprising that those who could afford to establish or endow monasteries were eager to do so, and it can also readily be appreciated why some nobles chose to retire to monasteries and be laid to rest in the habit of the order. Not only did they end their lives free from secular cares, but they hoped that the purity of life in their chosen monastery could offer them tangible benefits in the next world as well.

The wave of new ideas which spread through much of Scotland in the twelfth century has tended to obscure evidence for the survival of older religious communities, but it is clear that some of the latter died hard. The community of *célidé* at St Andrews is one example.[8] In the middle of the twelfth century it was proposed that its endowments should be transferred to the Augustinian cathedral priory as individual members of the older community perished, but this proved impossible to put into practice, partly because bishops replaced the *célidé* with their own servants. The original house of *célidé* evolved into the secular college of St Mary on the Rock, and came to be filled by royal clerks and episcopal nominees who had no connection or sympathy with the Irish church, but there was no clean break with old traditions, and the successors of the *célidé* claimed a role in episcopal elections until at least the end of the thirteenth century, albeit as a secular chapter rivalling the Augustinians rather than because of any legitimate precedent set by the earlier *célidé*. In Brechin, the older community developed into the secular

[8] See generally Barrow, *Kingdom of the Scots*, ch. 7.

chapter of the cathedral, while Iona became a Benedictine abbey. Elsewhere, some religious houses were 'reformed' by the adoption of the Augustinian rule, which was sufficiently flexible to enable it to envelop a variety of different traditions. This phenomenon can be discerned throughout Europe, and Scottish examples include Loch Leven, Monymusk and Inchaffray, where some form of regular life appears to have continued, albeit on a small scale, before the houses were refounded under the aegis of the Augustinian order. How much or how rapidly the lifestyle of those communities changed cannot be established, but a gradual evolution is more likely than a sudden rejection of the past. The fact that Inchaffray and Monymusk were still functioning in an unreformed state around 1200 or even later is further evidence of the continuation of traditional practices through and beyond the twelfth century.

The thirteenth century witnessed the foundation and development of the orders of friars, inspired by the teaching and example of men like St Francis and St Dominic. Unlike monks, the friars were committed to operating in the secular world, even though they were based in convents. They were, at least in theory, sworn to poverty, and sustained themselves through the offerings of the faithful. They swiftly gained a reputation as preachers and teachers, and were often highly educated and fully involved in theological controversies. By the later Middle Ages the orders of friars were being bitterly criticised in literature and sermons throughout Europe, and Chaucer's *Canterbury Tales* give a good indication of the suspicion with which they were viewed. They were accused of extortion, of making false promises of salvation, and of undermining the functions of the parochial clergy. That they were so vehemently attacked is a measure of their success, both financially and in impressing the populace. Donations to the friars and a desire to benefit from their ministrations remained common throughout society right up to the Reformation, while the friars' learning and their enthusiasm for argument made them spirited opponents of orthodox clerics and potential reformers alike. Their appearance in the thirteenth century coincided with a dwindling level of enthusiasm among lay donors for enclosed monasticism, which was generally less austere than it had been a century earlier, and the transfer of munificence from the monks to the friars enabled the latter to establish firm footholds in most European states.

The friars' work and lifestyle meant that their convents were normally in towns. Scotland had few towns in the thirteenth century, despite it being a period of widespread economic prosperity. Berwick was the most important trading centre, and all four major orders of friars – the Dominicans, Franciscans, Augustinians and Carmelites – were established there before the Wars of Independence. Elsewhere in Scotland, however, progress was somewhat slower than in more urbanised parts of Europe, although friaries continued to be founded in Scotland throughout the remainder of the Middle Ages. Many houses were poorly endowed and make only fleeting appearances in the records, but this should not lead us to underestimate the impact of the friars on Scottish society. Some became bishops, including Clement of Dunblane as early as 1233, just three years after the friars' first appearance in Scotland. At a more fundamental level, the friars must have brought improved standards of preaching and learning to many Scottish burghs, and they remained a small but significant element in Scottish town life until the upheavals of the middle of the sixteenth century.

For all the importance which has often been attached to the regular clergy, the fundamental unit of ecclesiastical organisation in the later Middle Ages was indubitably the parish. The parish church was the focus of the spiritual life of the local community, and those who ministered there acted as a direct link between the faithful and God. Little is known about the establishment of the parochial system in Scotland, although most parish churches owed their origin either to episcopal foundation or to the initiative of laymen. The Anglo-Norman penetration of Scotland in the twelfth century had the effect of increasing lay control over the church, as many former church lands came to be held by the new feudatories, for example in Clydesdale. In Annandale, lands previously possessed by the bishops of Glasgow were confirmed to the second Robert Bruce in the latter half of David I's reign, and the bishops had difficulty in retaining the patronage of those churches which had previously been established on their old estates, while Bruce kept the right to appoint incumbents to newly erected churches.[9]

It was during David I's reign that the creation of parishes became deliberate policy. A royal assize made the exaction of teinds

[9] Cowan, *Medieval Church*, 6.

compulsory, so that a tenth of all produce now had to be rendered to the parish church, including corn, young animals, products such as cheese, and, where appropriate, fish. In the past, local churches had been supported by an allotment of land of varying extent, and possibly in some cases by other dues, but the decree that definite renders should be made to a particular church was novel in the Scottish context, and the levy of teinds from the estate on which the church was built made the parochial unit an important legal and territorial entity. In heavily feudalised areas there was a close correlation between the parish and the secular unit of the vill, as was inevitable when the parish church was itself founded by an Anglo-Norman lord.

In the more remote parts of Scotland there is little direct evidence for parochial organisation for much of the Middle Ages, and some parishes appear in the records only at the Reformation. While the parochial system had probably reached most parts of the realm by the end of the thirteenth century, arrangements in some areas doubtless remained fluid for a while after this. In Argyll and the Isles, for instance, many surviving ecclesiastical buildings were first erected in the twelfth or thirteenth centuries, no doubt reflecting the generosity of the descendants of Somerled and other leading laymen of the area, but the building of stone churches does not presuppose a full parochial system, as some places of worship probably began as chapels of mother-churches which had jurisdiction over a wide area and were comparable to Anglo-Saxon minsters and Welsh *clas* churches. A remote example of such a mother-church is Snizort on Skye, which possibly originally served the whole or most of the island, and on occasions functioned as the cathedral church of the diocese of Sodor. By the time of the Reformation there were twelve parish churches on Skye, but it is likely that most of them originated as chapels and gradually broke away from the mother-church. The precise chronology of these changes will never be known.

The existence of chapels or pendicles complicated parochial arrangements in Scotland. In parishes which were geographically extensive it was sensible to provide alternative places of worship which were more accessible than the parish church to sections of a scattered population. The establishment of such chapels, however, threatened the teind income of the incumbent of the parish church, and detailed regulations were normally drawn up in an attempt to prevent the chapel ever developing full parochial status. In some cases, however, the chapels were of considerable antiquity, and in such instances the rather rigid parochial structure of later medieval Scotland may have been at variance with traditional loyalties and practices. Nor was there ever a straightforward correlation between beneficed clergy and individual parishes: some churches had more than one incumbent, while in other cases, particularly in the far north and west, it was normal for a single priest to serve more than one parish simultaneously. In such a system chapels, whether ancient or newly founded, fitted often uneasily into administrative arrangements which were sometimes much clearer in legal theory than in practice.

In its simplest form, each parish church was held by a rector or parson (the terms are synonymous), who was instituted by the diocesan bishop following nomination by the lawful patron of the benefice. The rector had security of tenure and enjoyed the right to receive the teind revenues derived from his parish. Scotland, however, never had a fully developed system of independent parsonages, because from a very early stage some of the revenues were diverted to cathedrals, monasteries and other institutions, by the process known as appropriation. In the twelfth and thirteenth centuries many lay lords granted the patronage of churches to newly established religious houses, and in due course most such monasteries sought leave to annex to themselves the revenues which would normally have gone to the rector. The appropriating corporation thereby legally became the rector, and the pastoral work in the parish was entrusted to a deputy, often a stipendiary chaplain appointed and removed at will. The Fourth Lateran Council of 1215 laid down that, where the rector could not reside, a perpetual vicar should be canonically instituted, enjoying secure tenure and a portion of the revenues of the church. In the wake of this conciliar decree large numbers of vicarages were established in appropriated churches, although the system had been evolving for many years before 1215 and was never fully effected even in the thirteenth century. The arrangements for vicarages varied widely. A basic principle was that the rector would receive the teinds of corn and the vicar the remaining revenues, but only rarely was the division of the fruits as simple as this. Appropriators sought to minimise the emoluments of vicars, and in many instances were successful in this aim, but numerous lawsuits ensued.

In Scotland the number of appropriations was abnormally high. By the time of the Reformation, 86 per cent of parishes had their parsonage revenues diverted to some other individual or corporation, and of these appropriated parishes 56 per cent had their vicarage revenues annexed as well. The practice was common even in areas which had few religious houses: in the northern dioceses of Ross, Caithness and Orkney every church came to be held by the bishop or cathedral chapter or provided income for prebendaries. Many annexed churches were served by ill-paid pensionary vicars, whose stipends were eroded by inflation and who were therefore encouraged to be rapacious in demanding mortuaries and other fees from their parishioners. The situation in the so-called 'free parsonages' was little better, because many of the rectors were habitually absent and likewise delegated their responsibility to underpaid chaplains. In the long run, therefore, the enthusiasm with which religious houses and cathedrals annexed the revenues of parish churches had serious effects on pastoral care, but it was justified by the appropriators on the grounds that they required increased income for the maintenance of their houses for the greater glory of God.

The delineation of parish boundaries inevitably sparked off a number of disputes, often concerning areas of marginal land. Where monasteries had appropriated the parishes in question, such disputes were frequently prolonged because corporations did not perish like individual litigants. The fervour with which religious houses pursued their claims to teinds and other rights sheds unfavourable light on the communities' supposed espousal of poverty and simplicity, but monasteries could justify their litigiousness on the grounds that they needed to ensure that their benefactors' wishes were being upheld. Also, records of litigation were more likely to be preserved than evidence of spiritual life, so the sources give only a partial, and sometimes misleading, picture. Nor should it be supposed that the regulars were the only ones to argue about revenues; it is just more likely that their archives have survived than those of the secular clergy and laymen.

Most lawsuits over teinds and other possessions ended in compromise, either through a division of the disputed revenues or by the promise of one of the parties to pay the other an annual pension in return for the surrender of its claims. Some suits were settled by agreement between the parties, others by arbitration, relatively few by formal judgement. Even where one of the parties emerged victorious, it was often difficult to put the sentence into effect, and so a compromise acceptable to both sides was the preferred solution. Litigation was thus often employed as a means of helping to bring the matter to a conclusion rather than as a final resort to be pursued at all costs, but it is through the records of litigation that we can most easily understand the nature of such disputes.

Many examples can be furnished of litigation between two monasteries over teinds. For instance, the Premonstratensian canons of Dryburgh appealed to the pope against the priory of May, claiming that the monks of May had deprived them of teinds belonging to their appropriated church of Kilrenny in Fife, and in August 1223 Pope Honorius III appointed three Scottish ecclesiastics to hear the case and pronounce judgement. In the judges' presence, Dryburgh alleged that boats mooring in the narrow stream which formed the boundary between the parishes of Kilrenny and Anstruther encroached on the bounds of Kilrenny parish, which extended to the middle of the channel, because they fixed their anchors within the bounds of that parish and remained there overnight. Dryburgh therefore alleged that half of the teinds of all the boats mooring there ought by right to pertain to Kilrenny, yet the monks of May received the whole amount in their capacity as appropriators of Anstruther. The suit continued for some time, but was eventually brought to an end by the judges with the assent of both parties. The monks of May would henceforth pay one silver merk annually, and in return would be free from future molestation from Dryburgh over the teinds, except that the canons would fully take teinds from those who attended the parish church of Kilrenny, dwelt in that parish and moored to that part of the shore. The monks of May were to receive the remaining teinds in full. This compromise was confirmed by the judges in December 1225 by the papal authority vested in them, and corroborated by the seals of the parties and of the abbot of Reading, since May was a dependency of that English house.[10]

[10] *Dryb. Lib.*, 137–8.

The appointment of papal judges-delegate, as in this example, was in fact the normal response of the pope to an appeal, and the practice had a number of advantages. Firstly, it was inherently sensible for the investigation to be undertaken by clerical judges who were aware of local conditions if not of the actual circumstances surrounding the case, and the strict rules which governed the maximum distance that defendants could be made to travel prevented parties from incurring expenses on the scale which a journey to Rome would have necessitated. Secondly, the judges often had a vested interest in restoring and maintaining harmony between their colleagues and neighbours, which must have inclined them towards seeking a compromise which both parties would find acceptable. Thirdly, the system suited those litigants who had possessions in more than one diocese or enjoyed exemption from episcopal authority and would have been afraid of setting an unfortunate precedent if they had approached the local bishop. Finally, although the plaintiffs normally chose the panel, there is no evidence that it tended to be biased in their favour, for papal justice had a reputation for being impartial and fresh appeals to the pope were always possible. Judges-delegate provided one of the most significant points of contact between Scotland and the papacy in the thirteenth century, and the fact that even some laymen had resort to them indicates the effectiveness of this form of justice.

Monasteries and other ecclesiastical corporations also had recourse to the pope when they sought apostolic confirmation of the grants and privileges which they had received. Sometimes the ensuing papal bull covered all the possessions of the house in question, as in the confirmations granted to St Andrews priory by successive pontiffs from 1144 onwards.[11] On other occasions a particular transaction or agreement was given papal corroboration: for example, the right of Dunfermline abbey to appropriate the churches of Hailes and Kinglassie was confirmed in January 1226.[12] Religious houses also asked the pope to bestow special favours on them: in 1289, for instance, Nicholas IV permitted the monks of Lindores to wear caps as a protection against the cold,[13] a concession which was doubtless appreciated by those who lived through

[11] There were six such confirmations in the twelfth century alone: R. Somerville, *Scotia Pontificia* (Oxford, 1982), nos. 25, 28, 37, 50, 119, 148.

[12] *Vet. Mon.*, 23.

[13] Ibid., 141–2.

the enforced austerity of a Scottish winter. Such contacts between monasteries and the papacy must not, however, be taken out of context, for religious houses understandably sought confirmation of their rights from all relevant authorities, lay and ecclesiastical, and their cartularies contain numerous royal and episcopal charters of confirmation as well as papal bulls, as houses sought to ward off any subsequent challenge by seeking the approval of the supreme powers in both church and state.

At the level of high politics too, contact between the papacy and Scotland became more frequent. We have seen how David I sought the establishment of a metropolitan see at St Andrews, and how the Scottish bishops achieved independence from York under the terms of *Cum universi*. In the thirteenth century Scottish kings endeavoured to obtain papal approval to be crowned and anointed, a mark of regal status which, if granted, would have undermined the claims of the king of England to feudal suzerainty. Attempts to secure papal permission for a coronation all failed, partly because successive popes were reluctant to make a decision on so politically sensitive an issue, and partly because of the unprecedented interest which the papacy had in the internal affairs of England following King John's submission to Innocent III in 1213. Papal backing was a significant factor in ensuring the succession of the young Henry III in 1216, and the continuing gratitude of Henry towards the Apostolic See was a notable feature of his long reign. It is not surprising that papal legates based in England pursued policies which were sometimes directly opposed to the political ambitions of Alexander II and Alexander III.

This was most apparent during the legation of Guala, who in 1216 laid Scotland under interdict in response to Alexander II's armed support for the opponents of John and Henry III. An interdict aimed to bring recalcitrant rulers to heel by banning normal church services, and was a sanction which was used, or at least threatened, with considerable frequency in this period. In this case, Guala displayed a degree of vindictiveness towards the Scottish clergy and the king's adherents which clearly demonstrated his pro-English attitude; in the fifteenth century the chronicler Walter Bower was to remark that he 'had to such an extent become an Englishman that it was as if he had been born in England'.[14]

[14] *Chron. Bower*, v, 133.

Subsequent legates were more circumspect, but tensions nonetheless remained. The bull *Cum universi* had laid down that no legate could serve in Scotland unless he was himself Scottish or had been sent specially by the Apostolic See. It did not prevent the appointment of a legate *a latere*, that is one nominated directly by the pope, but the Scottish government was often understandably reluctant to accept a legate who also had a commission for England, and Honorius III recognised this both by confirming *Cum universi* in November 1218 and by appointing his chaplain James as legate to Scotland in July 1220. There is some evidence, admittedly problematic, that Alexander II resisted the visit of Otto to his realm in the autumn of 1239, even though the legate had a separate commission specifically for Scotland, and Cardinal Ottobuono, who in 1265 was appointed legate to the whole of the British Isles, never entered Scotland, apparently because the king opposed his mission.

While some legates visited the British Isles for political reasons, most twelfth- and thirteenth-century missions were intended to institute reforms in local churches and were therefore part of the process whereby the papacy attempted to standardise ecclesiastical practices throughout Christendom. For example, in 1201 John of Salerno, like several of his predecessors and successors legate to Ireland as well as Scotland, suspended from office priests who had been ordained on a Sunday.[15] Thirteenth-century legates were frequently entrusted with the task of enforcing the reforms laid down by the Fourth Lateran Council of 1215, which had been attended in person by at least three Scottish bishops and the abbot of Kelso, with other prelates sending representatives. The Council decreed a wide range of measures designed to improve the quality of the clergy and end canonical irregularities, but the extent to which these reforms were effective is hard to assess. In the 1240s Bishop David de Bernham of St Andrews is known to have dedicated 140 churches,[16] which points to a desire on his part to ensure that the places of worship in his diocese had been properly consecrated, but we have no means of determining whether in this respect he was typical or unusual among the prelates of his day. When Honorius III instructed the Scottish bishops in 1225 to hold a provincial council, he clearly hoped that they would act to uphold the Lateran

[15] Ibid., iv, 429. [16] *ES*, ii, 520–6.

Council's statutes, but in many countries extra stimulus from papal legates seems to have been required. In England, the statutes of Otto and Ottobuono remained influential for the remainder of the Middle Ages, but it is unlikely that either legate had much lasting impact in Scotland. Otto's activities there appear to have been on a lesser scale than those of the papal chaplain James in 1221, which suggests that legates who were sent specifically to Scotland had a better chance of success than those who could be regarded as having had a Scottish commission tagged on to a visit to England. James certainly received a number of requests for assistance in his capacity as a direct representative of the pope's authority, including a request from Alexander II for coronation. The canons of Dryburgh abbey took advantage of his visit to settle several issues relating to the church of Gullane in East Lothian, and for good measure they also obtained from the legate a general confirmation of all their possessions.[17]

One of the most controversial consequences of the increasingly close links between Scotland and the papacy was the imposition of papal taxation. In the late twelfth and thirteenth centuries the Apostolic See frequently ordered ecclesiastics to pay a proportion of their incomes, such as a twentieth or a tenth, to help fund fresh crusades to the east to aid the now beleaguered settlements in the Holy Land which had been set up in the wake of the triumph of the First Crusade in 1099. These papal income taxes were levied throughout western Christendom, and necessitated widespread assessments of clerical wealth which, like all valuations for taxation, caused considerable resentment. However, collection was especially difficult in Scotland, partly because relatively few Scots were directly involved in the crusades, but more especially because of the fear that the money raised would be appropriated by the English king.

This fear was justified. When it came to crusading taxation, English monarchs regarded the Scottish church as a mere appendage of its English counterpart, despite the terms of *Cum universi*, and successive kings of Scots were concerned that the precedent of the king of England taxing the Scottish clergy might be used to justify a similarly subservient relationship in the secular sphere also. From the standpoint of the papacy, however, the administrative

[17] *CPL*, i, 83; *Dryb. Lib.*, 15–16, 17–19, 23–5, 171–3.

convenience of entrusting levies in Scotland to a collector based in England outweighed the political disadvantages, and the revenues were diverted to the English king only because there was a realistic prospect of him using the money to prepare for participation in a crusade. The Scots naturally saw the situation in a somewhat different light. They tried to resist Henry III's attempts during Alexander III's minority to raise taxes for his proposed crusade and his far-fetched plan to conquer the kingdom of Sicily under papal auspices, and this experience may well explain the later reluctance to allow the legate Ottobuono to enter Scotland, since he was seeking a triennial tenth for Henry III as well as procurations, sums which were levied on local churches for the expenses of papal agents and which always led to allegations of greed. Alexander III also impeded the collection of the tenth imposed by the Second Council of Lyons in 1274 because Edward I had been granted the proceeds, although opposition to the export of the money raised collapsed after the king's death in 1286. With the benefit of hindsight we can fully appreciate Alexander's reservations, but Edward did have a reputation as a crusader, and there had been a substantial Scottish contingent on his expedition in 1270–2, while others had joined Louis IX of France in his ill-fated attack on Tunis.[18] The difficulty lay in the fact that secular rulers often justified the use of crusading taxes for other purposes on the grounds that local problems had to be solved before they could leave their realm, and Edward I was not slow to claim such justification.

The impression that relations between Scotland and the papacy were dominated by politics, litigation and finance is not an entirely false one, although we must not underestimate the papacy's role in bringing church reform to Scotland. Our problem, as so often, is lack of source material. In the thirteenth century attempts were made to establish a series of synods involving representatives of the whole of the Scottish church, the equivalent of provincial synods elsewhere except that there was no Scottish archbishop to summon and preside over them. Such synodal statutes as survive, together with the pronouncements of papal legates, indicate that there was an awareness of canonical irregularities in the practices of the Scottish church and of misconceptions on the part of the faithful,

[18] A. Macquarrie, *Scotland and the Crusades, 1095–1560* (Edinburgh, 1985), 56–63.

but it is impossible to quantify these or assess their significance to spiritual life in Scotland. Repeated injunctions normally imply that the measures had been ineffective, and it would probably be fair to say that reform was slow to spread throughout Scotland. In the fourteenth century, for instance, there were numerous allegations by claimants to benefices that the current incumbent or one of his predecessors had not been ordained to the priesthood within a year of obtaining possession of the living. These claims cannot be checked, because there are no surviving lists of ordinands for any Scottish see, but there were significantly more such allegations in Scotland than in England, and in at least one English example there is every reason to believe that the claimant was telling the truth. It seems likely, therefore, that there was some veracity in at least a proportion of the allegations that men were holding benefices without having been fully ordained, which points to a rather casual attitude towards the niceties of canon law. Some of the clerks were said to have held their benefices for many years without due promotion, but they surely administered the sacraments during this period. Technically, they performed priestly functions without formally being ordained as priests, but it must be doubted that their flocks knew this or cared. Such laxity in abiding by the rules was apt to horrify reformers, but we must ask whether, in practical terms, it had as adverse an effect on the lives of parishioners as, for example, pluralism and non-residence, practices which the papacy often excused even if it did not actively encourage them.

Evidence for the educational standard of churchmen in the Middle Ages is elusive. There were presumably some local schools, mainly attached to monasteries or cathedrals, but there was no university in Scotland until St Andrews was founded in 1410. Scots ambitious for a university education had, therefore, to travel abroad, to Oxford or Cambridge or overseas, this last option being generally preferred after the outbreak of hostilities between Scotland and England at the end of the thirteenth century. The international connections made by these men helped to consolidate Scotland's place on the wider European stage, and allowed new ideas to enter Scotland through its educated elite. But it was an elite, and inevitably a small one. There were certainly not enough graduates to transform the educational standards even of the beneficed clergy, let alone the unquantifiable mass of ill-paid stipendiary chaplains and other members of the clerical proletariat. It has been calculated that out of about 1,100 parochial livings in Scotland, fewer than 300 had a university-educated man as an incumbent at any point during the thirteenth and fourteenth centuries, and even the favoured parishes did not necessarily actually benefit from the personal presence of a graduate who might easily find more lucrative openings for his talents in the service of the king, a noble or a bishop.[19] We must assume that most churches continued to be served by men of limited education and possibly of limited general ability. Most were probably drawn from a relatively local area and some no doubt shared in the disputes of their kinsfolk and partook of the activities of their home villages. Realistically they cannot have transcended the bounds of their own experience, but through the sacraments which they celebrated they could offer their flocks the means of grace, and help them to feel that they were members of a great Christian family which stretched far beyond the limited horizons of parish life.

This chapter has sought to outline the ways in which the Scottish church was transformed between the middle of the eleventh century and the end of the thirteenth. There can be no doubt that the ecclesiastical institutions of Scotland in 1300 were very different from those of two centuries earlier. There was a diocesan structure which reached the furthest parts of the realm, and a widely established system of parishes. Many monasteries had been founded, and the friars had brought their own version of spiritual renewal. Close links with the papacy had been forged and consolidated. In short, although the claims of York to metropolitan jurisdiction had been rebutted, Scotland was very much part of the universal church and offered a home to most of the great international religious orders. These achievements, considerable though they were, must not, however, be exaggerated, for many of the changes were on an institutional rather than a pastoral level. The spiritual requirements of the Scottish people probably differed little from the days of the Celtic churches, and many of the practices of both institutional and popular religion may have changed less between 1050 and 1300 than reformers such as Queen Margaret and her sons might have wished.

[19] D. E. R. Watt, 'Scottish university men of the thirteenth and fourteenth centuries', in T. C. Smout, ed., *Scotland and Europe, 1200–1850* (Edinburgh, 1986), 10.

Religious practice is often intensely conservative, especially in predominantly rural societies, and in medieval Scotland much of it was doubtless steeped in superstition and had its roots in a pre-Christian past. The parish clergy, who were in the most immediate contact with the common people, were often insufficiently well educated to attempt to change the outlook of their flock, even if they had wanted to. Popular adherence to holy sites and the ancient communities which served them is implied by the long survival of such communities and the distinct peculiarities of the ecclesiastical map of late medieval Scotland. The transformation of the Scottish church was, therefore, by no means total, and the reformers were unable to obliterate all traces of the Columban, Ninianic and Pictish brands of Christianity which had long held sway in Scotland.

4

THE CONSOLIDATION OF THE SCOTTISH REALM

The development of the Scottish state cannot be explained solely in terms of institutional and ecclesiastical changes, but must be viewed also from the standpoint of the kings' relations both with external powers such as England and Norway and with semi-independent potentates within the frontiers of the realm itself. Around 1100 large parts of Scotland were effectively beyond the authority of the king, and the incorporation of Moray, Ross, Argyll and Galloway, and ultimately of the Hebrides, was to be a major theme of Scottish history well into the thirteenth century, although control of the more peripheral regions was frequently elusive even into the early modern period. Consolidation of their own position within Scotland, and of Scotland's status in the wider European world, were complementary objectives of the kings of the Canmore dynasty.

The notion that England and Scotland were continuously at war during the Middle Ages is deeply embedded in popular consciousness. In the period before the Wars of Independence, however, relations between the two states were often peaceful, a point which is emphasised by the relatively small number of castles in the frontier regions. This was partly a result of frequent marriages between members of the respective royal lines, but more especially because king and barons alike belonged to an international aristocracy, where relationships were determined by feudal bonds. It was directly contrary to the interests of those twelfth- and thirteenth-century magnates who held land on both sides of the border to allow the rulers of England and Scotland to enter into a conflict in which the barons would forfeit their estates in the realm of the king whom they chose not to support.

Relations were, nonetheless, sometimes strained. As the kings of both Scotland and England sought to consolidate their territories, the issue of the location of the border became increasingly important. The kings of Strathclyde had claimed territory south of the Solway, traditionally as far as the Rere Cross on Stainmore and the river Duddon, although this frontier is not meaningful earlier than the tenth century and may not have been tenable in the eleventh. The area was certainly under Northumbrian control in MacBeth's reign, but Malcolm III may have recovered it and held it as late as 1092, when the English king William Rufus built a castle at Carlisle, and twelfth-century Scottish monarchs were heirs to these claims. In the east, conversely, the English kingdom of Northumbria had once stretched to the Forth, and there remained a cultural and linguistic unity which straddled the political border between England and Scotland as it developed in the eleventh and twelfth centuries. The Scottish kings, having securely incorporated Lothian, sought to extend their influence southwards to the Tyne or even the Tees, either through annexing these territories to their realm or, more realistically, holding the northern counties as a vassal of the English crown. Their ambitions were enhanced by David I's marriage to Matilda, daughter of Earl Waltheof of Northumbria, but were consistent with the policy of earlier kings of Scots and involved seeking not only an expansion of the Scottish sphere of influence, but also the security of a buffer-zone against possible future English aggression, for Lothian (as its inhabitants were to find on numerous occasions) was very vulnerable to English armies advancing along the east coast of Northumberland. The English too had a vested interest in a secure northern border, particularly when their kings were occupied with their lands in France, but tensions on the frontier could easily erupt into violence.

Another contentious issue was the feudal relationship between the two kings. Scottish monarchs were willing to pay homage to their English counterparts in respect of lands they held in England, whether in the northern counties or in the English Midlands, where David I had been granted the earldom of Huntingdon around

Christmas 1113 on his marriage to Matilda. Despite the fact that Matilda had sons by her first marriage to Simon de Senlis, David's descendants were to hold this honour, which had been another part of Earl Waltheof's territories, until the fourteenth century, although tenure was not continuous and the male line of earls died out in 1237. Performing homage for such lands did not necessarily imply that the kingdom of Scotland itself was a fief of the English crown, any more than the swearing of homage by English kings in respect of their French lands meant that the realm of England was feudally subject to the king of France. The very act of homage, a public symbol of a feudal relationship, could, however, send a strong signal as to the relative status of the individuals involved. It suited English commentators to portray the kings of Scots as vassals in respect of Scotland as well as of their estates south of the border, although the Scots inevitably saw the relationship in very different terms.

The outlook of Anglo-Norman chroniclers was naturally shaped by the types of feudal relationship which characterised the society in and for which they wrote. They therefore seized on incidents, some perhaps apocryphal, when a Scottish ruler had acknowledged the superiority of one of the Anglo-Saxon monarchs. The most famous such event took place in 973, when Edgar was reputedly rowed across the river Dee at Chester by a number of other kings, including Kenneth II of Scotland. This can be interpreted as one of a series of negotiations over frontiers, comparable to those held by Constantine II with the English kings Edward the Elder in 920 and Athelstan in 927; on this view of events, Edgar recognised Kenneth's occupation of Lothian in return for peace. However, Kenneth may still have acknowledged Edgar as an 'over-king' in line with the common practice of early medieval Britain. What is certain is that he did not enter into a feudal relationship in the Norman sense of the word. In implying that he did, the chroniclers are guilty of a serious anachronism.

In 1018 Malcolm II defeated the levies of the area between the Tees and the Tweed at Carham, after which Earl Eadulf of Northumbria seemingly conceded Scottish possession of Lothian. Inconsistencies in the sources have spawned much debate, especially because the accounts imply that the Scots had recently lost control of at least part of Lothian, perhaps in 1006 when Malcolm was heavily defeated in an attack on Durham. Although it is possible to reject altogether the tale of an invasion in that year and argue that Lothian had been securely under Scottish control since well before 973, the victory at Carham clearly impressed contemporaries and it is surely reasonable to postulate that Malcolm had launched some earlier expeditions southwards and sometimes met with reverses. It is in this context of thrust and counter-thrust, often obscured by the exiguous surviving evidence, that we must view Duncan I's abortive siege of Durham in 1040, the expeditions against MacBeth by Earl Siward of Northumbria, and the career of Malcolm III.

Several of Malcolm III's incursions into northern England can be regarded as expeditions in favour of the Anglo-Saxon opposition to William the Conqueror and his sons, deriving from his marriage into the old English royal house, but they can equally readily be seen as a continuation of the old policy of expansion southwards at the expense of an English king whose primary interests often lay elsewhere. Malcolm's campaigns were portrayed, at least by their victims, as needlessly bloodthirsty, and they were far from successful. In 1072 William drove the Scottish king back as far as Abernethy on the southern shore of the Tay, right in the heart of his realm, and forced him to become his man and give his son Duncan as a hostage. This was later taken as evidence of the feudal subjection of the Scottish monarchs to their English counterparts, and there can be little doubt that William saw it in this light, but no reason to suppose that Malcolm chose to interpret his submission in such terms. He certainly paid little heed to his supposed obligations, and launched several more savage raids into Northumberland. In 1080 he faced a counter-invasion by the Conqueror's son Robert and perhaps came to terms at Falkirk, and in 1091 he is said in English accounts to have sworn homage to William Rufus. Malcolm perished two years later, along with his eldest son, in yet another invasion of England.

The generally hostile chroniclers give few clues about what, other than the spoils of war, Malcolm III hoped to achieve by his frequent aggression. But it is clear that he did not regard himself as a feudal vassal of the kings of England, and probably saw his submission to them as no more than a mark of their, perhaps temporary, military superiority. His sons were in a rather different position. Following their flight in the aftermath of Malcolm's death, they were driven to accept support from the Norman kings in terms which clearly showed their vassal status. Duncan II and Edgar owed their throne to William Rufus, Alexander I married an illegitimate daughter of Henry I, while David I was a close confidant, personal friend and brother-in-law of the English king.

As we have seen, David I became a masterful ruler in his own right. He inevitably took advantage of the civil war which erupted in England after Henry I's death in 1135 between the late king's daughter and preferred successor, the Empress Matilda, and his nephew Stephen of Blois. Nominally acting on Matilda's behalf, David's real aim was to take over Cumberland, Westmorland and Northumberland, and possibly even Yorkshire, and it is likely that by the latter part of his reign he envisaged that these areas would be permanently annexed to the kingdom of Scotland. These territorial ambitions are sufficient explanation for his actions, although the recently developed silver deposits at Alston may have provided an additional incentive for David to retain Carlisle, which was granted to the Scots (who were already in firm control of the area) under the terms of a transient agreement with Stephen in 1136.[1] David was temporarily checked when his polyglot army was defeated at the battle of the Standard, fought on Cowton Moor near Northallerton in Yorkshire in August 1138, but he continued to hold Northumberland and Cumberland. In 1139 Stephen granted to David's son Henry the earldom of Northumbria, supposedly excluding Newcastle and Bamburgh although subsequently the Scots were in control of both, while in 1149, when David I knighted Matilda's son, the future Henry II of England, Henry promised that, should he succeed to the English throne, he would grant the Scottish king Northumbria from Tyne to Tweed, including Newcastle. In 1152, after the death of his son Henry, the aged king conducted his young grandson William to Newcastle to be acknowledged as earl. He took hostages from the leading men of the earldom, and this may suggest that Scottish rule was not widely accepted, which would be understandable if there is any truth in the English chroniclers' tales of brutality on the part of the Scottish army, although hostage-taking was not uncommon at this period as a means of persuading magnates to concur in a particular political programme.

[1] For the silver see *Chron. Stephen*, iv, 123; *RRS*, i, 156.

David's achievements proved short-lived, partly because the premature deaths of Earl Henry and Stephen's son Eustace materially shifted the balance in favour of Henry fitz Empress. The youthful Malcolm IV was no match for Henry II, who became one of medieval England's most powerful kings. Despite his extensive continental empire and his many difficulties with his quarrelsome sons, Henry succeeded in stifling Scottish ambitions regarding the northern counties and sought to define the relationship between the two monarchs in much more precise terms. He reneged on his agreement of 1149, and in July 1157 Malcolm resigned Northumberland, Cumberland and Westmorland in return for the earldom of Huntingdon which his grandfather had held. His brother William thereby abruptly lost his title to the earldom of Northumbria, a slight that, to his cost, he never forgot. Henry also took advantage of Malcolm's ardent desire to be knighted and so enter the charmed world of chivalry. It was most honourable for a king to be knighted by a fellow-king, but a clear demonstration of feats of arms was required first. This was why Malcolm IV joined Henry's expedition against the count of Toulouse in 1159, a move which has sometimes been interpreted as an acknowledgement of the English king's suzerainty. There is, however, no evidence that he was formally summoned by Henry, nor that he went involuntarily, although Henry cannot have been displeased at the apparent manifestation of Malcolm's dependence on his favour. The expedition was successful from Malcolm's standpoint, because knighthood was finally bestowed upon him, but he was criticised at home for leaving his realm and faced a rebellion on his return in 1160.

While there is no doubt that Malcolm submitted to the superior military and political power of Henry II, to the extent of giving his brother and other young men as hostages in 1163,[2] there is no firm evidence that he compromised his kingship by offering fealty and homage for Scotland as opposed to his English lands. Receiving knighthood from Henry did not make him a vassal of the English king, any more than Henry had become David I's vassal in 1149. The loss of the northern counties was a blow to Scottish prestige, but from the English standpoint can be regarded as no more than

[2] *Chron. Holyrood*, 141.

the return of David I's ill-gotten gains during the civil war of Stephen's reign. The respective strengths of the two monarchs, however, must have been evident to everyone.

William the Lion's relations with England can best be understood in terms of a desire to recover his father's earldom of Northumbria which amounted almost to an obsession. He availed himself of every diplomatic and military opportunity which promised potentially to further his aim, though always in vain. In 1173 he entered into an alliance with Henry II's rebellious eldest son, also named Henry, and the following year was captured at Alnwick. Rather than exacting a pecuniary ransom, which might have implied that William was an independent ruler, Henry II took the opportunity to force the Scottish king into a direct feudal arrangement in what is traditionally known as the treaty of Falaise. William became Henry's vassal, specifically in respect of Scotland as well as his English lands, and as a mark of this relationship five of William's major castles, namely Edinburgh, Berwick, Roxburgh, Jedburgh and Stirling, were to be held by Henry.

Fifteen years elapsed before William was able to purchase release from this uncomfortable subjection. Richard I, who succeeded to the English throne in 1189, needed to raise money for a crusade, and under the terms of the Quitclaim of Canterbury the treaty of Falaise was cancelled in return for a payment of 10,000 marks, and the castles of Roxburgh and Berwick were handed back to William.[3] But the Quitclaim merely restored the status quo as it had existed in the time of Malcolm IV, and left undefined the earlier ambiguities in the nature of the relationship, including William's claim to Northumbria. It may have suited both parties to be unspecific, and indeed it is unrealistic for us to expect that neat definitions would, or could, be inserted into such a document. William's primary motive was probably the recovery of his castles and the termination of the direct homage owed by his magnates to the English crown, both very tangible reminders of his capture at Alnwick. He may have been prepared to accept a vague English suzerainty as an inevitable consequence of the imbalance of power between the two realms.

[3] Henry II appears never to have taken possession of Jedburgh and Stirling, and Edinburgh castle was restored to William in 1186 on condition that it be assigned as the dower of the king's new wife: Howden, *Gesta*, i, 351.

William's loyalty to Richard I caused him to contribute towards the English king's ransom after his capture on return from the crusade, and to decline to support Richard's brother John when the latter sought to take over the government of England in 1193, but his attempts to recover Northumbria from Richard ended in disappointment. Negotiations continued after John acceded to the English throne in 1199, but the slippery English monarch outmanoeuvred William at every turn. Details of the relationship are obscure, but in 1209 William seems to have given up his claim to Northumbria, paid John a large sum of money, and allowed him to arrange the marriage of his daughters, the elder of whom was to wed a son of John, receiving in return acceptance of the destruction of a new English castle at Tweedmouth and a promise that the northern counties would form an English appanage for the heir to the Scottish throne when he came of age, as they had done for Earl Henry before 1152. Although the agreement promised an honourable marriage for William's daughters, it is hard to escape the conclusion that this was a disadvantageous peace for the Scots.[4] Further negotiations followed in 1212, when William allowed John to arrange the marriage of his heir Alexander and, according to an English document, both father and son promised to uphold the cause of John's son Henry. This document is a later forgery, but some peace agreement was certainly made, probably because the ailing Scottish king feared for the succession of Alexander while the ruthless John still ruled England and Ireland.[5] John's control over William is clear.

Shortly after his accession in 1214, Alexander II tried to take advantage of John's political difficulties by joining the baronial opposition. One of the clauses of Magna Carta gave him hope that he might recover the northern counties, but he also sought to make his claim good by force. In October 1215 he attacked the border fortress of Norham and received the homage of the Northumbrian barons. John responded with a major winter campaign and burned Berwick and Haddington, but Alexander counter-attacked in the west and took Carlisle in August 1216. He then went to Dover and joined Louis, the French prince who sought to replace John on the English throne, and did homage to

[4] For detailed discussion of the events of 1209 see Duncan, *Scotland*, 241–9.

[5] Ibid., 251–2; *ASR*, no. 4.

him. According to a French chronicler, this homage included Lothian,[6] although it is hard to see why Alexander would have compromised his feudal position in such a manner when England was in the throes of civil war, and it is almost certain that English Northumbria is meant. As with his father in 1173–4, however, Alexander backed the wrong horse. The victory of John's party, now working on behalf of the young Henry III, brought Alexander into conflict with the papal legate Guala, and he was forced to yield Carlisle and submit to papal authority in order to ensure that the interdict on Scotland was lifted.

Alexander did not abandon his hope of recovering Northumbria, which he claimed had been granted to him by King John as the dowry of his daughter, whom Alexander married in 1221,[7] but he also came under some albeit ineffectual pressure from the pope to renew his fealty to Henry III in line with the treaty of Falaise and other agreements. The treaty of York of September 1237 was a statesmanlike attempt to reconcile the conflicting interests of the two monarchs, although it has been variously interpreted. Alexander received English lands, for which he performed homage, but relinquished his claim to the northern counties. It can be argued that the treaty implicitly recognised that Scotland had an independent existence, but against this the ancient claim to Northumbria was sacrificed for lands of much more limited extent and without castles, and it was, moreover, several years before they were finally assigned to Alexander. It is unlikely, however, that the Scottish king saw the treaty of York as a final concession, and there are indications that Alexander III laid claim to the area between Tyne and Tweed in 1260.[8] Similarly, the question of homage for Scotland was not resolved, and the issue was to create further tension.

That relations between Alexander II and Henry III remained uncomfortable is due to Henry's suspicious nature and to appeals made to him by Scots who wished to take advantage of the ambiguities in the feudal relationship. In 1242 Walter Bisset, who was accused of involvement in the murder of Patrick, son of Thomas of Galloway, fled to England and claimed to Henry III that he should not have been disinherited by the Scottish king without the consent of Alexander's overlord. By 1244 two border fortresses, probably

[6] *ES*, ii, 412. [7] Paris, *Chron. Maj.*, iii, 372.
[8] *Flores Historiarum*, ed. H. R. Luard (3 vols., Rolls Series, 1890), ii, 459.

Hermitage and the earlier of the two castles of Caerlaverock, had been built by the Scots, and a major war looked imminent, although in the event conflict was averted and another marriage alliance arranged.

When Alexander III married Henry's daughter Margaret in December 1251, he did homage to his father-in-law for his possessions in the kingdom of England. Although one English chronicler includes Lothian among these lands,[9] it seems clear that Alexander declined to render homage and fealty for the realm of Scotland itself. Henry III used solicitude for his young daughter as an excuse to intervene in Scottish politics during Alexander's turbulent minority, but all sides in the factional disputes called on Henry for assistance when it suited their purposes, and relations between the two countries remained relatively stable. In 1278 Alexander did homage to Edward I at a parliament at Westminster, but specified only his lands in Tynedale and Penrith; he carefully reserved the question of homage for Scotland, claiming that he held his kingdom of God alone. For the time being Edward I did not press the point. His opportunity for direct intervention in Scotland was to come in due course.

The importance of relations with England frequently prevented Scottish monarchs, especially David I, Malcolm IV and William the Lion, from devoting their full energies to consolidating their power within their own realm. The crown's authority in the north, west and south-west was severely limited throughout the twelfth century and well into the thirteenth, and there was a series of claimants to the throne itself who enjoyed strong support in Moray and Ross. In the view of those historians who see the period as one of steadily advancing royal power, the military campaigns in the north and west were a response to rebellions and an opportunity to introduce feudalism and the institutions of centralised government in areas which were unreceptive to them. However, it is misleading to view twelfth-century Scotland in these terms. Men such as Fergus of Galloway, Somerled of Argyll and Harald Maddadson of Orkney saw themselves as independent potentates, freely negotiating with other rulers and at best acknowledging the king of Scots as a distant

[9] Paris, *Chron. Maj.*, v, 268.

overlord. Somerled and the earls of Orkney also owed obedience to the kings of Norway in respect of certain of their lands, and they exploited the situation to their advantage. These men surely did not regard themselves as rebels against the Scottish crown but rather as significant powers in their own right.

The rulers of Moray also had the capacity to be independent. The Mounth had long served as a barrier between the provinces of Moray, Mar and Buchan on the one hand and the heartland of the Scottish kingdom on the other. As we have seen, Bede drew a distinction in the eighth century between Picts who lived south of the mountains and those who dwelt beyond them, and geography must have played a major part in the political configuration of the peoples of early Scotland. It is likely that Moray was beyond the control of many kings of Scots, as is suggested by the number of tenth- and eleventh-century kings who perished in campaigns against its people, and the ruler of Moray could on occasion extend his authority southwards, as MacBeth had shown. Throughout the twelfth century this history of independence made Moray a potential threat to the centralising tendencies of David I and his successors, and contemporaries realised this. Irish and Scottish annals draw a distinction between 'men of Moray' and 'men of Scotland', while a fourteenth-century chronicler, probably relying here on a contemporary source, could refer to William I returning 'from Moray to Scotia' as late as 1214, indicating that Moray could still be regarded as being outside the Scottish kingdom.[10]

Moray was not only resistant to Scottish royal authority, but was also a haven for rival claimants to the throne. While the Mounth was a barrier to armies from the north as well as royal forces, rulers in Moray could nonetheless threaten the security of Angus and Mearns. Moray also boasted lines of communication with other areas which were troublesome to the Scottish kings. The Great Glen offered access to Argyll, the southern Hebrides and the Irish Sea world, which included Galloway, Man and Ireland, while the lowlands of Easter Ross enabled the earls of Orkney to extend their power southwards from their territories in Caithness. Throughout the Middle Ages, Scottish kings endeavoured, with varying degrees of success, to control the northern end of the Great Glen, through

[10] *Johannis de Fordun Chronica Gentis Scotorum*, ed. W. F. Skene (2 vols., Edinburgh, 1871–2), i, 279; Broun, 'Defining Scotland', 6.

which these lines of communication passed. To fail to do so was to offer an opportunity for rivals to unite and thereby strike from several different directions.

In 1130 Angus, earl of Moray, was killed in battle at Stracathro in Mearns. He was accompanied by Malcolm MacHeth, who perhaps had a claim to the Scottish throne, and their campaign south of the Mounth may have been intended to supplant David I as king of Scots. The defeat of the men of Moray, who were no match for the heavily armed knights who fought on behalf of the king, gave David and his successors the opportunity to extend their authority in the north. Major beneficiaries of this policy were two Flemish adventurers, Freskin and Berewald, who were given lands widely distributed across the province.[11] Freskin's descendants later took the surname 'de Moravia' (now Murray), and such an overtly territorial designation surely suggests that the crown regarded the family as taking the place of the former earls. In other words, David I and his grandsons replaced a native dynasty by one of proven loyalty to themselves, and the lands the Flemings received were perhaps the demesne territories formerly held by Earl Angus. The lands were granted on feudal terms, and before the end of David I's reign royal burghs had been established at Forres and Elgin, but the introduction of a new aristocracy and of the institutions of royal government was insufficient to pacify Moray. We must regard such developments as expressions of the king's intentions rather than as straightforward indications of his actual power.

The identity of Malcolm MacHeth remains a puzzle. He may have been an illegitimate son of Alexander I, as some English chroniclers assert, although his patronymic suggests a link with someone called Aed, perhaps the earl of Moray or Ross of that name who is attested in the early part of David I's reign, in which case Malcolm was probably connected to the branch of the royal house which had produced MacBeth. In any event, the fact that he was imprisoned rather than killed following his capture in 1134 indicates that he was of royal blood and, moreover, that there was some justice in his claim.[12] Certainly his sons persisted in their opposition to the Scottish kings, joining in a widespread campaign against royal authority in 1153 in alliance with Somerled of Argyll, who was

[11] *RRS*, ii, 198–9; *RRS*, i, 219–20.

[12] Duncan, *Scotland*, 165–6; Barrow, *Kingship and Unity*, 51.

Malcolm MacHeth's brother-in-law. Malcolm MacHeth was released from prison in 1157 and by 1162 had been created earl of Ross, which implies that Malcolm IV had chosen to negotiate with him in an attempt to detach him from Somerled, offering Ross either as a return of his inheritance or as a rump of the much larger earldom of Moray which his family had perhaps once possessed. The success of this manoeuvre is hard to evaluate because Malcolm MacHeth's sons never inherited the earldom of Ross and, indeed, largely disappear from Scottish politics, which may suggest that they continued to oppose the crown. That the problem in the north was not solved by the release of Malcolm MacHeth is also implied by the laconic remark in a contemporary chronicle that in 1163 'King Malcolm transferred the men of Moray'.[13] This comment has been variously explained, but the most obvious interpretation is that some of the inhabitants of Moray were forcibly transplanted; if this is so, then it points to continuing unrest in the north which Malcolm MacHeth either could or would not quell.

The MacHeth claim did not totally disappear on the death of Earl Malcolm in 1168. His daughter had married Harald Maddadson, earl of Orkney, a union which gave their son Thorfinn a claim to his grandfather's earldom of Ross and even conceivably to Moray and the Scottish throne itself. Harald was one of the most powerful of the Orkney earls, and the establishment of royal castles at Redcastle and Dunskeath in Easter Ross in 1179 makes most sense in the context of a threat from further north, presumably from Harald. The earl of Orkney was perhaps also involved in the serious rebellion of Donald MacWilliam, which began in 1181.[14] Donald was the grandson of Duncan II, son of Malcolm Canmore by his first wife Ingibiorg and briefly king in 1094. Although Duncan had sought the Scottish throne with Norman backing, and his son William had apparently been loyal to the crown, subsequent generations drew their support from the traditional elements in northern Scotland which had backed MacBeth, Donald Bán and, most recently, the MacHeths. It is questionable whether Donald MacWilliam was of legitimate birth according to canon law, but

[13] *Chron. Holyrood*, 142.

[14] Duncan, *Scotland*, 193. It is, however, possible that Howden has misdated the events of 1181, and that the royal expedition of 1179 was a response to a rebellion by Donald MacWilliam which had erupted in that year. *RRS*, ii, 11.

such considerations were of little moment in Celtic society in comparison with his royal blood. His mother is unidentified, although she may have been connected with the MacHeths or related to Angus, earl of Moray. In a thirteenth-century genealogy to illustrate the descent of lordships in Cumberland, where he had been given lands, William son of Duncan is described as earl of Moray; if this is correct, he may have been granted the dignity by the crown or (more likely) have assumed it by right of a putative first wife, heiress of Earl Angus and mother of the rebel Donald, whose claim to the throne may have been more cogent if traced through his mother rather than his father. This would explain why Donald chose to rebel when William had not, and give an indication of the sources of his support.[15] The king, preoccupied with his relations with Henry II of England and the dispute over the bishopric of St Andrews, was unable to launch a major expedition to the north until 1187, when Donald was fortuitously killed by Roland of Galloway.

There is no direct evidence for an active role being played by Harald Maddadson in Donald MacWilliam's rebellion, and his opposition to the king in the 1190s may have resulted from the increased level of royal authority in the north after Donald's death rather than any affinity to the alliance of MacHeth and MacWilliam supporters which had proved so threatening to the crown in the 1180s. It has even been argued that Harald had relatively little interest in his wife and son's claim to Ross.[16] But it is surely likely that he was at least prepared to fish in troubled waters, and the subsequent blinding and castration of Thorfinn while in royal custody, albeit in response to the mutilation of the bishop of Caithness by some of Earl Harald's army, implies that he was seen by the crown as a threat not merely in Caithness but in Ross and Moray as well.[17]

William the Lion's northern campaigns were not unsuccessful, but permanent control was elusive, even in Moray. Geography, distance and the existence of more pressing problems with the English kings combined to limit William's long-term achievement in the north, although the loss of some of his southern castles under the

[15] *RRS*, ii, 12–13. For William as earl of Moray see *The Register of the Priory of St Bees*, ed. J. Wilson (Surtees Society, 1915), 532.

[16] P. Topping, 'Harald Maddadson, earl of Orkney and Caithness 1139–1206', *SHR*, 62 (1983), 114–15.

[17] Duncan, *Scotland*, 195–6.

treaty of Falaise may have encouraged him to concentrate more on the peripheral regions of his realm. William's most successful period coincided with the reign of Richard I of England, who was too busy on crusade or in continental affairs to be greatly troubled with Scotland. As William's relationship with King John became more strained, so his problems in northern Scotland became more intractable. A serious rebellion broke out in Ross in 1211 under Guthred, son of Donald MacWilliam, who had perhaps been driven from Ireland by John. Guthred invaded Moray, probably with support from Orkney and the Hebrides but more especially from Gaelic Ulster. He was executed in 1212, but a further incursion followed three years later, involving men who claimed kinship ties with the MacWilliams and MacHeths, and again there was an Irish dimension. The timing of this rebellion is surely connected, as that of 1153 had been, with the recent accession of a young and inexperienced king.

Alexander II had to face several further threats from northern rivals. The MacWilliams continued to be troublesome until 1230, when a girl of that family was brutally despatched at the market cross in Forfar, and the rebels still received support from the chieftains of western Scotland such as Ruairi, grandson of Somerled, and from Ireland. Alexander was, however, more successful than his predecessors in controlling the north, albeit at the cost of granting wide powers to some of his leading subjects. We have seen how David I established Flemings in Moray, and in the early thirteenth century the descendants of Freskin pressed northwards, eventually acquiring for themselves the new earldom of Sutherland, probably in the 1230s. Royal control further north was restricted by the earls of Orkney, as the bishops of Caithness found to their cost. Bishop John was maimed at Scrabster in 1201, and Adam murdered at Halkirk in 1222, prompting his successor Gilbert de Moravia to reorganise his diocese so that he could base his administration further south at Dornoch. The impression is, however, that the crown's authority was becoming steadily more secure to the north of the Moray Firth.

The major beneficiaries of the crown's northern campaigns were the Comyns, who became the dominant family in thirteenth-century Scotland. Around the time of the rising of 1211–12 William Comyn became earl of Buchan through his marriage to Marjorie, the heiress of the last native earl, Fergus. Allowing an Anglo-Norman settler, for the first time, to obtain an ancient earldom must be seen as an element in a long-term strategy to stabilise royal authority in the north, a policy which is also seen in the early 1230s when the hitherto temporary expedient of a warden of Moray was replaced by the hereditary lordship of Badenoch, which was vested in another branch of the Comyn family. The grant of Badenoch gave the Comyns, and through them the king, control over two of the high passes into Atholl which could be used as a point of entry into the heartland of Scotia, and it is virtually certain that it is connected with the rebellion of Gilleasbuig MacWilliam and his sons in around 1229. Although other families such as the Durwards and the Bissets benefited from Alexander II's largesse, it was the Comyns who were most firmly established as royal agents in the north, a position which was to allow them to maintain a Scottish administration during the Wars of Independence and make them a major threat to the ambitions of Robert Bruce.

It is unhelpful to regard the northern uprisings as a Celtic reaction to Anglo-Norman settlement and the establishment of feudalism. Many members of the royal armies were equally Celtic: Roland of Galloway had killed Donald MacWilliam in 1187, and the leaders of the 1215 rebellion were defeated by a native magnate of Wester Ross. Earl Fergus of Buchan had some Anglo-Norman knights in his following, and his successor William Comyn successfully combined tenurial relationships of a feudal type with more traditional forms of social organisation. The rebellions cannot, therefore, adequately be explained in racial or cultural terms, and three features of them should be noted. Firstly, they were made in the interests of individuals who had a claim, however tenuous, on the Scottish throne and could mobilise support for that claim in northern and western Scotland and even beyond the boundaries of the kingdom. Secondly, and more significantly, the rebellions were a reaction against the assertion of royal authority by the inhabitants of provinces with a long history of effective independence from the Scottish crown. The opposition was not solely, nor even primarily, to feudalism as such, but rather to the influx of alien settlers and the threat to local particularism that they posed. Thirdly, these forces could be kept in check only when the king was able to devote sufficient attention to the matter without being preoccupied with

England. All the recorded expeditions were based on Inverness, suggesting that the stronghold of the king's opponents was in the wild mountainous country of western Moray and Wester Ross, an area which was too remote for a Scottish ruler whose primary interest lay in recovering lands from the Angevin kings. It is no coincidence that Alexander II, whose attitude to the earldom of Northumbria was less obsessive, was more successful in quelling the northern threat than his father had been.

The contacts of the MacHeths and MacWilliams with the family of Somerled have already been noted. Somerled is an important figure in Scottish history, through both his own actions and the fact that he was the progenitor of several clans which were to be prominent on the western seaboard, including the MacDonalds and MacDougalls. Different historiographical traditions have portrayed him as both a Highland hero and a rebel who endangered the process of royal centralisation. He had interests both on the Scottish mainland, especially in Argyll, and in the Hebrides, where he successfully intervened in the politics of the kingdom of Man and carved out for himself a semi-independent lordship which was effectively beyond the control of either the king of Scots or the king of Norway. His relations with David I seem to have been fairly smooth, but in Malcolm IV's reign he was frequently at odds with the Scottish monarch.

The alliance between Somerled and his nephews, the sons of Malcolm MacHeth, has been viewed as a challenge to the succession of Malcolm IV by traditionalists who did not accept the principle of primogeniture. There may be something in this, but it is surely not the whole picture, because it explains neither the continuation of Somerled's opposition to the king after the latter came to terms with Malcolm MacHeth in 1157 nor the later campaign in 1164 during which Somerled met his death at Renfrew. There is no need to postulate a distinctively Gaelic reaction to Malcolm IV's accession in 1153, since the actions of Somerled must be seen in the broader context of a sudden weakening of royal authority as the experienced David I was replaced by his twelve-year-old grandson. Somerled, along with other native leaders, must have felt threatened by the growing territorial and political power of the Stewarts in the area of the Clyde estuary through the largesse of David I. The opportunity presented by the succession of a youthful king was too good to miss.

The wider rebellion of 1160 must be viewed in the same light. On his return from Toulouse Malcolm was besieged in Perth by six earls led by Ferteth of Strathearn, ostensibly because he had left the kingdom. He also had trouble in Galloway, although after three expeditions there he forced its native lord, Fergus, to retire to Holyrood abbey. Somerled too appears to have continued his opposition until he came to terms with Malcolm IV in November 1160. The conclusion is that the king overcame a number of opponents, doubtless with the aid of Anglo-Norman feudatories, but the question remains of why there was such opposition to him at this juncture. Some native magnates may have been angered by his apparent submission to the feudal overlordship of Henry II, although it is uncertain that they understood the full ramifications of such a relationship and more likely that they objected simply to his absence from his realm. They may well, however, also have feared that closer contact with the English crown would increase the number of immigrants to Scotland, which was surely a factor in Somerled's final rebellion in 1164, when he gathered an army from Argyll, Kintyre, the Hebrides and Ireland. It is no coincidence that he landed at Renfrew, the centre of the Stewart lordship, but we must doubt whether he was fighting for the abstract concept of traditional values rather than merely in defence of his own interests.

Just as David I and his grandsons bestowed lands in Moray on Freskin and Berewald, royal grants to the Stewarts were intended to provide a bulwark between the heartlands of the Scottish realm and the uncontrollable inhabitants of more peripheral areas. Somerled and his successors had a Hebridean power base, and the Isles were beyond even the theoretical jurisdiction of the kings of Scots. In 1098 all the islands off the west coast of Scotland which could be circumnavigated by a ship with the rudder set had been ceded to Magnus Barelegs of Norway,[18] although the Norwegian monarchs could make their suzerainty effective only intermittently. The king of Man paid a tribute of ten merks of gold on the succession of a new king of Norway but owed no other service, and in 1219 King Ragnvald tried to evade even this obligation by offering an annual

[18] *ES*, ii, 112–13. The Norse sagas name the Scottish king as Malcolm rather than Edgar, which is probably an error of a type not infrequent in such sources, although it is possible that Magnus negotiated with a pretender to the Scottish throne; Malcolm III may have had a son called Malcolm from his first marriage.

payment to the pope and claiming that he had been invested in his realm by a papal legate.[19] In practice, Hebridean chieftains obeyed the Norwegian crown only when it suited them to do so or when a major expedition to the Isles concentrated their minds.

The thirteenth century witnessed the recovery of the Western Isles by the Scottish crown. As in the north, the initiative was taken by Alexander II. In 1222 he pacified the Clyde estuary, erecting Dumbarton as a royal burgh, depriving the rebellious Ruairi, grandson of Somerled, of his lands in Kintyre, and probably bestowing Cowal on Walter Stewart. A castle was built for Walter at Dunoon, and the period possibly saw the first phase of building at Tarbert castle and, much further north, at Eilean Donan.[20] Further west, the descendants of Somerled remained powerful, although internecine strife meant that the threat from them was much less monolithic than it may have seemed, while the building of stone castles testifies to the wealth and self-confidence of the peoples of the western seaboard. Alexander II died on an expedition against them in 1249. On a diplomatic level, the king had attempted in 1244 to purchase the Hebrides from the Norwegian crown, but his proposals were rebuffed,[21] and it was not until the reign of his son that the king of Norway agreed to cede the Western Isles. In 1263, in the face of renewed political and military pressure, Haakon IV made a final effort to exert his authority, but the expedition demonstrated the inherent weakness of his position. He campaigned down the western seaboard, had his ships dragged across the isthmus between Loch Long and Loch Lomond, devastated Lennox, and fought an inconclusive battle at Largs, but many of the native lords, especially south of Ardnamurchan, supported him only reluctantly. Haakon's death at Kirkwall in December marked the end of Norwegian attempts to hold on to the islands to the west of Scotland.

The treaty of Perth of 2 July 1266 provided for the sale of Man and the Isles to the Scots for 4,000 merks payable over four years and an annual tribute of 100 merks, although in the event the final instalment of the lump sum was rendered only in 1282 and the tribute was paid only intermittently. While the treaty can be seen as a triumph for Alexander III's diplomacy, the effect of the change of overlordship on the attitudes of the inhabitants of the western

[19] *Chron. Stephen*, iv, 229; *Vet. Mon.*, 11; cf. 21–2.

[20] McDonald, *Kingdom of the Isles*, 83–5.

[21] *ES*, II, 539–40.

seaboard remains difficult to ascertain. At the highest level of society, there is some evidence that the descendants of Somerled now acted as agents rather than opponents of royal authority and thereby facilitated the incorporation of the west into the Scottish realm, and it is significant that they were among the magnates who swore to uphold the right of Alexander's infant granddaughter Margaret in 1284, but lack of evidence prevents us from fully analysing the impact of feudalism in Argyll and the Isles. Certainly Robert I brought many chieftains into a closer relationship with the crown by granting or confirming lands in return for galley service, and in doing so he doubtless built on foundations laid by Alexander III. The expression of obligations in 'feudal' terms does not, however, imply that royal authority in the west was ever more than superficial, and even the use of feudal terminology by local chiefs does not prove that there had been major changes in the nature of landholding. The peaceful relations with England for most of the thirteenth century undoubtedly helped Alexander II and his son in their quest to control the periphery of their realm, but there is no reason to believe that social structures were fundamentally changed. Subsequent events were to prove how tenuous was the link between the kings of Scots and the independent-minded inhabitants of the maritime world of the western Highlands and Hebrides.

The Scottish kings faced a similar combination of local particularism and powerful native lords in Galloway, and again it was not until the reign of Alexander II that the crown obtained effective control of the area. While there is much controversy about the ethnic origins of the Galwegians, there is no doubt that they had closer links with other parts of the Irish Sea world, such as Ireland, Man and north-west England, than they did with the kingdom of the Scots. Lords such as Fergus in the twelfth century and Alan in the thirteenth exploited their geographical location to play a major role in the diplomatic alliances of the British Isles.

Fergus is unusual in that no source details his ancestry.[22] Nor is there any evidence for an independent power in the south-west prior to his emergence in the 1130s. The history of the lordship of Galloway thus starts abruptly, which makes it all the more remarkable that it was to prove such a thorn in the flesh of the Scottish

[22] See R. D. Oram, 'Fergus, Galloway and the Scots', in R. D. Oram and G. P. Stell, eds., *Galloway: Land and Lordship* (Edinburgh, 1991), 117–30.

monarchs for the next century. Fergus married an illegitimate daughter of Henry I of England, which suggests that he was a personage to be reckoned with, but there is no reason to suppose that he was of Anglo-Norman origin; his name and the support he gave to the conservative opponents of Malcolm IV in 1160 suggest that he was from a Celtic background, probably with some Norse ancestry thrown in.

A distinction must be drawn between the heartland of Galloway and the area east of the river Urr known as Desnes Ioan. There is considerable evidence that Desnes Ioan owed some subjection to the Scottish crown even in the twelfth century. It was in Glasgow diocese, so presumably formed part of the ancient kingdom of Strathclyde, now incorporated by the kings of Scots. In the late 1160s or early 1170s Uhtred of Galloway paid cain to the crown in respect of it, and his generosity in granting lands there to his followers strongly suggests that the district had become part of his territories only recently, perhaps as a result of a division of the lands of Ralph, lord of Nithsdale, between Uhtred and the king. While Malcolm IV had defeated Fergus and forced him to retire to a monastery, the grant of Desnes Ioan to Uhtred appears a sensible move. Following the loss of Carlisle in 1157, the king wanted to use the stronghold of Dumfries as a major base in the south-west, and this could best be accomplished by gaining the goodwill of the nearest great lord, namely Uhtred, whose establishment of knights in Desnes Ioan may well be linked with garrison service at Dumfries.

West of the Urr, however, royal influence was extremely limited. Although Galwegian troops fought in Malcolm III's armies, and gained a reputation for brutality in the campaign of 1138, there is no evidence that they were under any obligation to fight, and were probably hired troops. The revival of the diocese of Whithorn around 1128 has sometimes been attributed to David I, but was almost certainly a result of an initiative by Archbishop Thurstan of York. The Cistercian monastery of Dundrennan was probably founded by Fergus, perhaps to atone for the damage done by his soldiers in 1138. There is no reason to suppose that David was involved.[23] All the evidence suggests that the lordship of Galloway

[23] Oram, 'A family business?', 114–15.

under Fergus was a compact, self-contained unit based on two main centres at Cruggleton and Kirkcudbright, with its own bishopric and its own laws, owing no obedience to the Scottish crown.

The extent to which Galloway was 'feudalised' in the twelfth century is debatable, especially if Desnes Ioan is distinguished from the lands west of the Urr. The rebellion of Fergus in 1160 was probably connected with the more general unrest of that year, while the uprising of 1174 began in the wake of William the Lion's capture at Alnwick. These incidents were not, however, simply opportunistic attacks on a Scottish king who had done nothing to arouse the Galwegians' animosity, for the lords of Galloway, like Somerled, were doubtless concerned by the increasing authority of the Scottish crown and its policy of granting lands to immigrants. The murder of Uhtred by his brother Gilbert during the rebellion of 1174 certainly suggests internecine strife, but does not necessarily mark a native reaction against a feudalising lord, whatever lands Uhtred may have granted in Desnes Ioan and however much his marriage into the Cumbrian aristocracy had brought him into closer contact with Anglo-Norman attitudes. The well-informed English chronicler Roger of Howden tells us that the Galwegians expelled Scottish royal officials, destroyed fortifications erected by the king, and slew all the Englishmen and Frenchmen they could find.[24] This points to xenophobia rather than opposition to feudalism as such, although it implies that some mottes had already been constructed, and this suggests alien settlement. More importantly, it demonstrates a hatred for the agents of royal government.

Gilbert died in 1185 and was replaced by his nephew Roland, son of the murdered Uhtred. Only a few immigrants obtained land from Roland, and so his successful takeover was probably based largely on the support he received from natives, probably from Desnes Ioan, which he may already have controlled, or from his father's former following.[25] But increasingly the lords of Galloway were moving in an international milieu. Roland married into the powerful Moreville family, and the death of William de Moreville in 1196 brought him the extensive lands of Cunningham and Lauderdale as well as shares in some estates in the earldom of Huntingdon. Since the king had also apparently invested Gilbert's

[24] Howden, *Gesta*, i, 67–8. [25] Oram, 'A family business?', 128–9.

son Duncan with the earldom of Carrick, there was a danger that the house of Fergus would become predominant in a large area of south-western Scotland. The foundation of the sheriffdom, burgh and castle of Ayr in and after 1197 marks a royal reaction to this threat as well as to the continuing danger from the descendants of Somerled and the rulers of Man, and indicates the importance that the king attached to controlling the area. It is no surprise that William objected strongly to the unauthorised marriage between Duncan of Carrick and the daughter of Alan son of Walter Stewart in around 1200.[26]

Roland's son Alan, who succeeded to the lordship in 1200, had an influence on the history of the whole Irish Sea world. He was the hereditary constable of Scotland, married his illegitimate son Thomas to the daughter of Ragnvald, claimant to the kingship of Man, and was granted a vast fief in Ulster by King John after the fall of Hugh de Lacy, earl of Ulster, in 1210. It is sometimes suggested that Alan's role in Scottish politics was minor, but in fact he must be seen as Alexander II's chief lieutenant in the reassertion of Scottish control over Cumbria towards the end of John's reign,[27] notwithstanding the favour that the English king had earlier shown him in Ulster; Alan could doubtless draw on links between Galloway and Cumbria which had been strengthened by grants of land to Cumbrians by his father and grandfather.

The death of Alan without legitimate sons in 1234 gave Alexander II the opportunity to extinguish the semi-independent lordship. In line with feudal practice, Alan's lands were divided between his three daughters. The Galwegians sought to maintain their lordship as a distinct political entity, doubtless comparing it to Scottish earldoms, which were indivisible and could exist as territorial units even in the absence of an earl. They apparently asked Alexander to disinherit Alan's daughters and become their lord, but on his refusal rebelled on behalf of Alan's illegimate son Thomas, although his nephew Patrick was also a potential claimant.[28] Alexander put down the revolt and strengthened his position by intervening in a dispute over the bishopric of Whithorn on behalf

[26] Howden, *Chronica*, iv, 145.

[27] K. J. Stringer, 'Periphery and core in thirteenth-century Scotland: Alan son of Roland, lord of Galloway and constable of Scotland', in *Barrow Essays*, 89–92.

[28] *ES*, ii, 494; Paris, *Chron. Maj.*, iii, 364–6.

of Gilbert, a monk of Melrose who had, however, experienced Galwegian politics as abbot of Glenluce. Gilbert was the king's candidate and was presumably used as a royal agent in the same way as the northern bishops were. Furthermore, the deposition of the abbots of Dundrennan and Glenluce by the Cistercian general chapter in 1236, and their replacement by monks of Melrose, may be a reaction to the support possibly given by Galwegian monasteries to Thomas's cause. If so, it is further evidence of Alexander II's desire to use the church as an instrument for control in Galloway, and of his ability to influence the affairs of a great international religious order.[29]

Galloway remained, however, a potential source of disaffection, because its inhabitants retained a spirit of independence and a sense of loyalty to Fergus's descendants long after 1234. From the mid-1260s Galloway was dominated by the line of Dervorguilla, daughter of Alan and mother of the future king of Scots, John Balliol. Throughout the Wars of Independence the Balliol cause was widely upheld in Galloway even when it was all but lost elsewhere. The laws of Galloway still existed in 1384, when parliament agreed to preserve them against the provisions of a new statute, and in the late fourteenth and fifteenth centuries the Black Douglases, although not native lords, could still harness the traditions of Galwegian unity to build a virtually impregnable position for themselves in the south-west.

The tradition of independence from the Scottish crown thus died hard in Galloway, as it did in Moray. By Alexander III's reign, however, the kingdom of the Scots had been consolidated territorially and the authority of its monarchs was felt throughout the realm. Orkney and Shetland still pertained to Norway, but the Western Isles had been ceded to the Scottish king and the crown's influence in the north, in Galloway and along the rugged western seaboard was as great as it had ever been. The border with England had been stable for over a century, and while the northern English counties had never been brought under secure Scottish control the king had successfully avoided permanent feudal subjection to his

[29] Oram, 'In obedience and reverence', 96; D. Brooke, *Wild Men and Holy Places: St Ninian, Whithorn and the Medieval Realm of Galloway* (Edinburgh, 1994), 138; for the events of 1236 see *The Chronicle of Melrose*, ed. A. O. Anderson and M. O. Anderson (London, 1936), 85.

more powerful neighbour. Despite the tensions between Scotland and England and the centrifugal forces within the Scottish realm, the thirteenth century was predominantly a period of internal and external peace. But all the achievements of the Canmore kings were abruptly put in jeopardy with Alexander III's fatal accident in March 1286. Scotland was suddenly faced with a dubious royal succession and an uncertain future as an independent state.

5

THE WARS OF INDEPENDENCE

The death of Alexander III ushered in a period of crisis for Scotland, during which the English kings involved themselves in Scottish affairs on an unprecedented scale and there was a serious danger that Scotland would cease to be an independent realm. The establishment of institutions of government which could function even in the absence of a monarch and the sense of nationhood described in the Declaration of Arbroath were, or at least became, marks of Scottish identity and pride, and the long period of resistance to English imperialism has served as a watershed in the history of medieval Scotland. In the popular mind, the age of William Wallace and Robert Bruce is one of heroes and villains, patriots and traitors, victories won against overwhelming odds. No period in Scottish history has aroused so much passion or, it must be said, so many misconceptions.

The conflict with England which began in 1296 has traditionally been regarded as a war for Scottish independence, and in some respects it was indeed a struggle for the right to self-determination. In other ways, however, it was a civil war within Scotland between rival claimants to the throne who were prepared to seek or reject English assistance as circumstances dictated. The king of England, Edward I, was both willing and able to take advantage of the opportunity presented to him by the extinction of the direct line of Scottish monarchs, but it is not certain that he set out deliberately to destroy Scotland as a separate political entity and impose his own direct lordship on the whole of Britain. Some Scots supported Edward I and sought preferment from him; many others acquiesced in his apparent conquest for want of a more attractive alternative. The advantage of hindsight enabled late medieval Scottish writers to place a nationalistic emphasis on the events of the late thirteenth and early fourteenth centuries which was much less obvious at the time, and to condemn the Balliols and Comyns for feebleness and treachery while exalting the Bruces as the great victors that they turned out to be. The myth has become embedded in Scottish national consciousness.

Alexander III's sudden demise in March 1286 was especially tragic because all his children had predeceased him, and his only living descendant was his infant granddaughter Margaret, known as the 'Maid of Norway' because she was the daughter of the Norwegian king. In 1284 Alexander had prevailed upon his magnates to accept Margaret as his heir, although it seems unlikely that the Scottish nobility viewed the prospect of a female ruler with enthusiasm. This was not merely a manifestation of the prejudices of a male-dominated elite whose principal concerns were with martial exploits, but also a realisation that the succession of a ruling queen would inevitably raise the problem of whom she was to marry. Her future husband could expect considerable political power, which would arouse jealousy if he was taken from the local nobility and might lead to undesirable foreign entanglements if he came from outside the realm. There was the risk that a small kingdom like Scotland might become a mere appendage of another country, or in time even an integral part of it.

Despite these fears, the Scottish political community appears to have accepted Margaret as queen, although for some months after Alexander III's death there was a lingering possibility that his widow, Yolande of Dreux, might be pregnant. In any event, there was the prospect of a long minority, and the very real danger that, in an age of high child mortality, both Margaret and any heir born to Yolande might die, leaving an uncertain succession. In parliament in 1286 John Balliol and Robert Bruce, both descendants of David I and later rivals for the crown, engaged in bitter pleading. Bruce may have been disinclined to accept the succession of Margaret, but it is more likely that the argument was over who had the better claim if Margaret died and Yolande did not give birth to an heir.[1] The heir presumptive, after all, could expect a major role in any council of regency.

Memories of the factionalism during the minority of Alexander III doubtless encouraged the appointment of a panel of six Guardians to rule on behalf of the 'community of the realm' during the absence of an active monarch. Those selected comprised two bishops (William Fraser of St Andrews and Robert Wishart of Glasgow), two earls (Alexander Comyn of Buchan and Duncan of Fife), and two barons (John Comyn of Badenoch and James Stewart), a cross-section of the political community which has been seen also as constituting a delicate balance between the supporters of Balliol and Bruce.[2] Although it was prudent to try to ensure that the Guardians could command widespread support, this interpretation of the composition of the panel may owe too much to our knowledge of subsequent events, for the earl of Fife was not a Bruce partisan to the extent, for instance, that the Comyns were allied to John Balliol, whose sister had married John Comyn of Badenoch. The panel more accurately reflects the balance of political power in late thirteenth-century Scotland, with the Comyns and their supporters playing a pre-eminent, but not exclusive, role.

The aged Robert Bruce, lord of Annandale, doubtless felt excluded from the government of Scotland in the late 1280s. He was later to allege that Alexander II had named him as heir presumptive, but he had played a relatively small part in Scottish politics during Alexander III's reign and also retained extensive territorial interests in England. The rival Balliol claim was at this time vested in a woman, Dervorguilla, who died in 1290, and Bruce may have opposed the succession of Margaret through fear that admission of a woman's right to rule would prejudice his claim to the throne, although his hostility to the government was probably more a reflection of anxiety that he might suffer territorial reverses under a Comyn-led regime.

On 20 September 1286 Robert Bruce of Annandale, his son and namesake the earl of Carrick, and a number of other nobles met at

[1] N. Reid, 'Margaret "Maid of Norway" and Scottish queenship', *Reading Medieval Studies*, 8 (1982), 77–8.

[2] G. W. S. Barrow, *Robert Bruce and the Community of the Realm of Scotland* (3rd edn, Edinburgh, 1988), 15–16.

the castle of Turnberry in Ayrshire and concluded a bond of alliance, reserving their allegiance to the king of England, from whom many of the signatories held lands, and to the unspecified person who would inherit the Scottish throne 'in accordance with the ancient customs hitherto approved and used in the realm of Scotland'. This was not necessarily a rejection of the notion that a woman could succeed, but rather a cautious admission of the continuing uncertainty as to who might emerge as king if Margaret died without producing an heir. The inclusion in the Turnberry Band of Richard de Burgh, earl of Ulster, and of Thomas de Clare suggests that some enterprise in Ireland was contemplated, probably an attempt to conquer land in Connacht, although the promise of help was doubtless meant to be reciprocal, implying that the Bruces could expect military support from the named Irish magnates when required. The precise motivation of those who subscribed to the agreement will never be known, and some of their objectives were perhaps deliberately left vague so that they could be adapted to changing circumstances, possibly including a future Bruce claim to the Scottish throne. The Bruces were certainly determined to make life difficult for their Balliol rivals in the south-west, and violence between the two families was never far below the surface. Fourteenth- and fifteenth-century sources imply that Robert I rescued Scotland from years of faction-fighting and disorder, but the Bruces were in fact the principal disturbers of the peace in the years after 1286, launching a legal, territorial and military challenge to the Guardians.

The Guardians needed to secure the support of Edward I of England, whose beneficence towards Scotland was essential for stability and security. In 1286 Edward was preoccupied with the affairs of his territories in Gascony, and spent the period from May 1286 to August 1289 overseas, but he must have realised the potential advantages of a marriage between his own son and the young Scottish queen. The Guardians too saw merit in such an alliance, as it would persuade the English king to support those who ruled in his daughter-in-law's name and would thereby ensure strong government. The later rapacity of Edward I may make the Scots' overtures appear misguided, but there was a long history of royal marriages between the two countries and there had been a lengthy period of generally pacific relations between their respective monarchs. In the negotations which eventually led to the treaty of Birgham in July 1290, the Guardians sought and received from the English king a guarantee that Scotland would continue to be governed by its own laws and customs, despite the fact that its ruler was likely to spend most of her time in England. They were aware of the dangers of a marriage alliance, but equally they could not afford to ignore Edward I, still less antagonise him.

It was inevitable that Edward I would become involved in the affairs of Scotland, whatever promises he had made about the integrity of Scottish laws and institutions, but that does not mean that he already contemplated establishing direct lordship over the Scots. The death of the experienced Alexander Comyn, earl of Buchan, in the summer of 1289, and the murder of Duncan, earl of Fife, probably in September of the same year, had weakened the Scottish government at the very time that it most needed to be strong, while the failure to replace the two Guardians can be ascribed to a lack of consensus within the political community in the face of the continued opposition from the Bruces and their allies. Paradoxically, however, these events made an accommodation with Edward I all the more urgent, because of Edward's capacity to provide stability. Many Scottish nobles held land in England, and performed military service to the English crown in respect of it; some, moreover, had sought English backing in legal disputes over land in Scotland even during the reign of Alexander III. Links between the two realms were, therefore, close, and the prospect of Edward I taking an interest in Scottish affairs was not necessarily viewed with undue alarm.

In the event, all the negotiations were in vain. The young queen of Scots died in Orkney in September 1290, on her way to the country she had never yet visited. With her perished the prospect of a marriage alliance with the son of the English king and, more fundamentally, the direct line of monarchs who had ruled Scotland for two centuries. The fears of a bitter succession dispute had come to reality. Robert Bruce and John Balliol now aired their claims more openly, as eventually did a dozen other hopefuls, while Edward I, denied the chance to intervene in Scotland on behalf of his daughter-in-law, was still a powerful neighbour whose interests could not be ignored.

It was entirely understandable that the Guardians would look to

Edward I to assist in the settlement of the dispute over the throne, just as they had sought a marriage alliance with him while Margaret was still alive. But Edward wanted to do more than act as arbitrator. He was determined to judge the merits of the respective claims in a formally constituted court, using an established legal procedure, and this required that he was accepted as overlord of Scotland, with possession of the kingdom and its castles, so that he could execute the court's judgement in favour of the victor; he may deliberately have encouraged other potential candidates to submit claims in order to convert the dispute from a simple one between Bruce and Balliol (which might be settled by arbitration) into a more complex suit which required a formal judgement.[3] The representatives of the 'community of the realm', quite justifiably, were unwilling to commit themselves on the matter of overlordship in the absence of a king, but Edward simply required all candidates for the throne to accept it, and in July 1291 he ordered several English religious houses to insert the relevant documents into their chronicles as a permanent testimony that the Scottish king was feudally subject to his English counterpart. He was unable to understand the Scots' reluctance to concede that he was their superior lord.

From the Scottish standpoint, Edward I's demands in 1291 have always appeared high-handed, demonstrating a desire to exploit a crisis in a neighbouring state for his own selfish ends, although Edward had many continental interests and professed a desire to participate in a fresh crusade, so that Scotland was probably not his chief priority at this stage. Hindsight has driven some historians to see a deliberate policy of English imperialism in all of Edward I's actions with regard to the Scots, Welsh and Irish, a view that perhaps pays too little regard both to his generally friendly relations with Alexander III and to the fact that his intervention in Scotland was actively encouraged by the Guardians of the realm. The Guardians were the leading secular and ecclesiastical magnates of the kingdom with a wealth of experience behind them, and from the moment of Alexander III's death they regarded the pursuit and maintenance of cordial relations with England as their primary objective in external policy, and for good reason. A marriage alliance offered the best

[3] A. A. M. Duncan, 'The process of Norham, 1291', in P. R. Coss and S. D. Lloyd, eds., *Thirteenth Century England V: Proceedings of the Newcastle upon Tyne Conference, 1993* (Woodbridge, 1995), 215.

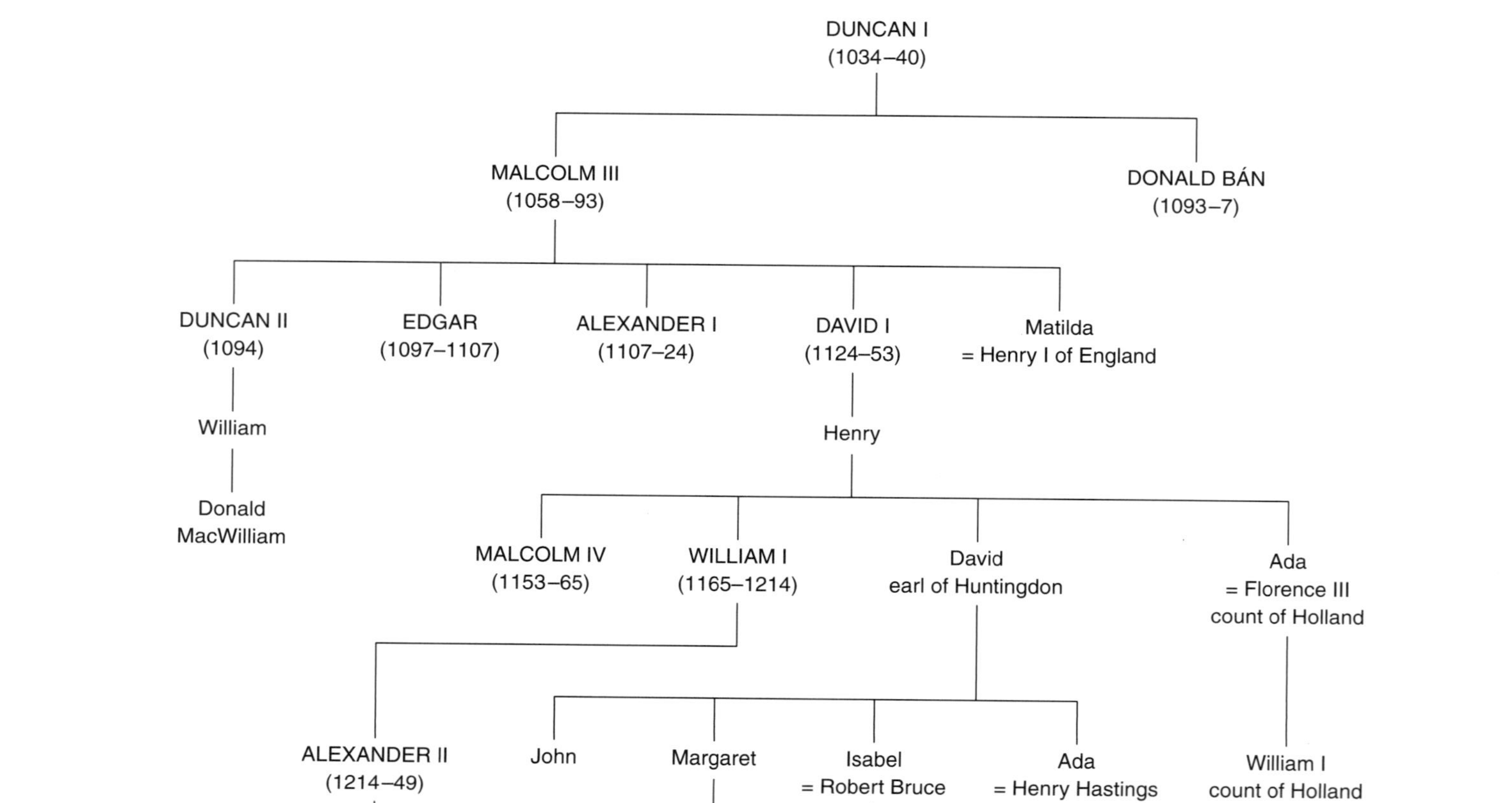
DUNCAN I
(1034–40)
MALCOLM III
(1058–93)
DONALD BÁN
(1093–7)
DUNCAN II
(1094)
EDGAR
(1097–1107)
ALEXANDER I
(1107–24)
DAVID I
(1124–53)
Matilda
= Henry I of England
William
Henry
Donald
MacWilliam
MALCOLM IV
(1153–65)
WILLIAM I
(1165–1214)
David
earl of Huntingdon
Ada
= Florence III
count of Holland
ALEXANDER II
(1214–49)
John
Margaret
Isabel
= Robert Bruce
Ada
= Henry Hastings
William I
count of Holland

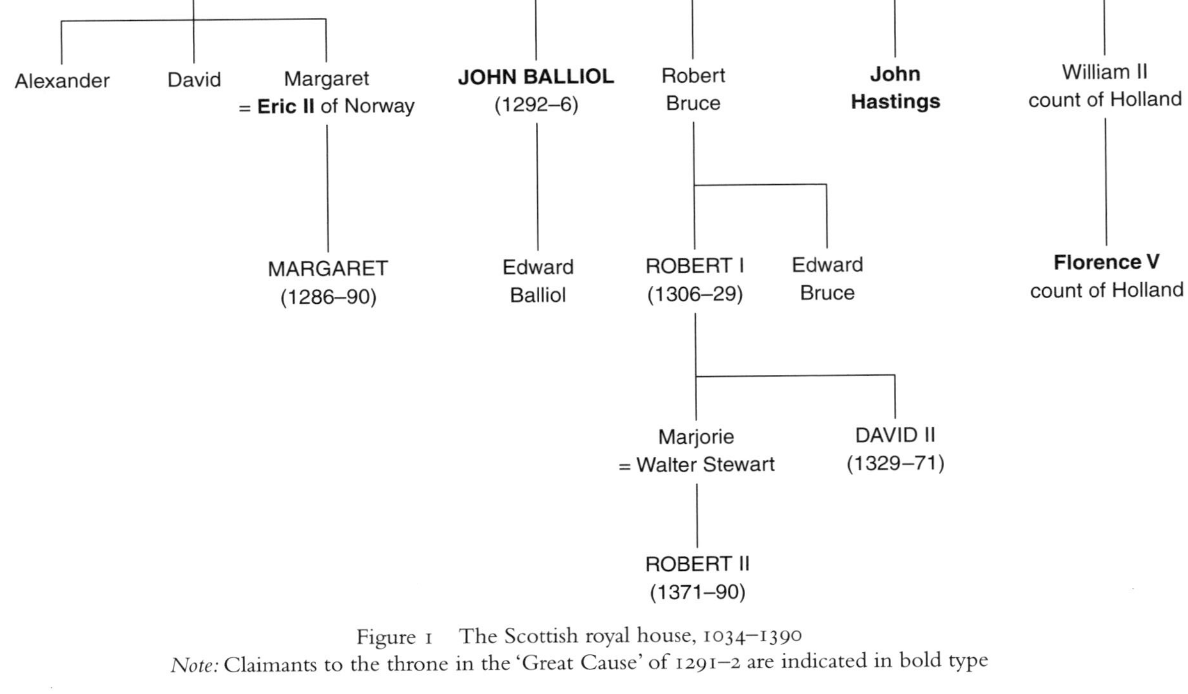

Figure 1 The Scottish royal house, 1034–1390
Note: Claimants to the throne in the 'Great Cause' of 1291–2 are indicated in bold type

hope of political stability, and after 1290 the judgement of the rival claims to the throne by a respected monarch such as Edward I must have seemed infinitely preferable to the prospect of a civil war which would extend to the whole realm the violence already stirred up by the Bruces in the south-west. The policy of seeking assistance from the masterful English king was not without its risks, but the alternatives were surely more unpalatable still.

This is not to exonerate Edward I from the charge that he took advantage of Scottish weakness to press far-reaching claims to feudal suzerainty in Scotland. As well as his own claim to the throne through Henry I's marriage to Matilda, daughter of Malcolm Canmore, which was abandoned when the other competitors acknowledged his authority to judge the case, there was also the possibility of arguing that the realm of Scotland had escheated to the overlord in the absence of either a direct heir to Margaret or any other close relatives. There is some evidence that Edward considered the latter option. On 1 August 1291 six Scottish magnates, including James Stewart, were offered lands in England 'if it happens that the realm of Scotland shall remain in the possession of the king and his heirs'. This was probably an attempt to see whether the Scottish political establishment would be willing to accept such a plan, but it aroused little enthusiasm, and the 'Great Cause' therefore proceeded.

Some of the candidates may simply have wished to place their claim on record for possible use in any subsequent contest, lest failure to articulate a claim in the 1290s be used by future opponents as an argument against its validity. Bids for the throne on the basis of illegitimate descent from earlier kings were almost certain to fail, as was the unusual and belated claim by King Eric II of Norway on the grounds that he was the father of the late queen. John Comyn of Badenoch, the most powerful lay magnate in Scotland, could claim descent from Malcolm III's brother Donald Bán, who had briefly been king of Scots in the 1090s, but was unlikely to prevail and so chose to support his brother-in-law John Balliol. In registering a claim, however, Comyn ensured that, should the male line of the Balliols become extinct, his own descendants by John's sister would inherit a double claim to the Scottish throne, and so the link with Donald was well worth articulating at this stage. But the main contenders were all descendants of David I's son Henry, earl of Northumbria, who had died in 1152.

Three claimants, John Balliol, Robert Bruce and John Hastings, were descendants of Earl David of Huntingdon, the younger brother of Malcolm IV and William the Lion. Earl David's estates had passed to his surviving son John, but he had died in 1237 without issue, whereupon his lands were divided between his sisters. Balliol, who was the grandson of the eldest, Margaret, based his claim on the grounds of seniority of line, in other words on primogeniture. Bruce, who was descended from Earl David's second daughter, Isabel, argued that his claim was superior to Balliol's because he was Isabel's son and so a generation closer to their common ancestor. He also said that Alexander II had named him as his heir. Hastings, the grandson of the third daughter, Ada, had no viable claim to the kingship but could allege that Scotland should be partitioned like Earl David's other lands, an argument which, if accepted, would have brought about the destruction of Scotland as a political and territorial entity. The court eventually decided that a kingdom, like a Scottish earldom but unlike an English one, was indivisible. Edward I did not wish to bring about the extinction of the Scottish realm on terms which might set an evil precedent for kingdoms everywhere.

Another claimant was Florence, count of Holland, who was descended from Ada, daughter of Earl Henry. He alleged that Earl David had quitclaimed his and his descendants' entitlement to the throne in return for succession to the lordship of Garioch, and later supplemented this with a statement that David had been forfeited for felony against Henry II. It is highly unlikely that the brother of William the Lion, who at that time had no legitimate son, would have abandoned his rights in so cavalier a manner in favour of a sister who had married a foreign count; if he had, then we might expect a claim to have been lodged by Humphrey de Bohun, earl of Hereford, descendant of another (and possibly older) sister.[4] Florence's arguments were, however, taken seriously by the court, and a long adjournment was granted to allow a search to be made in Scotland for documentary evidence of David's quitclaim. This strengthens the hypothesis that he was receiving direct encouragement from Edward I, whose daughter was contracted to marry Florence's son, although it has also been suggested that Bruce at

[4] Barrow, *Robert Bruce*, 40.

times backed and perhaps partly concocted Florence's claim in the hope that it might defeat Balliol even if his own arguments could not.[5] In November 1291 the prior of Pluscarden and the bishop of Moray both issued what purported to be certified copies of David's resignation; these were never produced in court and it is easy to dismiss them as forgeries. But could there be more to Florence's claim?

In 1195 William the Lion, who was suffering from illness, proposed that his eldest daughter Margaret should inherit the kingdom along with her prospective husband Otto, son of the duke of Saxony, thereby passing over the claim of Earl David. This idea was opposed by a group of influential Scottish nobles, who argued that custom dictated that a daughter should not succeed while the king's brother and his son were still alive. William's plan involved a treaty with Richard I of England whereby the newly married couple would receive Lothian from the king of Scots, and Northumberland and Cumberland from the king of England, and so should be seen in the context of William's long struggle to re-establish Scottish control over the northernmost English counties.[6] It does not, of course, prove that Earl David had renounced his right to the throne, and indeed the aristocratic reaction on his behalf may suggest that he had not. But William's proposal for the Scottish throne to pass to his daughter and her husband is unexpected, particularly when he appears to have had generally good relations with his younger brother. It is probably more likely that, if Florence's argument had any factual basis at all, it derived from a memory of Earl David's acceptance that his nephew Alexander had a prior claim to his own,[7] but there remains a nagging element of doubt that Florence was correct in stating that David had renounced his rights of succession.

Florence of Holland was the only claimant in the fray able to displace Bruce and Balliol. They had always been the principal candidates, which was recognised when each was entitled to provide forty

[5] J. A. Kossmann-Putto, 'Florence V, count of Holland, claimant to the Scottish throne in 1291–2: his personal and political background', in G. G. Simpson, ed., *Scotland and the Low Countries, 1124–1994* (East Linton, 1996), 23–4; Barrow, *Robert Bruce*, 43–9.

[6] Howden, *Chronica*, iii, 298–9, 308.

[7] K. J. Stringer, *Earl David of Huntingdon, 1152–1219: A Study in Anglo-Scottish History* (Edinburgh, 1985), 42–3, 284 n.92.

auditors to hear the case, along with twenty-four nominated by Edward I. The names of Balliol's auditors indicate that the geographical basis of his support was more extensive than that of Bruce, as could be expected in view of the widespread interests of his Comyn allies, and he could also boast a higher level of ecclesiastical representation. Bruce's case was, moreover, inherently weaker than his rival's. He could produce no written proof that Alexander II had nominated him as his heir presumptive, and failed even to make clear whether the alleged acknowledgement of his right had been in 1237–41, before the birth of Alexander's son, or in around 1249, when the king may have made arrangements for the succession in the event of the death of both himself and his young heir; although in 1291 Bruce was explicit that Alexander had not had a son at the time, he stated elsewhere that the king was going to war in the Isles.[8] Now that Dervorguilla Balliol was dead, Bruce could no longer allege precedence over her on the grounds of gender, and his claim therefore depended on the fact that he was of an earlier generation than John Balliol, a concept that was unfamiliar in contemporary feudal society in Britain and raised a host of problems. What would happen when the aged lord of Annandale died, as he surely must? Would his son's claim take precedence over that of his Balliol cousin in the same generation? Under Roman law he had a case, and could propose that the only relevant issue was who was closest in degree at the time of the vacancy, but in practice the horrendous potential for conflict was a serious flaw in his argument, and Bruce surely realised this. In desperation he came to an arrangement with Florence whereby each promised to compensate the other in the event of victory, and took up Hastings's argument that the kingdom was divisible. It was all to no avail. On the grounds of primogeniture, the court decided for Balliol on 17 November 1292, saving the rights of the English king, and he was duly inaugurated at Scone on St Andrew's Day. The homage he swore at Newcastle on 26 December may have been a humiliation, but it symbolised the fact that he had the favour of Edward I, who was duty bound to protect his vassal against his numerous rivals. If that was a comfort to King John, then it proved to be of short duration.

[8] E. L. G. Stones and G. G. Simpson, eds., *Edward I and the Throne of Scotland, 1290–1296: An Edition of the Record Sources for the Great Cause* (2 vols., Oxford, 1978), ii, 144–5, 170.

It is important to remember that John Balliol received the kingdom of Scotland by due legal process, and that his case was cogent. Furthermore, Balliol was supported by much of the political establishment in Scotland, most notably by the powerful Comyn family. The problems he experienced at the hands of Edward I have made King John seem like a puppet of the English monarch, but there is no reason to suppose that the Bruces would have acted appreciably differently, or have been able to resist the inevitable retribution of Edward I had they chosen to defy him.

Edward made it abundantly clear that his perception of overlordship over John Balliol was different from the feudal relationship which had prevailed under Alexander III. He expected the king of Scots to serve him militarily in France, and he heard appeals against the judgement of Scottish royal courts. Resistance to these demands was to be punished by the confiscation of key castles and, ultimately, of the realm itself. Such a relationship was unprecedented, at least since 1189, and Edward I's interest in Scotland was more direct, and therefore much more threatening, than Henry II's had been. Edward may deliberately have sought to humiliate King John, even to make his rule in Scotland untenable; by pursuing a policy which he knew the Scottish king and his magnates would find unbearable, he would have the legal right to seize Scotland as a fief forfeited to the overlord by a recalcitrant vassal. He can hardly have been totally unaware of John Balliol's sensibilities, for the English monarch himself was feudally subject to the king of France in respect of his duchy of Aquitaine; at the very time that he was imposing his overlordship on the hapless Balliol, Edward I was chafing under the similar restrictions placed on him by Philip IV of France, and he too faced the confiscation of his fief. But if he did realise the difficulties under which Balliol was labouring, he was unsympathetic to them. Moreover, his actions undermined the authority of King John within his realm, whereas Philip could threaten Edward only in respect of a French duchy which was not an integral part of the kingdom of England, merely a further territory held by its ruler.

Pro-Bruce accounts have painted a very gloomy picture of John Balliol's short reign, and the image has endured in the popular imagination. Even his ultimate resistance to Edward I has been criticised, its futility emphasising his inadequacies as a king. John has, therefore, been condemned both for obeying Edward I's demands and for resisting them. The alliance he made with France, which in the later Middle Ages was to be the cornerstone of Scottish foreign policy, was attributed to the counsel of others, it being unthinkable that so miserable a failure could ever have had the spirit to invoke Edward I's wrath in such a manner. This bias in Scottish sources is matched by a somewhat different bias in contemporary English ones, for to the English Balliol was a traitor, a man who had defied the legitimate demands of his overlord. Attempts to rehabilitate him have to penetrate this marked hostility of the sources.

In 1293 King John created three new sheriffdoms on the western seaboard, thereby consolidating the advances in royal power under Alexander II and Alexander III. The sheriffdom of Skye was entrusted to William, earl of Ross, while the local magnate Alexander MacDougall was granted that of Lorn and James Stewart received Kintyre. The new arrangements did not last because of the long crisis which followed John's deposition, but when Robert I subsequently established a sheriffdom in Argyll he was merely building on John Balliol's foundations on a more modest scale.

A number of English chroniclers note that during the parliament which met at Stirling in July 1295 the government of Scotland was taken out of the king's hands and entrusted to a council of twelve magnates, comprising four bishops, four earls and four barons, and thus reflecting, albeit on a larger scale, the arrangements made for the guardianship in 1286. The chroniclers draw parallels with French practice, but the example of the baronial revolt against Henry III of England in 1258 is perhaps more pertinent. The presumption is that the king was considered unfit to rule by the leading secular and ecclesiastical lords, who therefore took action to preserve the integrity of the realm, although it is equally likely that John sought the support of his principal magnates against the overbearing arrogance of Edward I. The sources are contradictory on whether the embassy to France was sent by John or by the aristocratic council, but its purpose was probably commercial rather than political, aiming to prevent the reimposition of a French trade embargo on the British Isles which threatened Scottish wool exports to Flanders.[9] Evidence for John's diplomacy is found in a

[9] A. Stevenson, 'The Flemish dimension of the Auld Alliance', in Simpson, ed., *Scotland and the Low Countries*, 33–5.

tale that he sent envoys to Pope Celestine V, requesting that he be absolved from his homage to the English king on the grounds that it had been extorted by force.[10] Celestine was pope for a few months in the second half of 1294, and so an approach to him demonstrates that John was seeking to rid himself of an uncomfortable bind long before the parliament of Stirling. The story may have no factual basis and merely reflect propaganda against a perfidious Scottish king who had long plotted against his overlord, while the fact that Celestine apparently acceded to Balliol's request could be dismissed on the grounds that the simple-minded hermit, who had unwillingly accepted an office to which he was palpably unsuited, had been misinformed. The tale cannot, however, be arbitrarily dismissed. It is uncorroborated by record sources, but may suggest that King John was less subservient to Edward I than his reputation would allow.

John Balliol's recalcitrance came at a difficult time for Edward I, who was at war with the king of France over Aquitaine, and had had to face a revolt in Wales. It is improbable that Edward desired a breach of relations at this juncture, and more likely that the Scots took advantage of his discomfiture to express their disapproval of the breaches of the guarantees laid down in the treaty of Birgham, which Edward had annulled in January 1293 because the proposed marriage with which it had dealt was no longer possible. On 26 March 1296 they attacked Carlisle, where Robert Bruce, son of the Competitor who had died the previous year, was in charge of the garrison. Edward's invasion was not long in coming. It could be justified on the grounds of the Franco-Scottish alliance, which had been ratified in February, or as the culmination of the appeal to the English royal courts by MacDuff of Fife and others, the Scots king having refused to attend court or hand over the three castles and towns which he had been sentenced to forfeit. Berwick was stormed and many of its inhabitants killed, the Scottish force was crushed at Dunbar, and Edward proceeded through Scotland without encountering serious opposition. King John had little choice but to submit. Edward apparently considered granting him an English earldom in return for his quitclaim of Scotland, but this

[10] *The Chronicle of Walter of Guisborough*, ed. H. Rothwell (Camden Society, 1957), 270; *The Chronicle of Pierre de Langtoft*, ed. T. Wright (2 vols., Rolls Series, 1866–8), ii, 220–2.

offer, if it was ever formally made, was withdrawn. Balliol was ceremonially divested of his royal garments and led away to an English prison, a pathetic figure. Edward also removed to England the Stone of Destiny, upon which Scottish kings were traditionally inaugurated, the royal archives, and Scotland's holiest relic, the Black Rood of St Margaret. More than 1,500 people are recorded to have sworn fealty to him. Whatever his original intentions, the realm of Scotland had fallen into Edward's hands.

The English administration set up in the wake of King John's surrender was soon regarded as oppressive, partly because Scottish procedures were deliberately replaced by English ones. The Scots were not used to paying taxes, and were therefore all the more angered by the very successful collection of revenue by Hugh Cressingham, Edward I's treasurer in Scotland. This success was, however, short-term. Opposition to the occupying regime was encountered in several parts of Scotland, with leaders who included William Wallace and Andrew Murray, the latter having escaped from Chester, where he had been placed in custody the previous year. Their early activities are difficult to trace in detail, but their combined force succeeded in defeating a major English army at Stirling Bridge in September 1297. Cressingham was slain, and his skin cut up to make souvenirs for the victorious Scots. Murray and Wallace wrote on 11 October to merchants of Lübeck and Hamburg announcing that it was once again safe to trade with Scotland, the realm having been 'recovered by war from the power of the English'. Murray died soon afterwards of the wounds he had received at Stirling Bridge, leaving the younger son of an insignificant knight as the unlikely Guardian of the kingdom and commander of the army.

William Wallace has rightly become a folk-hero. Unlike Robert Bruce, the future king, whose activities were influenced by the need to defend his broad territorial interests and to preserve his chance of receiving the Scottish crown with Edward I's blessing, Wallace could concentrate on the task of freeing Scotland from English control, whether in battle or through diplomacy. He came to prominence through his successful involvement at Stirling Bridge, although he had clearly proved himself as a military leader before this. His political power stemmed from this success on the field of battle and his leadership of the savage raids into northern

England which followed his victory at Stirling, but was likely to continue only for as long as he retained that aura of invincibility, since he was not the natural leader of the Scottish aristocratic community. Even after his defeat, however, he was not an insignificant figure, as Edward I's obsession with his capture amply testifies.

News of the disaster at Stirling Bridge reached England at a period of political crisis caused by the incessant demands of Edward I for money to finance his wars and his disregard of traditional conventions. The realisation that the settlement of Scotland had been put in such serious jeopardy concentrated minds wonderfully, and the army which Edward led to Scotland in 1298 was probably one of the largest ever mustered by a medieval English king. Wallace used the tactics which Robert I was to employ in 1322, namely of adopting a scorched-earth policy and withdrawing northwards, hoping to draw the English force beyond the limits of its logistical support. English armies advancing along the east coast could be supplied from the sea, but in 1298 provisions were in short supply and Edward was contemplating retreat when he learnt that the Scots were at nearby Falkirk. It remains unclear why Wallace chose to stand and fight so large an English force. Presumably he believed that he could defeat it, especially when it was rumoured that the large Welsh contingent might desert; perhaps the fundamentally conservative attitude of the age persuaded him to seek glory in a pitched battle.

The battle of Falkirk on 22 July proved, however, to be a shattering defeat for William Wallace. He had drawn up his army in a series of *schiltrons*, circular formations which presented a hedgehog-like wall of spears from all directions. Such units were impregnable against charges by mounted men-at-arms, but very vulnerable to attack from archers, especially when the Scottish cavalry had left the field and was no longer in a position to harass the English bowmen. The departure of the Scottish mounted knights has often been seen as treachery on the part of nobles who resented Wallace's pre-eminence and so were prepared to abandon him and his army to Edward I's superior firepower. This explanation is unsatisfactory, for many leading Scots had in fact shown themselves willing to join Wallace. It is much more likely that the Scottish cavalry fled in terror in the face of the more numerous men-at-arms on the

English side.[11] Whatever the reason, the victory belonged to the English. Shortly afterwards Wallace resigned as Guardian, apparently voluntarily, although it would have been virtually impossible for him to maintain his political leadership now that Edward I had destroyed the highly trained infantry army on which he had relied.

The victory at Falkirk did not restore the English position in Scotland to the state in which Edward I had left it in 1296. The next few years saw a series of inconclusive campaigns and a continuous struggle on the part of English administrators to maintain more than a vestige of authority north of the border. Money was short; the supply of provisions was irregular; it was difficult to recruit troops for campaigns or garrison duty, and even more so to retain them in the king's service when there was often no pay to prevent them deserting; potential royal officials were frequently reluctant to serve in Scotland. Any extension of English control exacerbated these problems because it was not matched by a corresponding increase in the number of troops or the availability of money or supplies. The Scottish government in the north was probably more successful, and the fact that it could hold a parliament as far south as Rutherglen in May 1300 shows that it could operate across a broader swathe of the kingdom than the English occupying forces were able, even nominally, to control. Scotland had become a running sore for Edward I.[12]

Those who governed the parts of Scotland outside English control did so on behalf of the deposed King John. They also actively sought international support, especially in France and at the papal curia. The French king, Philip IV, was favourably disposed to the Scots in view of his own difficulties with Edward I, but the attitude of Pope Boniface VIII was less predictable. Boniface was a bad-tempered and aggressive man who during his pontificate managed to antagonise most secular rulers, and the support which he offered to the Scots was partly a mark of his bitter opposition to Edward I's taxation of the English clergy, although he may have been genuinely convinced by the learned pleading of Master Baldred Bisset and other Scottish advocates. In June 1299 he composed a bull, *Scimus fili*, to Edward, supporting the Scottish position, declaring that

[11] Barrow, *Robert Bruce*, 102.

[12] The issues discussed in this paragraph are treated in detail in F. Watson, *Under the Hammer: Edward I and Scotland, 1286–1306* (East Linton, 1998).

Scotland was a possession of the Roman church and not feudally subject to the king of England, and pointing out that during the negotiations for Queen Margaret to marry his son, Edward had promised that Scotland would be free. Boniface ordered the release of imprisoned Scottish clerks, and told Edward to make the case for his right in Scotland within six months.[13] Some of these arguments could easily be disproved, especially the claim that Scotland belonged to the Apostolic See, although in 1291 the Scots may have sought papal protection or at least confirmation of Edward I's concessions.[14] The bull was, nonetheless, a clear indication of papal support for the Scottish cause, if not specifically for John Balliol, who was referred to merely as the man to whom Edward was said to have committed the kingdom. This suggests that the envoys to the curia had different priorities from those who were influential at the French royal court, where there was support for Balliol in person.

Scimus fili was probably not delivered until spring 1300, but it placed Edward in a dilemma. He received advice that to respond to the bull might be portrayed as a recognition of the papal claim to judge temporal matters. On the other hand, failure to answer the points raised by Boniface might serve indirectly to confirm the pope's belief in the veracity of the Scottish case. So in May 1301 he replied, arguing that the English kings had enjoyed suzerainty over Scotland since ancient times, and that more recently also Scottish leaders had sworn fealty to him; furthermore, the competitors for the throne had asked him to intervene, and Balliol had specifically surrendered Scotland into Edward's hands.[15] Like the Scottish claims which this statement sought to refute, Edward based his arguments on a combination of legendary history and more recent events.

By 1302 there seemed a realistic chance that John Balliol would return to his kingdom and resume the mantle of government. He had been released from the papal custody into which Edward I had handed him in 1299, and could count on French support, perhaps even on a French military expedition in his favour. In 1301 the official acts of the Scottish government began to be issued directly in the name of King John and be dated by his regnal year, with the

[13] *ASR*, no. 28. [14] Duncan, 'Process of Norham', 228–9. [15] *ASR*, nos. 29, 30.

Guardian, John de Soules, attesting merely as a witness. This was a more modest position than that of earlier Guardians or army commanders, who since 1297 had issued documents under their own names, albeit on behalf of the absent monarch. It is unlikely that the change of style was merely cosmetic, and it probably demonstrates that the government expected the king to return to Scotland. Moreover, this expectation seems to have been shared by Edward I and by the Bruces. Probably early in 1302 Robert Bruce, earl of Carrick and grandson of the Competitor, returned to Edward's peace and received from the English king a vague and coded promise to uphold the right that Bruce claimed. The exact significance of the terms agreed between the two men is much disputed, but it is possible that Edward was considering the option of pressing the Bruce claim in the event of John Balliol's return, which at the very least would have stirred up hostilities in south-western Scotland and given Edward the opportunity to fish in troubled waters. He had already entered into a disadvantageous truce with the French, which is best explained on the grounds that he was seriously concerned by the prospect of Balliol's restoration. He feared the further erosion of his authority in Scotland, while Bruce feared the loss of his Scottish lands. Robert may have committed himself to the English cause out of dislike of the Comyns, who were still dominant in the Scottish government, but this does not fully explain the timing of his submission, since John de Soules had been sole or at least principal Guardian for nearly a year. It is much more likely that he felt that such a course of action would be the only guarantee of his continued possession of the earldom of Carrick and his succession to the lordship of Annandale after his father's death.[16]

Balliol's hopes were dashed by the crushing defeat of the French forces at the battle of Courtrai in July 1302, which impelled Philip IV to seek a settlement with Edward I. Furthermore, a deterioration in Franco-papal relations hindered the Scots' diplomatic efforts on John's behalf and caused the mercurial Boniface VIII to take a pro-English line. He withdrew from the position he had articulated in *Scimus fili* and now accused the Scottish prelates of causing the war, naming Bishop Wishart as the principal culprit.[17] By the

[16] Barrow, *Robert Bruce*, 121–4; Watson, *Under the Hammer*, 144–7.

[17] *Les registres de Boniface VIII*, ed. G. Digard, A. Thomas, M. Faucon and R. Fawtier (4 vols., Paris, 1884 1934), nos. 4725–6.

summer of 1303 the grip of the English administration in southern Scotland was clearly being tightened, and early the following year, after Edward I had overwintered in Scotland, it became evident to his opponents that further resistance was, for the time being at least, pointless. The general submission negotiated by the Guardian, John Comyn, was made on terms which were not vindictive or ungenerous, partly because Edward could not afford to keep his army in the field for much longer. With a very few exceptions, the Scottish lords were allowed to retain their lands and thereby much of their local political influence, and although their capacity to make decisions at the centre of government was inevitably reduced, Edward was clearly prepared to work with the natural leaders of Scottish society in making new constitutional arrangements for Scotland. He did not repeat the mistakes he had made in the aftermath of his triumph in 1296.

The arrangements made by Edward I after the Scots' submission in 1304 were, however, likely to arouse hostility among some of his supporters. In the past, he had granted Scottish lands to a number of magnates as an incentive to fight in what had become an unpopular and unproductive war. Few of the intended beneficiaries had been able to conquer their new territories, let alone make a profit from them, but the effective revocation of these grants may still have caused some resentment. The change of policy was nonetheless wise. If Scots had been dispossessed, they would have been less inclined to accede to English rule and the task of establishing widespread English control would have been rendered much more difficult. Edward had realised that he could not hope to conquer Scotland as he had Wales, nor could he convert Scotland into an English colony. Only at Berwick, where the inhabitants had been massacred during the invasion of 1296, was an English community established, and even then Edward was slow to grant it privileges; elsewhere, for example at Roxburgh, English burgesses had to live alongside Scots. Edward I's best chance of maintaining a vested interest in Scotland was to work with the political community which had resisted him so stubbornly and so effectively.[18]

[18] M. Prestwich, 'Colonial Scotland: the English in Scotland under Edward I', in R. A. Mason, ed., *Scotland and England, 1286–1815* (Edinburgh, 1987), 13–16.

There is little doubt, however, that the realm of Scotland had ceased to exist in English eyes. During the Great Cause it had been determined that Scotland was a kingdom and could not be divided, and even after Balliol's forced abdication and the removal of the Stone of Destiny and the royal archives, English documents still describe Scotland as a realm. The same designation was used when the English tried to justify Edward I's position to Boniface VIII in 1301. Yet by 1305, when an ordinance was drawn up for the government of Scotland, it is referred to merely as a 'land'. Although Edward did not add the lordship of Scotland to his lengthy list of titles, it appears that the former kingdom was being relegated to a status similar to that of Ireland. English control over the British Isles seemed assured.

Edward I's plans for the future government of Scotland must have disappointed the earl of Carrick, in whom the Bruce claim to the throne was now vested after the death of his less ambitious father in 1304. Whatever may have been promised when he submitted to Edward in 1302, it was now clear that the English king had no intention of installing him on the Scottish throne. Even so, his decision to seize the crown in the early part of 1306 appears a desperate gamble, especially when the Bruces had never enjoyed widespread support in those parts of Scotland which had successfully resisted English aggression.

Robert Bruce's intentions in the years before 1306 are difficult to determine. Periods of loyalty to Edward I had alternated with periods of resistance, and the reconciliation of 1302 probably came about because both Bruce and Edward feared the restoration of their common foe, John Balliol. Balliol lived until 1313, and his claim was passed on to his son, but after the submission of the Comyns and his other allies in 1304 there was little prospect that he would return to Scotland. Bruce's continued attachment to the English cause could not, therefore, be taken for granted, for the youngest Robert had inherited his grandfather's burning determination to be king of Scots. At Cambuskenneth on 11 June 1304, at the very time when he was with the English army at the siege of Stirling and was performing homage to Edward I as the heir of his late father, Bruce entered into a bond of mutual friendship and alliance with Bishop Lamberton of St Andrews. The terms were very vague, but no mention was made of allegiance to the king, and it may be that Bruce was already planning to seize the throne and was seeking support from the bishop who had received his see under the auspices of William Wallace. Certainly Lamberton was a supporter of Bruce from the time of his inauguration, but we must be wary of reading too much into this earlier bond of friendship. Like the Turnberry Band of 1286, later events may cause it to appear more significant than it really was.

Opinions differ as to whether Bruce's coup was planned in advance. On 10 February 1306 he met John Comyn in the Franciscan friary in Dumfries, and after an argument Comyn was murdered. The purpose of this meeting is obscure. Later writers tell a much embellished romantic story that Bruce and Comyn had entered into a pact that Bruce should take the crown with Comyn's support, Comyn receiving Bruce's lands in return; Comyn, who was later invariably regarded as a traitor, then revealed the plot to Edward I. There is no contemporary evidence for such an arrangement, and in its full form the story is clearly fictional, but such tales usually contain a basis of fact. Some English chroniclers suggest that Comyn was murdered because he would not join Bruce's treason, Edward I made similar allegations in a letter to the pope denouncing Bishop Lamberton, and there are suggestions that Bruce may indeed have accused Comyn of reporting his treason to Edward.[19] If Bruce did intend to usurp the throne, then the support of the Comyns and their numerous connections would have been invaluable, and so he may have been prepared to take the considerable risk of revealing his plans to John Comyn even though the latter had been a strong supporter of Balliol. It is not, however, apparent why Bruce, who potentially had never been richer or more highly favoured by the English king, was prepared to gamble on seizing the Scottish throne while the formidable Edward I was still alive, nor is it known whether he had discussed the matter with Comyn before February 1306. There must have been some reason for the meeting in Dumfries, but it is inconceivable that Bruce set out with the specific intention of murdering a rival within the confines of a consecrated church. There is good evidence that Comyn was killed in two stages, doubtless because Bruce realised

[19] Barrow, *Robert Bruce*, 139–41.

that he had now compromised himself so hopelessly that he had nothing further to lose from despatching Comyn and thereby silencing him.

Bruce's inauguration at Scone on 25 March 1306 has all the hallmarks of being a hastily arranged ceremony. The Stone of Destiny was, of course, in England, but the level of improvisation went beyond the need to supply a substitute. In the absence of the earl of Fife, to whom fell the traditional right of placing the new king on the stone, this crucial task was performed by the late earl's sister, Isabel countess of Buchan, who thereby committed herself to Bruce's cause even though her husband was a Comyn. Two days later Bishop Lamberton celebrated a solemn mass.[20] He must have known about the impending inauguration because he had left the English king's council 'secretly and by night', and Bishop Wishart of Glasgow was even more enthusiastic for Bruce. He and the bishop of Moray were to liken fighting for Robert's cause to participation in a crusade, and other clerics may have supported him because of Edward I's policy of promoting Englishmen to Scottish benefices. It has been argued that the inauguration was not only 'the private revolution of an ambitious man', but 'much more momentously . . . the political revolution of the community of the realm', and that it was in effect a sort of election marking the revival of Scottish kingship,[21] but the level of support for Robert in 1306 should not be overestimated. The impression is that the ceremony was attended by a number of Bruce partisans and inveterate opponents of English rule, but did not mark a revival of Scottish kingship upon which even a majority of Scots were willing to pin their hopes; after all, the violent death of John Comyn had destroyed any chance of Bruce gaining the support of his kinsfolk and connections. It is hard to escape the conclusion that the murder of Comyn precipitated Bruce's seizure of the throne, as he realised that his best chance of salvation lay in his becoming king, thereby drawing on the natural loyalty which was attached to the cause of a legitimate monarch and tapping into the considerable antipathy towards the English which undoubtedly existed in Scotland. Whatever interpretation we place on the events of early 1306, Bruce was now irrevocably committed to the cause of Scottish independence.

[20] On these events see *RRS*, v, 127–9.

[21] Barrow, *Robert Bruce*, 144; cf. p. xii.

The first few months of Robert I's reign were unhappy ones for the new king. After defeats at Methven and Dalry, he was forced to flee from Scotland, and his movements during the winter of 1306–7 remain the subject of speculation. In the meantime several members of his family and close supporters had been delivered to Edward I's implacable wrath. His captured brothers were executed, including Alexander Bruce, dean of Glasgow, whose clerical orders might have been expected to save him from the death penalty. Bruce's sister Mary was placed in a specially constructed cage in Roxburgh castle, while the countess of Buchan was similarly confined at Berwick for her effrontery in participating at his inauguration. Edward I has rightly been criticised for his brutality against Bruce's family and connections, particularly the women, but the usurpation of the throne had again put in jeopardy all he believed he had achieved in Scotland, and his angry reaction to the treachery of a man towards whom he had shown favour was only to be expected. On 7 July 1307 Edward, determined on yet another expedition to Scotland, died at Burgh-by-Sands on the southern side of the Solway. His son, Edward II, was to prove a much less vigorous adversary.

Edward I had accomplished much in Scotland, but had been unable to give his administration sufficiently firm foundations to achieve lasting English rule north of the border. Despite the fact that for most of his reign he enjoyed widespread support among his magnates and presided over a highly effective bureaucratic and military machine, he was unable to give his adherents a large enough economic or territorial stake in Scotland, and found it difficult to provide sufficiently large numbers of men or regular enough supplies finally to overcome Scottish resistance. The moderate settlement which followed John Comyn's surrender in 1304 offered the best opportunity to bring the political community of Scotland to an acceptance of English rule, but Bruce's usurpation of the throne once again plunged the country into war before the new constitutional arrangements had had chance to work. The level of continuing resistance to the English became apparent during Robert I's reign, but it drew strength from the Scottish king's striking successes and cannot be measured quantitatively or qualitatively at the end of Edward I's reign. Many Scots must have felt excluded from central government after 1304, and the choice in autumn 1305 of John of

Brittany as Edward's lieutenant was poor, because John was in no hurry to take up his appointment, leaving the English administration somewhat rudderless. But it was Bruce's rebellion, apparently not expected by Edward I, which darkened the final days of the formidable old king. Edward had clearly misjudged Bruce, but it would have been hard for him to have accommodated the ambitions of a man who felt that he had an hereditary right to a throne which in Edward's eyes was no more.

The ineptitude of Edward II, and the serious political problems he faced at home, allowed Robert I to consolidate his position in Scotland, especially after his decisive victory over the Comyns at Inverurie in 1308, after which he devastated the earldom of Buchan. This savage harrying or 'herschip' shows that Bruce was fighting a civil war against his internal enemies at least as much as a patriotic one against the English, and indeed the defeat of his Scottish foes was an essential prerequisite for any campaign against the English occupying forces. In alliance with the MacDougalls of Argyll, the Comyns could use their possession of key castles to control the main Highland passes and thereby render Scotland effectively ungovernable by the new king. The Comyns had been strengthened in their allegiance to the English by the violent events in the Greyfriars at Dumfries, but this was less an act of treachery than a reflection of common hostility to the Bruces. It was far from clear in the immediate aftermath of Robert's inauguration that he would ultimately enjoy the military triumphs which cemented his reputation, and there was no reason for the Comyns and their allies to support him. The 'herschip' of Buchan was the price they had to pay when the Bruce cause so spectacularly revived.

This is not the place for a detailed narrative of the war. It is a tale of daring deeds, such as the night assault on Perth in January 1313, when the king himself took the lead in wading through the icy moat and storming the ramparts. It is also a tale of the steady consolidation of royal authority, including the holding of a parliament at St Andrews in March 1309, when the clergy and nobles formally accepted the rectitude of the Bruce claim to the throne. The war was taken on to English soil, with two major raids in 1311 setting the scene for later, even more destructive plundering campaigns. Robert I's success during these years was striking, and owes much to his use of the resources of manpower from northern and western

Scotland on which he could draw. That was the area in which he had sheltered after the disasters of 1306, and of all the Scottish medieval kings he had the closest relationship with the chiefs of the area and their followers. The men he recruited were instrumental in the successes of the years up to 1314, and probably also in the subsequent invasion of Ireland; it was only after the great victory at Bannockburn that Robert was able to draw his armies principally from the more populous areas in the south and east.[22]

Bannockburn is a very famous battle, inevitably and rightly so. It was rare indeed for a full-scale English army to be defeated by the Scots, especially when that army was led by the king of England in person. Edward II's disastrous expedition is usually explained by the need to relieve Stirling castle, the key to Scotland, after its commander, Sir Philip Mowbray, had agreed with Edward Bruce that it would surrender if it had not been relieved by 24 June 1314. Edward Bruce, the king's warlike brother, has been blamed for issuing a rash challenge to which even Edward II would have to rise. It has, however, now been argued that the English campaign was not planned because of the threat to Stirling, but rather because in October 1313 Robert I proclaimed that his enemies had a year in which to come to his peace or suffer perpetual disinheritance, a move which would lead to widespread desertion among Edward II's supporters in Scotland unless he showed that he was prepared to uphold their interests. Three independent English sources place the start of the siege of Stirling in Lent 1314, and the agreement about the relief of the castle was made in the knowledge that Edward II was planning a campaign in the summer.[23]

To oppose the English army directly was a risky strategy, for defeat would have jeopardised the considerable achievements of the preceding years. Serious thought was given to making a strategic withdrawal into Lennox, the upland district west of Stirling, in the knowledge that Edward II would be unable to keep his force in the field for any length of time. The battle of Bannockburn might, therefore, never have taken place. But it did, and the victory sealed Robert I's reputation as both a military leader and a Scottish patriot. The success also allowed the Scots to embark on a new strategy,

[22] C. McNamee, *The Wars of the Bruces: Scotland, England and Ireland, 1306–1328* (East Linton, 1997), 12.

[23] A. A. M. Duncan, 'The war of the Scots, 1306–23', *TRHS*, 6th ser. 2 (1992), 149–50.

characterised by increasingly lengthy raids into northern England, concentrated military pressure on Berwick and Carlisle, and intervention in Ireland. The expeditions into England were led mainly by two of Robert's most trusted supporters: James Douglas, ancestor of a family which was to play a crucial role in late medieval Scotland; and Thomas Randolph, upon whom the king had bestowed the long-dormant earldom of Moray in 1312. The invasion of Ireland was under the command of Edward Bruce.

Scottish involvement in the troubled affairs of Ireland was no new phenomenon. Mercenaries from western Scotland, the so-called 'galloglasses', were a familiar feature of Irish warfare, and the Turnberry Band of 1286 had shown that the Bruces were prepared to dabble in Irish politics in return for unspecified support. English rule in Ireland was largely restricted to the south-east, and the invasion by Edward Bruce in 1315 increased the already considerable pressure on it. It is very unlikely, however, that Edward's ambition extended no further than the opening of another front against the English, for on a hill outside Dundalk in May 1316 he had himself proclaimed king of Ireland, and there is some evidence that he also sought to raise the Welsh in a pan-Celtic alliance. The notion of such an alliance may seem fanciful and romantic, but the rebellion of Llywelyn Bren in Glamorgan, which erupted in February 1316, coincided with a winter campaign in Ireland by Edward Bruce which seems incomprehensible unless it was intended to be an element in a broader plan.[24] Certainly Edward Bruce attempted the conquest of Ireland with almost indecent haste, and we should be in little doubt that conquest was his aim, for the pursuit of more limited strategic objectives would not have necessitated such extensive military expeditions. It is true that Ireland was an important source of supplies and troops for the English invasions of Scotland and the defence of north-west England, and the need to cut these lines of communication would explain the occupation of Ulster and perhaps the attempt to reduce English authority in Leinster, but not the campaigning further west. There is also little doubt that Edward Bruce was personally ambitious. Relations between him and his elder brother appear sometimes to have been strained, and Robert was doubtless glad to give him the opportunity to expend his

[24] McNamee, *Wars of the Bruces*, 193–4.

energies outside Scotland. While Robert supported the invasion of Ireland and personally participated in it, he could readily spare troops only in the winter months and Edward could achieve little outside Ulster without such reinforcements.[25]

This is not to say that the invasion of Ireland was merely a side-show, still less a luxury which the victorious Scots could now afford, for the opening of a new front was risky in view of the much greater resources of the English state. Although the relevant records are incomplete, there is clear evidence that the import of food from Ireland to Carlisle's port at Skinburness had been on a considerable scale in Edward I's reign, and continued to be a vital element of the English war effort until after Bannockburn. Provisions were again arriving at a significant rate by the early 1320s.[26] The Irish expedition, therefore, helped build up pressure on Carlisle, the capture of which may have been one of Robert I's objectives in the years after 1314, but ultimately the intervention in Ireland was a failure. Edward Bruce was defeated and killed at the battle of Faughart in 1318, and is remembered not as the agent of a grand Celtic alliance against the English, but as the source of great destruction in Ireland in a time of famine.

The famine which began in 1315 was widespread throughout Europe. A series of disastrous harvests, followed by an epidemic among cattle, may have marked the end of a long period of rising population. Its impact on Scotland is hard to gauge, and its effects may have been mitigated by successful plundering and extortion by Scottish armies in northern England. Communities were prepared to pay large sums for immunity from attack, and this must have lubricated the Scottish economy. Certainly, the high prices of Scottish commodities suggest that a good deal of bullion was in circulation, doubtless as a result of the successful war as well as booming wool exports. However, Robert I clearly did not regard the attacks on northern England as an end in themselves, nor as a strategy which could continue indefinitely. While he rejected a truce proposed by the pope in 1317, not permitting the papal nuncios to enter Scotland because their bulls did not address him as king, an action for which he was excommunicated the following

[25] R. Frame, 'The Bruces in Ireland, 1315–18', *Irish Historical Studies*, 19 (1974), 11. Frame's assessment of the relationship between the two brothers is more positive than that offered here.

[26] McNamee, *Wars of the Bruces*, 127, 189–90.

year, Robert made several overtures for peace. This was sensible, for the fortunes of war are unpredictable, and there was always the danger of an English counter-attack, such as the major campaign of 1322 which was met by a withdrawal north of the Forth and a scorched-earth policy in Lothian, moves which were hardly likely to improve the economic prospects of the south-eastern corner of the realm. In January 1323 Robert concluded a treaty with Andrew Harcla, earl of Carlisle, by which the Scottish king offered security for northern England and the payment of 40,000 merks over ten years in return for a simple recognition of Scottish independence. These very generous terms were angrily rejected by Edward II, and Harcla was executed for his presumption in agreeing terms with the king's mortal enemy. Edward was not prepared to admit defeat by recognising Robert I as king of Scots.

The fact that Robert was prepared to pay so handsomely for recognition of his title indicates his vulnerability. He was not accepted as king by the English, who were still formidable opponents despite Bannockburn, nor by the papacy, which remained convinced by the English version of events and unimpressed by the record of a man who had murdered a rival in a church and defied the papal truce of 1317. He had no direct male heir until the birth of his son David in March 1324, while his eldest daughter Marjorie had died, probably in 1317. In 1315 he had nominated his brother Edward as his successor, but the latter's death at Faughart necessitated fresh arrangements, and so in 1318 the king's infant grandson Robert, son of Marjorie Bruce and Walter Stewart, was named as heir presumptive. The Bruce dynasty was, therefore, by no means secure. Furthermore, although military victory had strengthened his hand, Robert I still faced potential challenges from former allies of John Balliol and the Comyns. It is in this context that we must view Robert's search for internal security and external recognition.

The desire to persuade international opinion of the justice of the Scottish cause is most clearly identified by the Declaration of Arbroath, which takes the form of a letter to the pope, dated 6 April 1320, purportedly from thirty-nine named lay magnates 'and the rest of the barons and freeholders and the whole community of the realm of Scotland'. It describes the legendary history of the Scottish nation and the migrations which eventually brought it to Scotland, stressing forcefully, if inaccurately, that the Scots had never been subject to any other people. Moving on to more recent events, the Declaration paints a lurid picture of the oppression wrought by Edward I, who had taken advantage of the Scots' temporary weakness, and upholds the cause of Robert I, who had become king by divine providence, the laws and customs of the realm, and the consent of the people. This combination of heavenly favour, legal right and popular assent was, however, to be of no avail if he were to forsake the principles which underpinned his rule, and especially if he were to subject himself or his people to English dominion; in such circumstances he would be expelled by the community of the realm, 'for it is not glory, nor riches, nor honours, but liberty alone that we fight and contend for, which no honest person will lose except with his life.' The pope is urged to use his influence to prevail on the king of England to leave Scotland in peace, since it is a small kingdom on the very edge of the inhabited world.

Although the Declaration of Arbroath was sent in the name of the lay baronage, it was almost certainly a product of the royal chapel. Stylistically and conceptually, it is much more polished than the similar remonstrance sent by the Irish in 1317, but shares with it a hostility to English rule and an appeal to a mythical past as well as to recent history. The author may have been Bernard, abbot of Arbroath and royal chancellor, although a case has also been made for Alexander de Kininmund, later bishop of Aberdeen.[27] The Declaration is a famous assertion of Scottish independence and nationhood, but it should be seen not as a unique document but merely as one of a lengthy series of initiatives to try to win the support of the pope and to justify Robert I's seizure of the throne and the extinction of John Balliol's claim. In the changed international circumstances, it was in fact much less effective than the approaches to Boniface VIII had been.

The unanimity implied by the Declaration of Arbroath was much more apparent than real. Like the assertion of Bruce's right to the throne by the St Andrews parliament of 1309, the Declaration was primarily a piece of propaganda, directed at an audience both within and outside Scotland. The circumstances of Robert I's seizure of the throne had exacerbated the already deep

[27] Barrow, *Robert Bruce*, 308. For Bernard's career see *RRS*, v, 198–203.

fissure in Scottish society between the followers of the Bruces on one side and the adherents of John Balliol and the Comyns on the other. The selective use of violence, as in the harrying of Buchan, and the inspiration engendered by the victorious war against the English combined to boost the support which Robert I received from all classes, but the king remained fundamentally insecure. His dynastic claim was relatively weak so long as the Balliol line remained, and his position depended largely on his military success, which might easily be reversed in the same way as Wallace's victory at Stirling Bridge had been avenged at Falkirk. In order to rule, Robert required the adherence of many magnates who had previously supported John Balliol, and their loyalty could not be relied on.

Throughout his reign, Robert pursued the principle that disinheritance should befall only those who were not prepared unreservedly to swear allegiance to him, which after 1314 meant that individuals had to choose whether they wished to be Scottish or English landowners. This finally severed the cross-border lordships which had been such a feature of the thirteenth century, although it did not mark a major upheaval among the personnel of the Scottish landed class. Although forfeitures led to significant redistribution of land, there was no 'new nobility' as a result of the Wars of Independence, but there were some disinherited and embittered exiles as well as individuals within Scotland who still hankered for a Balliol restoration and were at best unreliable. Both groups were to threaten to undermine Robert I's triumph.

The king's nervousness is seen in his desire to include the leading men of his realm in initiatives such as the Declaration of Arbroath and to require their assent to the arrangements for the succession made in 1315 and 1318. The disinheritance of intransigent opponents pronounced at the Cambuskenneth parliament in November 1314 did not remove the danger of internal divisions. The existence of opposition is most clearly revealed in a conspiracy against Robert in 1320 which centred on William de Soules, whose name is on the Declaration of Arbroath. The rebels were betrayed and duly condemned in parliament in August. The details are obscure, but the plot was probably much more serious than Bruce propaganda allowed; there may even have been military action. The origin of the conspiracy may lie in the collection of seals by the royal chapel for the purpose of appending them to the Declaration, a policy which may well have aroused resentment if the magnates concerned were unsure of the government's true intentions; the attempt to test loyalty was, therefore, both effective in identifying potential traitors and yet counter-productive in that it precipitated a conspiracy against the king. On the other hand, it is possible that the plot had been germinating for rather longer in the minds of those, especially in south-west Scotland, who felt themselves disadvantaged by Robert's territorial settlement since Bannockburn and saw their chance in the dynastic uncertainty which had followed Edward Bruce's death in Ireland. According to some sources, the intention was to place Soules on the throne, but this is unlikely, for although he was the son of one of the competitors of 1291 he had no realistic claim to the Scottish crown. He is said to have been imprisoned rather than facing the execution which would surely have been his fate if he had sought personally to supplant Robert I, although he may have escaped from Scotland only to die at the battle of Boroughbridge in 1322. The plot makes sense only if the conspirators were seeking to uphold the interests of Edward Balliol, son of the late King John, who was then in England and may have been promised help by Edward II; many of them had earlier had links with the Balliols and Comyns. This continuing threat from his bitter rivals serves to explain Robert's eagerness to make a final peace with England.[28]

The opportunity to end the long conflict with a formal recognition by the English crown of Scottish independence came amid the chaos which accompanied the deposition of Edward II in 1327 and his replacement by his son, Edward III, who at the start of his reign was under the influence of his mother Isabella and her lover Roger Mortimer. Despite his many political problems and numerous mistakes, Edward II had stubbornly refused to accept Robert I's title, an attitude exemplified by his execution of Andrew Harcla. One chronicler suggests that in the autumn of 1326 Edward II hoped to escape to Ireland and raise troops who would then invade England with Scottish collaboration, the price of Scottish support being Edward's recognition of Robert as king of an independent realm and the cession of much of northern England to him. Even

[28] The fullest account of these events is M. Penman, '*A fell coniuracioun agayn Robert the douchty king*: the Soules conspiracy of 1318–1320', *IR*, 50 (1999), 25–57.

if this account is true, and there is no independent corroboration of it, the offer was surely one made in desperation which might just as easily be rescinded if Edward II's fortunes improved. In any event, however, dissensions in England gave the Scots a favourable opportunity to renew the war, hence Robert's fresh intervention in Ireland in order to try and force the English to come to terms. In the Borders, an unsuccessful English campaign against a raiding Scottish force in 1327 was followed by an assault on Norham by Robert and rumours that the Scots intended to occupy Northumberland. The change of regime had enabled Robert to intensify the pressure on England.

This diplomatic and military pressure bore fruit in March 1328 with the treaty of Edinburgh, subsequently ratified at Northampton two months later. Peace between the two realms was declared, with Scotland's independence and Robert I's status as king both recognised by Edward III, and the English king further promised to work towards the lifting of the sentence of excommunication on Robert, which was accomplished in October 1328. The Scots were to pay £20,000, probably in reparations, although much of this ended in the hands of Isabella and her friends and did not secure widespread support in England for what was seen as a shameful peace. A marriage was arranged between Robert's young son David and Edward's sister Joan.[29] However, the issue of the so-called Disinherited was left unresolved.

Those whose lands had been forfeited by Robert I were inevitably the most obdurate opponents of peace. The negotiations which preceded the treaty of Edinburgh certainly included discussion of their concerns, but the issue proved too intractable. Robert probably later agreed to restore the Scottish lands of Henry Percy, Henry Beaumont, William la Zouche and Thomas Wake, or at least allowed them to sue for them in Scottish courts, although he may have yielded on this point only on account of his advancing illness. The youthful Edward III could afford to play for time. The dying Robert, knowing that he would be succeeded by a minor, could not. The treaty was the culmination of all that Robert I had striven for, yet it contained within itself the seeds of its own destruction and was, moreover, subscribed to by an English king who was desperate

[29] *ASR*, no. 41; *Vet. Mon.*, 240–2.

to avenge the humiliations of his father's reign and keen if possible to resume direct lordship in Scotland in the manner of his grandfather.

Robert I died on 7 June 1329. The Guardian of the realm on behalf of the new king was Thomas Randolph, earl of Moray, whose experience and long tradition of service to the crown made him an eminently suitable candidate for the office, but his death in July 1332 precipitated a great crisis within Scotland. The new Guardian was Donald, earl of Mar, who was probably chosen because he was the king's cousin and nearest adult male relative rather than on account of any ability he may have been believed to possess. Mar had spent most of his adult life in England, and was strongly suspected of being sympathetic towards the Disinherited and even of having an association with Edward Balliol. His appointment coincided with an expedition into Scotland by the Disinherited which proved unexpectedly successful. Mar was defeated and killed at Dupplin Moor near Perth as a result of poor generalship exacerbated by his desire to disprove allegations that he was a traitor. On 24 September Edward Balliol was solemnly crowned at Scone, and although he soon withdrew southwards his triumph had been striking. He was not widely accepted as the new monarch, and indeed the only armed uprising in his favour was in the traditional Balliol stronghold of Galloway, but the government of David II was in disarray and, perhaps more importantly, the door was open for Edward III to intervene in Scotland.

Edward III had offered only covert support for the expedition of 1332, but Balliol's success encouraged him to back his cause more openly. For his part, Balliol acknowledged his benefactor as lord superior in Scotland, and promised him extensive Scottish lands, all of which were to be permanently annexed to England. Although Balliol was soon driven out of Scotland, an army led by the English king in 1333 besieged Berwick and won a great victory at nearby Halidon Hill. It seemed that both the Bruce cause and the treaty of Edinburgh were dead, and that a relationship had been established between the two realms which was not dissimilar to that prevailing between John Balliol and Edward I, although in March 1334 the English king made concessions over personal attendance at parliaments and his right to hear appeals from Scotland.[30] As part of these ongoing negotiations, in June 1334 Edward Balliol fulfilled his earlier promise and formally granted to Edward III the sheriffdoms of Berwick, Roxburgh, Selkirk, Peebles, Edinburgh and Dumfries, the constabularies of Linlithgow and Haddington, and the forests of Ettrick and Jedburgh. As the price of English support, Balliol was prepared to divest his kingdom of some of its economically most productive territories, although in truth he had no other viable option.

It is difficult to assess the level of support enjoyed by Balliol in the kingdom, or the extent to which the Bruce party was able to restore effective government. The sources are meagre and tell us more about how military campaigns were organised than about the ebb and flow of politics. In the period immediately after Halidon Hill, the Disinherited and inveterate adherents of the Balliol cause were doubtless joined by those whose policy throughout the Wars of Independence was to attempt to join the winning side, and so the outwardly impressive list of those present at Balliol's parliament at Holyrood in February 1334 is no more conclusive as an indication of political allegiances than is the list of magnates named in the Declaration of Arbroath. David II, despite his youth, possessed a number of inherent advantages. He was the son of a great hero and liberator, while his opponent had not so much capitulated to English military might as positively encouraged its intervention, and he was upheld primarily by it. The success of David's cause depended, however, on effective resistance to Balliol and his English allies. A major campaign by Edward III in 1335 almost snuffed out this resistance, but it was revived when William Douglas and Andrew Murray defeated a force of Balliol supporters under David de Strathbogie at Culblean on Deeside in November. As in 1296 and 1304, the English offensive of 1335 had failed to secure final victory.

Opinions differ as to the effectiveness of the English administration in southern Scotland after 1334. The problems which had dogged Edward I's attempts to impose his authority there – financial difficulties, shortages of supply, over-extended lines of

[30] R. Nicholson, *Edward III and the Scots: The Formative Years of a Military Career, 1327–1335* (Oxford, 1965), 155.

communication, local hostility – must equally have impaired his grandson's prospects of bringing to full effect the annexation of the lands ceded by Balliol. Some revenues were, however, collected by English officials in southern Scotland, especially from the sheriffdom of Edinburgh and the constabularies of Haddington and Linlithgow, which produced annual receipts of over £300 in 1335–6 and 1336–7. Here at least, English authority must have possessed some meaning.[31] But such authority was transitory, and depended on Edward III continuing to be interested in Scotland, which from 1337 was not his priority. In that year Philip VI of France confiscated the duchy of Aquitaine, hereditary possession of the English kings, and precipitated the long series of Anglo-French conflicts now known as the Hundred Years War. The old issue of sovereignty in Aquitaine was now complicated by Edward III's claim to the French throne through his mother, the sister of Charles IV, the last king of the direct Capetian royal line, who had died in 1328. Scottish affairs played an important role in both causing and prolonging the Hundred Years War, but the field of English military ambitions now moved to France, and Edward Balliol's star consequently waned rapidly. By 1341 Scotland was thought to be safe enough for the return of David II from a seven-year exile in France.

The reputation of David II has suffered from his being too often compared with his father. In contrast to Bannockburn, David's principal foray into Anglo-Scottish conflict was a disaster. In 1346, invading northern England in support of his French ally, he was defeated and captured at the battle of Neville's Cross, near Durham, spending the next eleven years as a prisoner of Edward III. The negotiations between the two kings have sometimes been regarded as proof of David's treachery to the cause of Scottish liberty, as a betrayal of all that his father had supposedly stood for, but this is unfair to him. The details of medieval diplomacy are notoriously difficult to establish, as often we are forced to rely on what was essentially the negotiating stance of one or other of the parties. David was in a difficult position. Absent from his realm, he was unable to put the personal stamp on government which was an essential prerequisite for effective royal power in medieval Scotland.

[31] B. Webster, 'Scotland without a king, 1329–1341', in *Barrow Essays*, 230.

His lieutenant and heir presumptive, Robert Stewart, was an ineffectual ruler whose lukewarm participation at Neville's Cross smacked of treachery; furthermore, he had briefly submitted to Edward III in September 1335 following the latter's invasion of Scotland and an attack on the Stewart lands by a force from Ireland. Edward Balliol was still alive, and in theory remained the English king's candidate for the Scottish throne, although he too was an uninspiring figure whom Edward III would back only for as long as it suited him to do so; Balliol's formal surrender of his claim to the English king in January 1356 was no more than a recognition of the inevitable. There was even the possibility that the Scots would find an alternative candidate rather than ransom David, upholding the words of the Declaration of Arbroath that freedom from the English yoke was more important than loyalty to a particular monarch. On the other hand, David was Edward's prisoner and had to negotiate on that basis.

Those who have castigated David II have done so primarily because he was apparently prepared to consent to an English prince, or even Edward III himself, succeeding to the Scottish throne in the event of his dying childless. In other words, he was willing to see Robert Stewart displaced as heir presumptive, which in view of the antipathy between the two men is hardly surprising nor, in the final analysis, unreasonable. Whatever might be suggested by items of propaganda such as the Declaration of Arbroath, notions of exclusive national identities and ethnic purity were alien to the fourteenth-century mentality. The Wars of Independence had served to emphasise recognisable differences between the Scots and the English, and there is no doubt that those on both sides of the border who had suffered from the ravages of plundering raids were acutely aware of those differences and viewed their adversaries with bitter hatred, an attitude which must have been reinforced by a steady hardening of English policy towards the Scots between 1296 and Edward III's reign and increasing use of deliberate devastation as a military tactic. However, such considerations did not in themselves preclude the succession of an English prince to the Scottish throne, any more than similar feelings among the French towards English invaders necessarily ruled out Edward III becoming king of France. An English succession was not the ideal option, but neither, from David II's standpoint, was the accession of Robert Stewart, who may have delayed the king's release by his understandable opposition to Edward III's proposals. David, moreover, still hoped to produce an heir of his body.

The uncertainty over who would be David II's heir may have contributed to a rebellion in 1363 led by Robert Stewart and the earls of Douglas and March. Although it soon fizzled out, the alliance of three of the major magnates of the realm against the king calls for comment. Robert's poor relations with the king probably made him fearful for his place in the succession, since the idea that David might be succeeded by an English prince had been mooted in negotiations as early as 1350 and was still being considered. In 1359 the king had granted the earldom of Moray to Henry, duke of Lancaster, with his two daughters succeeding, for their lifetimes only, if the aged duke did not produce a son.[32] Henry's younger daughter was to marry John of Gaunt, third surviving son of Edward III, so the charter gave the ambitious English prince the prospect of a territorial foothold within the Scottish kingdom, a fact of obvious significance to Robert Stewart and his prospects of the crown. By advocating the succession of a younger son of the English king, David was clearly appreciating the need to protect the identity and separate standing of the Scottish realm, although it is unclear what, if any, protection was envisaged against the prospect of a future union of the crowns if the senior lines of descent from Edward III should fail. When Robert submitted to David II in the wake of the rebellion, he swore fealty 'under pain of losing all right of succession to the kingdom of Scotland', and it may be no coincidence that in the following spring parliament debated, and decisively rejected, the latest English proposals. This does not prove that the rebels were concerned about the succession, but the fact that David used the pretext of Robert's insubordination to intensify the threat against him suggests that the issue was not far below the surface. In addition, David's wife had recently died, and in January 1363 he made it clear that he proposed to marry Margaret Drummond, widow of Sir John Logie, a move which might produce a direct heir. It is, therefore, surely likely that the succession was at least one element in the cocktail which led to the revolt of 1363.

[32] *RRS*, vi, 240–1.

However, the rebels also had other, more immediate, grievances. Their dominance during David's captivity was called into question when the king returned. Robert Stewart had built up his power base in northern Scotland between 1346 and 1357, for example by making marriage alliances with the earl of Ross and the lord of the Isles. On his return, David initially had little choice but to ratify Robert's gains, despite his ambivalent performance at Neville's Cross and the fact that his lieutenancy appears to have been marked by a deterioration in the royal finances and in law and order. It was not surprising, however, that the king soon sought to reward his own supporters, and this threatened the power and patronage of those who had been prominent during his absence. Robert's hopes to gain control of the earldom of Fife through the marriage of its heiress Isabella to his son Walter were thwarted when Walter died late in 1362, enabling the king to allow Isabella to marry his favoured knight Thomas Bisset, a clear indication that David was prepared to act against the interests of his leading nobles. The king was also showing signs that he was prepared to take decisive, even arbitrary, action against individual magnates. Following the murder of his mistress Katherine Mortimer in the summer of 1360, he imprisoned Thomas Stewart, earl of Angus, who was suspected of involvement in the crime, in Dumbarton castle, where he died in 1362, possibly of the plague which was raging in that year. The king also seized the earl of Mar's castle of Kildrummy and sent him into temporary exile, perhaps because he had become the liege man of Edward III in 1359, although it is likely that the underlying issues were much more complex than this. Such actions must have alarmed other members of the nobility, unfamiliar as they had become with assertive action on the part of the crown, and Douglas had particular reason to be concerned by the attack on Mar because he was the childless earl's brother-in-law and heir presumptive. The contemporary *Scalacronica* states that Douglas rebelled because he felt that the king 'did not show him as good lordship as he would have wished'. In other words, despite the fact that David II had created an earldom for Douglas in 1358, he felt that he was no longer receiving the rewards appropriate to his station. The exclusion of Robert Stewart and his allies from the king's intimate councils must have increased their sense of alienation, while the heavy taxation necessitated by the king's ransom may have been a further encouragement to rebel.

In the years following his return from England, David restored much of the machinery of government and increased the yield of crown revenues. He was personally interested in administration and the execution of justice, and his lengthy periods of residence in Edinburgh after 1357 aided the development of centralised institutions. Comparisons between the period of his active rule and the years when Robert Stewart was lieutenant are unflattering to Robert, but this is hardly surprising, because Robert could not exercise the full authority of a king, and his reputation generally has suffered from the persistent belief that he was ineffectual throughout his career. Robert's relationship with David II after the revolt of 1363 is hard to assess. On the one hand, the marriage of Annabella Drummond, the queen's niece, to Robert's eldest son John probably marks acceptance by the king that the crown would pass to the Stewarts if he failed to produce an heir, especially in view of the fact that in June 1368 David granted John the earldom of Carrick, which he himself had held prior to his accession in 1329. On the other hand, Robert and at least one of his sons were arrested in the winter of 1368–9, and Robert was probably temporarily deprived of his earldom of Strathearn. The hand of Queen Margaret can be seen in these events. We have observed how the prospect of her marriage to David II had been one of the causes of the rebellion of 1363, and her antipathy towards Robert and the threat posed by her family's ambitions to Stewart interests in Menteith served also to poison his relationship with the king. Her difficulty was that she had failed to provide David with an heir, even though there was no doubt about her own fecundity. Around the time when the Stewarts were imprisoned, possibly at her instigation, she fell from grace and the king proceeded to divorce her, probably with the intention of marrying the latest woman in his life, Agnes Dunbar. Margaret was a spirited and charming woman, and she took her case to the papal curia, so impressing Pope Gregory XI that he not only bestowed gifts on her but even paid for her funeral when she died in 1375. Her determination to defend her rights even brought upon Scotland the threat of interdict, but in the context of Scottish politics her departure enabled Robert Stewart partially to return to the king's favour. When David II suddenly died in February 1371, Robert was at last able to claim his inheritance.

The death of David II, and with him the direct line of the Bruces, provides a suitable point at which to discuss the nature of the conflicts which had scarred Scotland since 1286. At one level, the events which followed the death of Alexander III can be seen as a civil war within Scotland, primarily between Bruce and Balliol, with the Comyns throwing their considerable political weight behind the latter. Although both the Bruces and the Balliols held Scottish lands, they also had significant interests in England, and as a result were less prominent in thirteenth-century Scottish politics than families such as the Comyns and Stewarts. They were thrust into the limelight through their common descent from Earl David of Huntingdon, and the bitter squabbles between them, even during the notional reign of Margaret, owed much to the fact that they had both inherited portions of Earl David's lands and, moreover, had conflicting interests in the still volatile south-western corner of Scotland. The careers of the Bruces up to 1306 can best be understood in terms of an anti-Balliol policy rather than an anti-English one, although the future king was at best ambivalent in his relationship with Edward I, and his service as Guardian after Wallace's resignation implies recognition of John Balliol as a legitimate king, since the guardianship was exercised in John's name. The early years of Robert's reign can again be seen as a period of civil war, marked by the bitter hostility between Bruce and the MacDougalls of Lorn and by the 'herschip' of the Comyn earldom of Buchan. Even after Robert's victories and the consolidation of his authority throughout Scotland, he still faced internal opposition, as seen in the Soules plot, and the threat from disinherited exiles. The war between Edward Balliol and the adherents of the young David II must be regarded as a continuation of a long-running, essentially internal, struggle between two families who cannot in either case be regarded as unambiguously Scottish; rather, they belonged to an aristocracy whose interests were not constrained by the peaceful border which ran between England and Scotland in the thirteenth century.

The wars, however, also had a national dimension, and this is how they are regarded in the popular imagination. Indeed, the very term 'Wars of Independence' implies that this was a struggle for liberty, for the right to self-determination. The inspiring rhetoric of the

Declaration of Arbroath emphasises that freedom was the Scots' ultimate aim, in the cause of which they were prepared to depose even the mighty Robert himself if he should dare to offer allegiance to the English tyrant. And there was indeed development of a sense of national identity and hatred towards England which dominated Scottish foreign policy well into the fifteenth century. Historians must, however, be cautious before they ascribe to medieval men and women a concept of the 'nation state' which was alien to contemporary mentalities. By the late thirteenth century, the realm of Scotland was a well-defined territorial, legal and administrative entity with a long history and firmly established political boundaries. It was the integrity of that realm which both necessitated and facilitated the appointment of Guardians to govern during Margaret's short reign and in subsequent crises, and the need to preserve that integrity was an essential point of discussion in the negotiations which led to the treaty of Birgham and, for that matter, in the diplomatic exchanges between David II and Edward III. But the existence of a state does not necessarily imply the existence of a nation in the narrow, ethnic sense of that word as it is used in the Declaration of Arbroath.

Who or what, then, was the 'community of the realm' in whose name the Declaration was sent to the pope? No doubt the term was employed to stress to John XXII that the Scots were solidly behind their king and united in their desire to resist English oppression, and it echoes many other medieval political programmes which were based on the supposed will or alleged interests of a community, whether it be of a whole state or merely a township. The concept was not articulated in a Scottish context before 1286, and may have come into prominence then because of the absence of a monarch and the Guardians' need to communicate with Edward I in terms with which he was familiar.[33] The use of the word 'community' does not, of course, imply unanimity, nor even that any attempt had been made to seek the views of the populace at large. In Scotland it is surely unlikely that many people, at least below the class of magnates, saw their primary loyalty as being to the crown as opposed to their village, burgh or province. Even if they were aware of Scotland as a realm, with a king whose agents and representatives were to be

[33] F. Watson, 'The enigmatic Lion: Scotland, kingship and national identity in the Wars of Independence', in Broun, Finlay and Lynch, eds., *Image and Identity*, 22.

found in each sheriffdom, their adherence to the lordship of Galloway, the earldom of Buchan or the burgh of Aberdeen was almost certainly stronger than their attachment to the much less tangible concept of the state, and probably eclipsed such loyalty as they felt to the individual person of the king. The great lords operated on a larger stage, sometimes pursuing interests well beyond the borders of Scotland, and they could both comprehend and be faithful to the idea of the realm as a political and legal entity. It is a much more difficult matter to say whether the long resistance of many of their number to Edward I was determined by 'patriotism' or by a more selfish desire to maintain their own influence in society.

If Scottish nationhood did indeed develop in the late thirteenth and fourteenth centuries, then it was forged on the anvil of English aggression. Resistance to Edward I and his successors was the unifying force which encouraged the inhabitants of Scotland to regard themselves as different from the English, and compelled those who had interests on both sides of the border to make a final choice of where their allegiance would henceforth lie. Edward I could not, of course, unwittingly have created the nation of the Scots if the kingdom of Scotland had not already been providing the political and administrative framework under which the Scottish people could unite. Edward underestimated the strength of the Scottish realm, and he grossly overplayed his hand as lord superior of John Balliol. He neither realised that the absorption of Scotland within his territorial empire would meet with stubborn resistance, nor understood that his objectives could be achieved only by persuading the Scottish magnates that the extinction of the kingdom of the Scots would not greatly harm their own territorial interests or local influence. For all his lack of sympathy for Scottish sensibilities, however, Edward I possessed too many advantages to pass over the opportunity to intervene in the affairs of the northern kingdom. He could seek a marriage alliance, and then could arrange to be the judge of the Great Cause. He could rely on a certain degree of support within Scotland, especially from those who held lands in England as well and realised the superior financial and military might of the English state, and after Robert Bruce's murder of John Comyn he could, at least in the short term, be sure of the allegiance of the most important political grouping in Scotland. Those who adhered to Edward should not be regarded as 'unpatriotic', but rather as determined to maintain their landed possessions and personal authority by acknowledging his superior power. That was always the aristocratic priority, and it explains why even Robert Bruce submitted to the English king when it suited his interests to do so, and why Robert Stewart briefly acknowledged the authority of Edward III, but equally it makes comprehensible the reluctant adherence to Robert I of former Balliol partisans. It also explains why Edward Balliol was prepared to cede part of his kingdom in return for English assistance. We can see this policy as unwise, even treacherous, but if we condemn Edward Balliol for being a puppet of Edward III, we must also condemn the actions of the aged Robert Bruce in 1292 when he was prepared to countenance the division of the kingdom and to make a deal with Florence of Holland in a desperate attempt to foil John Balliol.

It is too simplistic to say either that English intervention in Scotland was a naked act of aggression on the part of a more powerful neighbour, or that the English did no more than participate in a civil war at the invitation of particular parties, but it would be incorrect to dismiss either idea out of hand. The crisis which Alexander III unwittingly brought about on that stormy March night presented a range of opportunities to those both within and outside Scotland. Edward I and Edward III were both happy to fish in troubled waters, but at least some Scots were equally content to invite English intervention, just as both factions in the 1250s had sought the help of Henry III when it suited them. The Wars of Independence were in some respects just what the name implies, a struggle for liberation, but the events of this period of crisis are much more complex than the selective rhetoric of the Declaration of Arbroath and other propaganda, Scottish and English, might suggest.

6

THE STEWART KINGS

The dynasty inaugurated by Robert Stewart's coronation at Scone on 26 March 1371 was destined to rule Scotland for well over three centuries, and after 1603 its kings added the realm of England to their dominions. Despite a series of lengthy royal minorities, fifteenth- and sixteenth-century Stewart monarchs displayed great vigour in building up their power in Scotland, presided over the further development of central administrative and legal institutions, and sought to play a role in international diplomacy which complemented and assisted their ambitions to consolidate royal authority at home.

The first two Stewart kings, however, had difficulty in asserting themselves, partly because their dynasty was new to kingship and needed to establish itself. Despite the fact that his claims had long been recognised, Robert II's succession provoked opposition from the earl of Douglas and families such as the Leslies and Lindsays who had prospered under David II's patronage and feared the accession of a man towards whom their former benefactor had shown considerable antipathy. Although Douglas probably hoped merely to win concessions from the new king, he claimed to be upholding the rights of the Comyns and Edward Balliol, who had died in 1364, thereby threatening a return to the civil wars of the earlier part of the century and raising the spectre of possible English intervention. There was no

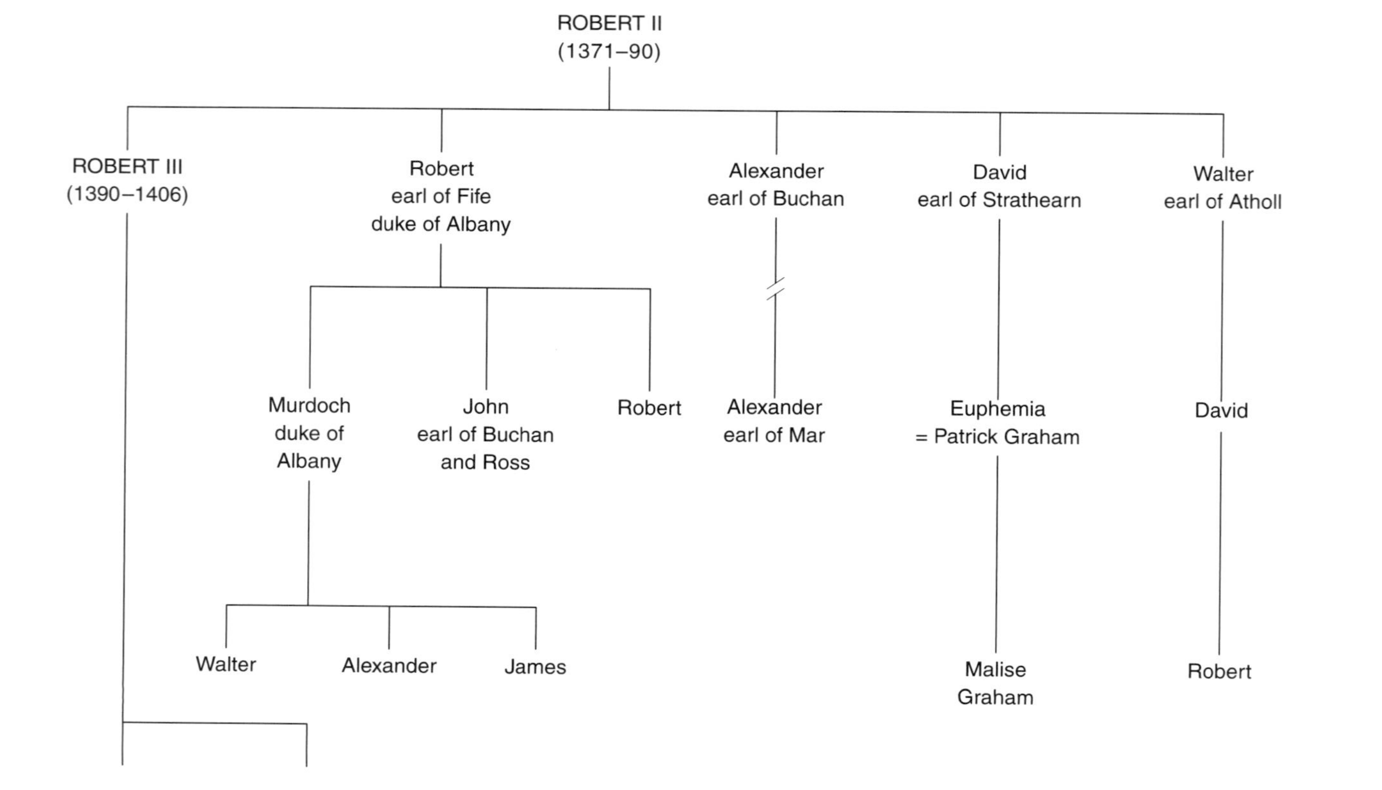
ROBERT II
(1371–90)
ROBERT III
(1390–1406)
Robert
earl of Fife
duke of Albany
Alexander
earl of Buchan
David
earl of Strathearn
Walter
earl of Atholl
Murdoch
duke of
Albany
John
earl of Buchan
and Ross
Robert
Alexander
earl of Mar
Euphemia
= Patrick Graham
David
Walter
Alexander
James
Malise
Graham
Robert

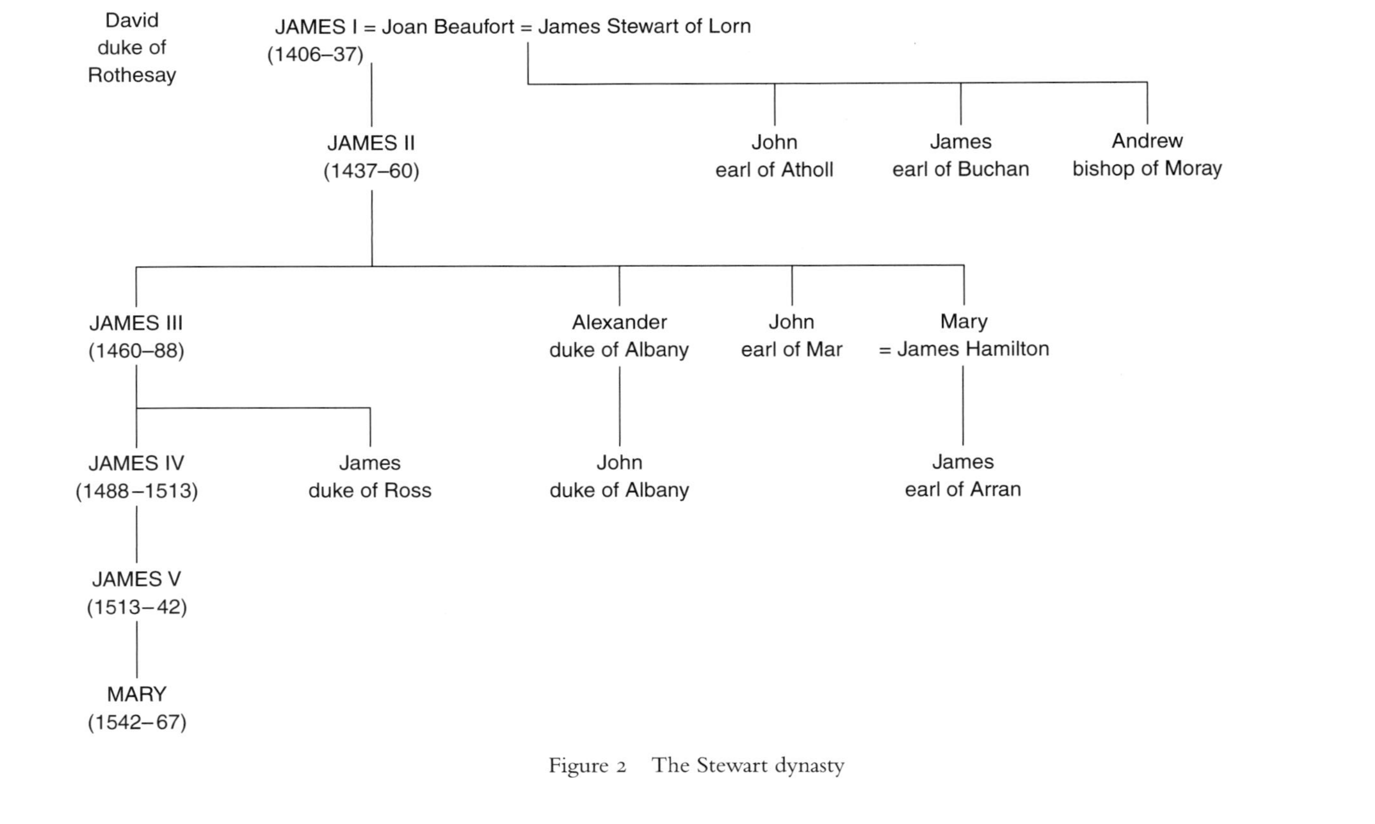

Figure 2 The Stewart dynasty

claimant to the throne other than Robert who was likely to attract widespread support, and Douglas received no backing from some of David II's closest adherents such as Sir Robert Erskine and the earl of March, but the king still moved to conciliate the rebels, thereby demonstrating the inherent weakness of his own position.

Robert II's undistinguished record of service to his predecessor also cast a shadow across the new reign. He had been ineffective as royal lieutenant, had submitted to Edward III in 1335, had allegedly left David II exposed to capture at Neville's Cross, and had joined the rebellion of 1363. His position of authority in David's reign had sprung not from his inherent abilities but solely from his position as heir presumptive. Because his priority was to maintain that position and enhance his own territorial lordship, he not unnaturally viewed with some ambivalence the return of the king from captivity, the negotiations with Edward III, and the recovery of royal authority and revenues through the employment of those whom David favoured, and Robert's manoeuvring to preserve his rights as heir doubtless made him appear indecisive, narrow-minded and lacking in conviction, if not actually treacherous. It has been argued that, by the time he succeeded to the throne, Robert was too old to rule, but it was his past record rather than his age which proved more troublesome for him.

Unlike David II, Robert Stewart had been very successful in producing children. His adult sons all now wanted increased political power and wealth for themselves, and their rivalries explain much of the turbulence of the reign, especially the crises of 1384 and 1388. Robert had five surviving legitimate sons from his two marriages: John, Robert and Alexander from the first; and David and Walter from the second. In 1371 John, earl of Carrick, was named as the king's heir, and in 1373 parliament approved the creation of a tailzie (equivalent to the English entail) which provided for the descent of the crown through male lines. These detailed arrangements for the succession have sometimes been seen in the context of a potential threat to the rights of Robert's sons from his first marriage to Elizabeth Mure. Most royal and aristocratic marriages required a papal dispensation to excuse the fact that the parties were too closely related to marry legitimately under canon law, and such dispensations were readily granted on request. Many couples sought papal approval in advance, but others claimed that the impediment had become known to them only subsequently. It was not until 1347 that Robert, with the backing of the kings of France and Scotland and an impressive array of bishops, petitioned the pope for dispensation, by which time his elder sons had been born. Whether this was as significant an issue to contemporaries as some historians have suggested is, however, doubtful. Under the terms of the dispensation, as was normal, the children were declared legitimate, and there is no reason to believe that the detailed settlement of the succession in 1373 was intended primarily to resolve the issue of whether John, Robert and Alexander had been born in wedlock, even though the principles of canon law did not necessarily apply in secular contexts. Rather, it was an attempt to consolidate the position of the new dynasty by clarifying the line of descent and by declaring that, in the absence of sons, brothers and other male relatives would succeed in preference to daughters. Rivalries between Robert's children doubtless made it desirable to make such provisions.

Robert II's policy in the 1370s was to build up the territorial and jurisdictional power of his family while endeavouring to fulfil the ambitions of his sons. In doing this, he was acting like any other medieval magnate in similar circumstances, indeed continuing the ruthless aggrandisement which had marked his career under David II. That ultimately he lost effective control of the realm to his sons is a reflection of his own comparative weakness rather than of flaws in the policy. The fact that central institutions in Scotland were relatively undeveloped meant that great nobles could frequently be dominant in their own areas; and it was inevitable that Robert would wish to strengthen the position of his dynasty by giving, where possible, these positions of dominance to his own sons or sons-in-law. The plan appears unusual in the Scottish context only because recent kings had not had to make widespread provision for adult relatives. Robert I might have faced this difficulty, but lost much of his close family in the wars against England and was able to encourage his potentially troublesome brother Edward to pursue his ambitions in Ireland. Robert II had to accommodate his sons' hopes within his own realm.

Robert II based himself largely in Perthshire and the old Stewart lands in Renfrew, Ayrshire and Bute. His authority outside this area was exercised principally through the agency of his sons. John, earl of Carrick, became the dominant member of the family in southern Scotland, while Alexander, lord of Badenoch and later earl of Buchan, was made lieutenant over much of the north. Alexander, who was involved in a long and often violent dispute with the bishop of Moray, and was nicknamed 'the Wolf of Badenoch', was widely accused of using bands of Highlanders to foment the disorder he was supposed to quell, and the king's inability to curb his excesses was used as a pretext for Carrick's appointment as Guardian of the realm by a general council at Holyrood in November 1384. It is significant, however, that, despite a range of complaints against him in April 1385, Alexander continued to hold the position of royal lieutenant even after Carrick's coup, which suggests that another factor was at play, namely relations with England.

The continued English occupation of Berwickshire, Roxburghshire, Teviotdale and Annandale was of particular concern to border magnates, especially the earl of March, most of whose lands were under English control. While it was important not to provoke large-scale English retaliation by attacking major strongholds such as Berwick, there was intermittent warfare on the border for much of the second half of Robert's reign. Payments of David II's ransom ceased after the death of Edward III in 1377, and in July 1378 the king transferred control of the priory of Coldingham in Berwickshire from Durham to Dunfermline. In 1384 Archibald Douglas of Galloway, nicknamed 'the Grim', took Lochmaben castle and the earl of Douglas re-established Scottish control in Teviotdale with the exception of Roxburgh and Jedburgh. The king probably approved of these attempts to expel the English from the conquests they had made in the early years of Edward III's reign, but his age and earlier lack of military success meant that it was his sons, John earl of Carrick and Robert earl of Fife, who played a more prominent role in Anglo-Scottish warfare and diplomacy. In 1384 an English invading force under John of Gaunt destroyed Haddington, and the desire for retaliation on the part of Carrick and the young second earl of Douglas helped create the political crisis in Scotland which was to see the king sidelined. However, Carrick's seizure of power was little more than a manifestation of his ruthless ambition and a reflection of the rivalries between himself and his brothers, and Robert II's indecisiveness in the face of English aggression was exaggerated by propaganda designed to justify his removal. It is significant that four years later the earl of Fife used similar tactics in order to replace Carrick.

Carrick's policy of aggression towards England was marked by an attack across the border in 1385, which provoked very destructive retaliation in Lothian under the personal command of the English king, Richard II. In 1388 the Scots launched another two-pronged raid into England, probably with the primary intention of ravaging the countryside, although it is possible that the original aim was to isolate Carlisle and occupy Cumberland in order to persuade the English to make concessions regarding the lands they still held in southern Scotland. At Otterburn the Scots won a famous victory, but the second earl of Douglas was slain. A dispute followed over his lands between Malcolm Drummond, who was married to the late earl's sister and heir and was Carrick's brother-in-law, and Archibald Douglas of Galloway, who decisively produced a charter of 1342 limiting the descent of most of the Douglas estates to male heirs and naming him specifically in the tailzie, despite his illegitimate birth. Drummond was afraid to come to a general council in April 1389 because the earl of Fife would not guarantee his safety.

Drummond's discomfiture came about because in the aftermath of Otterburn there had been another political coup. On 1 December 1388 Carrick was replaced as Guardian on the grounds of his lax exercise of justice, especially in the north, and because he was thought to be unable to deal with the English invasion expected the following year. We have here the first mention of Carrick's infirmity, which apparently derived from his having been kicked by a horse. Given that he played no part in the 1388 campaigns, it is likely that his disability was incurred before they were launched, although his physical incapacity only became a political issue when Fife felt strong enough to supplant his brother, which was not until he had lost his ally Douglas at Otterburn. Fife retained the guardianship until 1393, even though Carrick had become king in the interim.

Fife now took action against his brother Alexander, earl of Buchan, who had continued to enjoy considerable formal power in northern Scotland. At some point between 1385 and February 1387 he had even become justiciar north of the Forth, which indicates that he still enjoyed the support of the king and that Carrick's

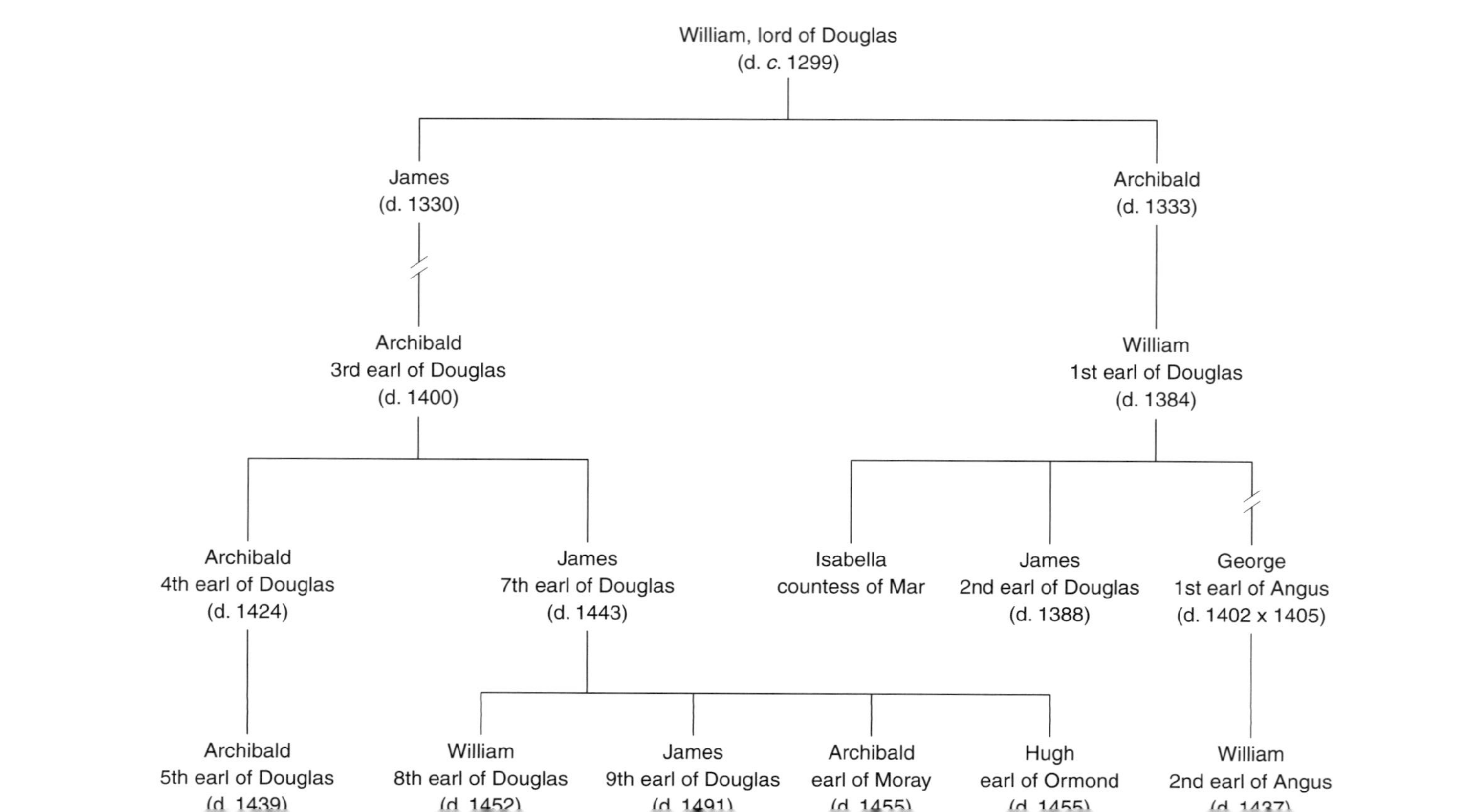
William, lord of Douglas
(d. c. 1299)
James
(d. 1330)
Archibald
(d. 1333)
Archibald
3rd earl of Douglas
(d. 1400)
William
1st earl of Douglas
(d. 1384)
Archibald
4th earl of Douglas
(d. 1424)
James
7th earl of Douglas
(d. 1443)
Isabella
countess of Mar
James
2nd earl of Douglas
(d. 1388)
George
1st earl of Angus
(d. 1402 x 1405)
Archibald
5th earl of Douglas
(d. 1439)
William
8th earl of Douglas
(d. 1452)
James
9th earl of Douglas
(d. 1491)
Archibald
earl of Moray
(d. 1455)
Hugh
earl of Ormond
(d. 1455)
William
2nd earl of Angus
(d. 1437)

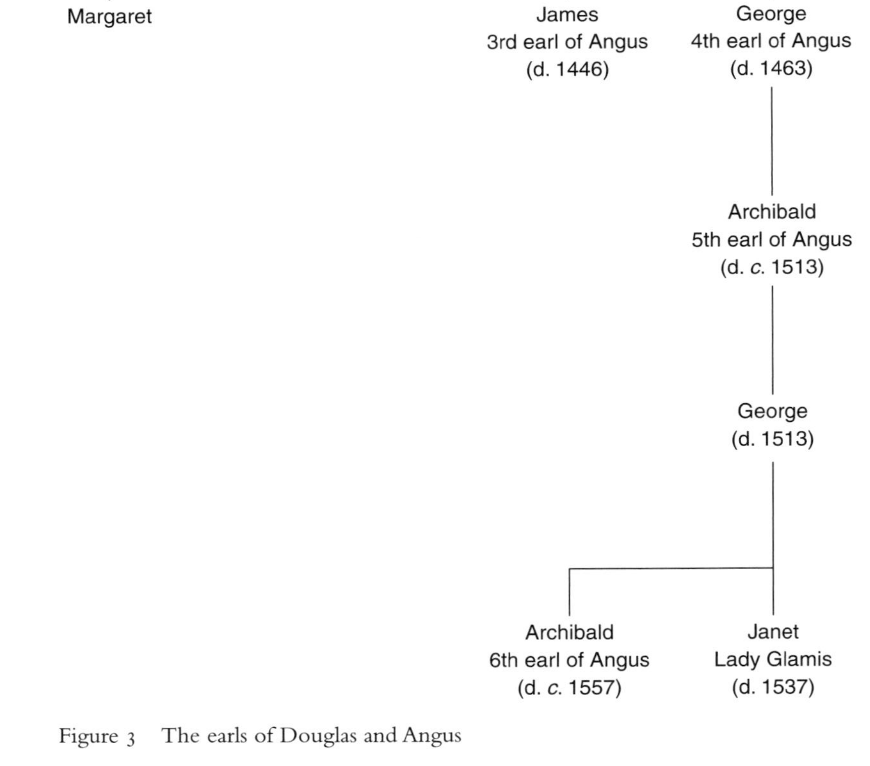

Figure 3 The earls of Douglas and Angus

primary interests were concentrated in southern Scotland. In December 1388, however, Alexander was removed from the office of justiciar as part of a co-ordinated assault against his position, through which Fife and his son Murdoch extended their influence at his expense. Murdoch himself was appointed justiciar in April 1389, indicating that the campaign against Buchan, and indeed that against Carrick, were part of a policy whereby Fife sought aggrandisement for himself and his son. In the meantime Scotland was included in an Anglo-French truce which had been concluded in June 1389, thus freeing the Guardian to impose his authority in the north.

Robert II thus apparently ended his life on the sidelines, the victim of his sons' unbridled ambitions. It is tempting to see him as a king who was unable to build on the administrative and fiscal advances of the latter part of David II's reign and squandered the inheritance which his predecessor had bequeathed to him. However, David's position after 1357 was much easier than Robert II's. David had no children or brothers, and so was able to rule through men he had chosen himself and who were loyal to him, rather than having to oblige members of his close family. Robert had different priorities and preoccupations, and can be seen as a full participant in the crises of the 1380s, supporting Buchan against Carrick and perhaps undermining his eldest son to the extent that Fife could take over in 1388. But it is hard to escape the conclusion that he was joining in the rivalries of his sons rather than standing above them. Throughout his long political career, Robert never appeared to have the consistency of purpose required in a medieval monarch.

Whatever the overall assessment of Robert II's reign, his heir cannot be regarded as a forceful ruler. With the assent of parliament, Carrick chose to alter his name from John to Robert, perhaps because his original name was thought to be unlucky in a king or else because he wanted consciously to identify himself with Robert I, although the move also avoided the problem of whether he would reign as John I (thereby ignoring Balliol) or John II (recognising a claim which was now vested in the English king).[1] In any event, this

[1] S. Boardman, *The Early Stewart Kings: Robert II and Robert III, 1371–1406* (East Linton, 1996), 176–7.

cosmetic change could not hide the fact that for most of his reign he was effectively controlled by his younger brother Fife. Indeed, Robert III's coronation was delayed until Fife had ensured that he would keep his position as Guardian, an unusual sequence of events considering that there was no direct military threat to the realm and the new king, for all his faults, was neither senile nor insane. At the same time the burning of Elgin cathedral by the Wolf of Badenoch emphasised the threat to law and order, and was probably timed to demonstrate the continuing importance, for good or ill, of Alexander Stewart, who doubtless hoped that the new king would offer him support to offset Fife's growing influence in the north, even if he was not strong enough to end Fife's guardianship. The events of 1390 were, therefore, simply a manifestation of the strife between the royal brothers, which did not augur well for the new reign. Fife used his dominance to extend his influence throughout northern Scotland, for example by marrying his son Murdoch to the heiress to the earldom of Lennox, and his territorial power was not seriously impaired by the termination of his guardianship in 1393.

Robert III's attempts at personal rule after 1393 proved disastrous. The king was widely treated with contempt, and his failings were typified by his inability in the autumn of 1398 to persuade a maverick cleric named Walter Danielston to surrender the great royal castle of Dumbarton, despite laying siege to the fortress. Earlier in the same year, amid complaints about the ineffectiveness of the royal administration in the north, Fife was created duke of Albany and the king's son David duke of Rothesay, and the two men were appointed to lead an army against the lordship of the Isles. Although royal patronage had been reversed, the inclusion of Rothesay in this command can be seen as something of a triumph for Robert III, for from the start of his reign the king had sought to counteract his younger brother's power by developing David's household as an active agency of royal government. He did this partly by granting heritable pensions to a number of nobles in return for service to himself and David, and thereby slowly reconstructed the affinity on which his dominance in southern Scotland before 1388 had been based. The adherence to David of the supporters of the second earl of Douglas threatened the position of his illegitimate cousin and successor Archibald the Grim, who was an ally of Fife. By building up David's authority in southern Scotland, the king hoped to put pressure on Fife's position, although it should be noted that Fife himself was granted a pension from the customs to retain him in service to David.[2]

Robert III was to be disappointed in his attempt to create a counterweight to his brother. In January 1399 Rothesay was created lieutenant of the realm for three years, with the apparent support of Albany and Douglas. Rothesay was thus outwardly co-operating with his father's political opponents in an attempt to remove him from effective power, even though he owed his own position to the king's initiative on his behalf, but the alliance between Rothesay and Albany was always more apparent than real. Although descriptions of his conduct may be derived from hostile propaganda, from all accounts Rothesay was an impetuous youth, reluctant to listen to advice and intent on behaving like the king he expected to become. From the middle of 1401 he ignored his father's court and Albany's allies on the council, while the deaths of Archibald, third earl of Douglas, the experienced Walter Trayl, bishop of St Andrews, and Queen Annabella Drummond, all within the space of a year, created dangerous instability within Scotland.

This instability was exacerbated by fresh tensions on the border with England, where Richard II had been deposed by his cousin Henry, son of John of Gaunt. Henry IV invaded Scotland in August 1400, having reasserted the old English claim to overlordship. He was encouraged to intervene by the actions of George Dunbar, earl of March, who had expected to see his daughter marry Rothesay only to witness the heir to the throne choosing instead the daughter of his bitter rival, Archibald earl of Douglas. Rothesay doubtless saw political advantages in a marriage alliance with the most powerful magnate in southern Scotland, but it had the effect of propelling March into treasonable dealings with the English. The English threat also had the effect of emphasising the importance of the Douglases for the defence of the border.

Towards the end of March 1402 Rothesay died in Albany's castle at Falkland in Fife. While it is possible that he perished of natural causes, it is much more likely that he was murdered, perhaps by starvation as tentatively suggested by the chronicler Walter Bower.

[2] *The Exchequer Rolls of Scotland*, ed. J. Stuart and others (23 vols., Edinburgh, 1878–1908), iii, 348.

Rothesay was clearly not at his uncle's castle voluntarily, and his imprisonment and death were probably the result of an arrangement between Albany and the new earl of Douglas, both of whom must have viewed with alarm the prospect of Rothesay succeeding to the throne; even if they could impose a settlement on him, it would be nullified when he became king. In late 1401 Douglas interests were dictating Scottish foreign relations: the earl was seeking the dismemberment of the earldom of March, and was both looking for French military aid and supporting an impostor who claimed to be the deposed king of England, Richard II. At a meeting between the two men at Culross, Albany probably agreed to support Douglas in his ambitions on the border in return for his support, or at least his neutrality, in the elimination of Rothesay and possibly also of Malcolm Drummond, lord of Mar, who was arrested at around the same time and perished in similar circumstances. Although an indemnity was granted to Albany and Douglas in May 1402, exonerating them from blame for Rothesay's death, its very existence suggests that they were already being accused of murdering the heir to the throne. That they could escape the consequences of their actions says much both for the weakness of royal justice and the ruthlessness with which great magnates might suppress any threats to their own position.

The defeat of a Scottish force at Humbleton Hill on 14 September 1402 complicated the political situation. The capture of Douglas, Albany's son Murdoch and other notables left a sudden political vacuum, with few adult earls or important regional lords who were capable of playing a role in the politics of the kingdom. Albany was thus unwillingly forced into a rapprochement with Alexander earl of Buchan and his illegitimate son Alexander, whose sudden marriage to the countess of Mar was grudgingly accepted by the lieutenant, and he was fortunate that a rising by the Percys against Henry IV prevented the English from taking full advantage of Humbleton. Albany's lieutenancy was renewed for a further two years from May 1404, although the king now made another attempt to assert his authority.

Robert III's latest plan was to create a power base for his surviving son James, who was still only a child but presented the best hope of arranging an effective focus of opposition to Albany. Robert placed his faith in men such as Henry Sinclair, earl of Orkney,

Sir David Fleming and Henry Wardlaw, bishop of St Andrews, all of whom were at some time guardians of the young prince and were keen to further their own interests in southern Scotland during the enforced absence of the fourth earl of Douglas. In December 1404 a regality was created for James, comprising all the Stewartry lands, Cowal, Knapdale and Carrick, and Ratho and Innerwick in Lothian. This removed the possibility that Albany would alienate these lands, and took them out of the control of the justiciar south of the Forth, an office probably held hereditarily in the Douglas family. Despite the failure of this policy in the case of Rothesay, the king was again endeavouring to create an independent source of power for his heir.

Once again Robert III's scheme was to end in disappointment. Early in 1406 James was sent into exile to France for his own protection. The traditional interpretation of these events has been questioned, on the grounds that the prince was taken on a risky military expedition through Fife and Lothian before waiting a month for a ship on the Bass Rock, an island fortress at the entrance to the Firth of Forth. Had James's exile been planned in advance, he would surely have set out in a ship from St Andrews, where he had been staying in the custody of Bishop Wardlaw, and it is likely that the expedition was an unsuccessful attempt on the part of Fleming and Sinclair to demonstrate the prince's authority and to further their own opposition to Douglas interests in southern Scotland. By this interpretation, the campaign ran into difficulty and James was sent to the Bass in order to avoid his capture by the Douglases, who killed Fleming in an engagement at Long Hermiston Moor, and the decision to send him into exile was spawned by the sudden emergency; after all, the removal from the realm of the heir to the throne suggests desperation on the part of the king and his supporters.[3] In any event, James was captured by pirates and spent eighteen years as an unwilling guest at the English court. Robert III died soon afterwards. He is said some years earlier to have expressed a desire to be buried in a midden, with the epitaph, 'Here lies the worst of kings and the most wretched of men in the whole kingdom.' The story may be apocryphal, invented by Bower to demonstrate the king's humility, but it serves to summarise Robert III's reign. Physically

[3] Boardman, *Early Stewart Kings*, 291–6.

incapacitated since before his accession, and psychologically unable or unwilling to assert himself, he was driven to oppose his more vigorous younger brother by building up the position of his sons, and even in that ambition he had been thwarted.

The death of Robert III and the enforced absence of his successor left Albany in control until his death in 1420. His rule has often been characterised as that of an 'over-mighty subject' interested only in his own advancement and neglectful of the rights of the king in whose name he governed. His policies and achievements require reappraisal.

Albany has been accused of failing to negotiate the release of James I, while arranging the return of his own son Murdoch in 1416. This has been regarded as treachery, and no doubt it appeared so from James's standpoint. The release of prisoners was not, however, a straightforward matter, even when, as in this case, the king had not been taken in battle. Any negotiations leading to James's return would have to be supported by the English king, and Henry V in particular was not prepared to enter into such arrangements. He used the king of Scots in his continental campaigns, making the Scotsmen fighting on the French side technically guilty of treason since their legitimate monarch was present, even if perhaps unwillingly, in the English army, and so long as Henry lived he was unlikely to want to release James. The Scots and French were allies against him, and Henry and Albany were supporting different popes in the great papal schism. The international situation, therefore, made the return of James to Scotland a distant prospect. Murdoch was in a different league, and his release was in exchange for Henry Percy, who had fled to Scotland during his family's rebellion against Henry IV; even then the negotiations were tortuous. It is understandable that Albany sought the release of his own son more enthusiastically than he did that of a king who was likely to ask awkward questions when he returned, but that does not mean that he was consistently indifferent to James's fate. In 1414 he persuaded Pope Benedict XIII to grant him half the sums due from certain papal taxes over a five-year period, the proceeds to be used for the ransom of James and Murdoch,[4] and it might be unduly

[4] *Copiale Prioratus Sanctiandree*, ed. J. H. Baxter (Oxford, 1930), 241–2.

cynical to suggest that this was merely a ploy to raise money from the church, although undoubtedly it had this effect. Albany was reluctant to impose taxation directly: when money was needed in 1409 for the destruction of the recently recaptured Jedburgh castle, the Governor preferred to make an assignment from the customs rather than court unpopularity.[5] This has been criticised as slack rule, but James I's problems when he attempted to tax his subjects show that Albany's methods were at least expedient.

Another allegation made against Albany concerns his indenture of friendship with the earl of Douglas on 20 June 1409. Albany has been accused both of accepting Douglas as an equal, thereby compromising the royal authority he represented as Governor, and of harbouring ambitions to be king, since the agreement was to expire if he succeeded to the throne. However, such indentures were not necessarily signs of weak government; they often merely regulated how disagreements between the parties or their supporters, or crimes committed by their followers, would be dealt with. Seen in this light, the agreement with Douglas in 1409 was a pragmatic step aimed at preserving order in the realm, although the very fact that it was made surely hints at previous tensions between the two men. That the arrangements were to lapse if Albany became king was perfectly natural. Even as Governor, Albany was merely a leading magnate, as was Douglas; but such an agreement between equals could not continue to prevail if one of the parties became king, because the relationship would then be different. As for Albany's ambition, it was, to say the least, a reasonable precaution for the prospect of his succession to the throne to be taken into consideration, for only James stood in his way. It takes a major leap to argue that, by making provision for this eventuality, Albany actively sought the elimination of James.

Albany certainly allowed magnates to appropriate royal revenues from the customs, and his policy was generally one of appeasement. His confirmation in 1410 of a grant by the earl of Orkney of land in free forest implicitly recognised the right of barons to create forests, even though the principle had been established in David I's reign that this was a royal monopoly.[6] In this and other ways, Albany

[5] *Chron. Bower*, viii, 73; *Exchequer Rolls*, iv, 115, 117.

[6] Gilbert, *Hunting and Hunting Reserves*, 183, 187; *RMS*, i, 403–4.

did not confront his fellow-nobles, preferring to keep them on board by concessions and agreements such as that with Douglas in 1409. The Douglases had further consolidated their power in the south-west in that year when the fourth earl was granted the lordship of Annandale by George Dunbar, earl of March, as a condition of the latter's return from exile, and they continued to dominate southern Scotland. In the north Alexander, earl of Mar and son of the Wolf of Badenoch, enjoyed wide powers, especially after his victory over Donald, lord of the Isles, at Harlaw in Garioch in 1411. Realising that he was the only effective bulwark against Donald's ambition, both Albany and his son Murdoch entered into agreements whereby Mar obtained a share of the profits of justice, the revenues of certain crown lordships, and grants from the customs. Whether allowing great magnates further to build up their power was a flawed policy depends on whether Albany could in practice have acted more forcefully without provoking the sort of opposition which might have led to anarchy and a long-term breakdown of the crown's authority. If the jury is still out on Albany, he did at least preserve the kingdom intact for James eventually to return to. Given his own and his son's prospects of succeeding to the throne themselves, this is scarcely surprising.

The relative success of the governorship of Duke Robert can be gauged by the difficulties experienced by Murdoch, who succeeded him in 1420. Like Robert II, Murdoch had trouble with unruly sons, and the ensuing disorder, together with the early death of Henry V of England, encouraged negotiations for the release of James I. The fourth earl of Douglas worked for the king's return, although he departed for France before James entered Scotland. On the other hand, Walter, Murdoch's eldest surviving son, violently opposed the negotiations and fomented disorder in Lennox which was to persist through the early months of James's active rule. By the treaty of London of December 1423, James was to be released in return for the sum of £40,000, payable in instalments, although a sixth of this amount was later remitted as the dowry for his new wife, Joan Beaufort. It was subsequently agreed that no further Scottish soldiers would be sent to France. The payment was not technically a ransom, because James had not been a prisoner of war, and so it was termed a payment for the hospitality which he had enjoyed during his eighteen-year sojourn in England. The significant point was that James had incurred a major financial responsibility, and for this both an increase in royal revenues and extraordinary taxation would be required; the noteworthy burst of parliamentary activity from 1424 is closely connected with the king's need to raise money.

Just as David II's release in 1357 had marked the beginning of troubled times for Robert Stewart, so James I's return to Scotland in 1424 must have been viewed with apprehension by those who had benefited during the Albany regime, and particularly by Murdoch himself, as well as by those who had been involved in the suspicious death of Rothesay. David II had initially had little choice but to ratify Robert Stewart's gains in northern Scotland during his lieutenancy, and James too had to tread warily. Royal authority had been in abeyance for many years, and he lacked both experience of Scottish politics and a secure territorial or personal power base. His participation in Henry V's campaigns may have made him the object of suspicion in some quarters, and he must have been aware of the presence of substantial Scottish forces in France, the return of which might pose difficulties for his fledgling regime. But he was a man with big ideas. He had seen at first hand the advanced administrative machinery of the English state, the most centralised in Europe, and had witnessed the methods and successes of one of England's most masterful medieval kings. Inevitably, James's programme of legislative and administrative reform drew heavily on lessons he had learnt during his captivity. His problem was going to be implementing his reforms in a realm with different traditions and much stronger regional identities.

The traditional view of James I is strongly influenced by the eulogistic, though not invariably unquestioning, account of his reign by the chronicler Walter Bower. Bower was a contemporary observer who extended his history of Scotland to 1437 in order to draw moralistic lessons from James's life and murder. But James's reign was not seen in so favourable a light by other contemporaries, particularly among the nobility. One of his murderers, Robert Graham, tried to justify the deed on the grounds that James was a tyrant, while Aeneas Silvius Piccolomini, the future Pope Pius II, who visited Scotland in 1435, described the king as 'irascible and eager for revenge', and commented on his having had a number of Scottish lords executed; the papal collector in England, writing shortly after the king's death, endorses the view that he was a tyrant.[7] James was undoubtedly a much more vigorous ruler than his father or grandfather, and did much to enhance the image of the Scottish monarchy at home and abroad, but his attempts to rebuild royal authority were understandably resented by those who stood in his way.

Bower described James as 'our lawgiver king'. To many medieval writers and more recent commentators, describing a ruler as a great legislator was a conventional way of expressing approbation, and we must be cautious before we over-emphasise the impact of James's constitutional, legal and administrative reforms or his stated intention to restore royal justice; even Bower comments on the undesirability of introducing new laws which cannot be kept.[8] On the other hand, we must not allow the limited long-term effectiveness of his legislation to conceal the fact that his proposed reforms were on an unprecedented scale.

The broad range of legislation in James's early parliaments suggests some advanced planning rather than a capacity merely to respond to events, although many of James's enactments, for instance those concerning the burghs, may have been based on the necessity to boost royal finances. Some statutes were designed to improve the quality of those who administered justice in lower courts, ordering their removal if they were inefficient or lacked knowledge of the law. Others aimed to improve law enforcement throughout the realm, and prevent powerful individuals intimidating courts by bringing along armed men. An act of 1426 laid down that none of the king's subjects was to live under particular laws or special privileges, and that everyone was to submit to the king's statutes. The origin of the central Court of Session can be attributed to this year. Some measures had a military purpose, for example encouraging archery and banning pursuits such as football, while in 1426 landowners north of the Mounth were ordered to repair or rebuild castles and other fortifications. Legislation was introduced to control the activities of those who sought preferment at the papal curia, and to combat heresy. Weights and measures were controlled, the export of bullion restricted, seasons for hunting defined, the killing of wolves and destruction of rooks' nests ordered, and the

[7] *The Dethe of the Kynge of Scotis*, ed. M. Connolly, *SHR*, 71 (1992), 66; *Copiale Prioratus Sanctiandree*, 284–5; R. Weiss, 'The earliest account of the murder of James I of Scotland', *EHR*, 52 (1937), 479–91.

[8] *Chron. Bower*, viii, 257.

dress of different sections of the community laid down. In many instances, this legislation either repeated earlier measures or was aimed merely at ensuring that the existing system worked more efficiently, and it would be misleading to suggest that it was fundamentally innovative. Its bulk and scope, however, must have made an impression on contemporaries.

On the constitutional side, James I tried to make the unicameral Scottish parliament conform more closely to the English model. The parliament of 1426 laid down that its members should come in person, rather than by proxy, unless they could show a lawful reason for absence. In 1428 a statute declared that the lesser barons and free tenants were no longer to be obliged to attend parliament and general council; in their place each sheriffdom was to send a fixed number of representatives according to its size, these persons being elected at the head court of the sheriffdom and having their expenses defrayed by the sheriffdom. Prelates and secular nobles were to be personally summoned by brieve (a royal letter similar to the English writ). These reforms were ineffectual, perhaps primarily because of the innate conservatism of the Scottish political classes, but the 1428 act has been seen as an attempt by parliament to end the fining of freeholders for non-attendance (under the statute of 1426) while ensuring that some representatives of this class would be present, even though magnates would surely have had a major role in their election. There may also have been a fiscal motive in the king's desire to regulate parliamentary attendance.

James found his subjects reluctant to grant taxes. Unlike their contemporaries in England, where direct taxation on movables and clerical incomes had become fairly regular during the course of the fourteenth century, the Scots had little experience of royal demands for extraordinary revenues. In order to help the king meet his obligations to the English, the parliament of May 1424 permitted a complex tax of 12d in the pound for two years on both clergy and laity, as well as a customs duty of 40d in the pound on the export of bullion. Bower, who was one of the auditors of the 1424 tax, tells us that much less was collected in the second year than in the first, and later attempts to levy taxation through the political community in parliament, for instance in 1431, had only limited success. A tax of 1433 to pay for a mission to France to arrange a marriage for the king's daughter Margaret led, according to Bower, to great murmurings and had to be abandoned, although it is improbable that the money collected was returned to the payers as Bower suggests.[9] After 1431, therefore, James raised money primarily from individuals by legal judgements and by forced loans such as those in 1436 which funded the journey of Princess Margaret into her unhappy marriage to the French Dauphin. Relatively little of the money raised by these methods ever found its way to England, much of it being used for the king's building projects and other measures designed to enhance his domestic and international reputation; but the difficulty James experienced in levying direct taxes is indicative of one of the most fundamental differences between Scotland and England.

James also launched enquiries into crown lands and the activities of officials during his absence, and grants from customs duties were revoked if the king felt that they were unjustified. One of the principal victims of these measures was the earl of Mar, who lost the annuities from the customs, most importantly those of Aberdeen and Inverness, which he had used to enhance his control of the north-east, and saw his position further undermined by the king's support for his enemy, the lord of the Isles. Such enquiries were also an obvious threat to Murdoch and his family, and it is likely that James saw the weakening of the Albany Stewarts as his primary objective in the first year of his active reign.

Paradoxically, James's security was strengthened by a heavy Scottish defeat in France. On 17 August 1424 a force under the earls of Douglas and Buchan was crushed at Verneuil, removing the threat to the king from the potential return of those troops and temporarily weakening the Douglases. Buchan was the half-brother of Murdoch, duke of Albany, and the king prevented his estates, which included the earldom of Ross as well as that of Buchan, passing to his brother Robert, so weakening the power of the Albany Stewarts in the north. Alexander earl of Mar was now prevailed upon to detach himself from Murdoch, although James distrusted him and was probably not prepared to grant him major concessions in return for support. James's actions are best explained in terms of a determination to crush the Albany Stewarts, even at the expense of enhancing the power of the lord of the Isles, whose claim to Ross

[9] Ibid., 241; for some cautionary remarks see E. W. M. Balfour-Melville, *James I, King of Scots, 1406–1437* (London, 1936), 109–10.

the king now supported. It may not be coincidence that in the parliament of March 1425 James was reminded that Highlanders could not be trusted to make restitution to victims of their violence.[10]

During the same parliament James had Murdoch and his son Alexander arrested. After trial in a subsequent sitting, they were executed, along with Walter Stewart, the most hostile of Murdoch's sons, and the former Governor's father-in-law, the aged earl of Lennox. Since the arrest of Murdoch did not take place until nine days into the parliamentary session, it is unlikely that the assembly had been called primarily to deal with the Albany Stewarts, and there remains some doubt as to the precise grounds on which they were seized and executed. The intensification of the rumbling rebellion in Lennox by another son of Murdoch, James the Fat, and the burning of Dumbarton on 3 May may well have sealed the fate of the rest of the family, as well as inspiring legislation in 1426 to prevent unauthorised contact with Ireland, where James had taken refuge; but in itself it does not fully explain either the arrest or the savagery with which the Albany Stewarts were despatched. After all, they could have been used as hostages in England for the king's debts there. It is likely that the king acted partly from long-standing resentment of his powerful kinsmen, dating right back to the death of Rothesay, and partly from a desire to increase royal revenues by securing control of their extensive territories in central Scotland; he realised that the profits of crown estates constituted his most important source of income. James exploited the poor relationship between Murdoch and his son Walter, and there can be little doubt that he was determined to extirpate the family as soon as he felt strong enough to do so. The crown was enriched by the revenues of the forfeited earldoms of Fife, Menteith and Lennox, a lesson which was not lost on James, nor on his opponents; writing after his death, the Englishman John Shirley commented that many felt that James's actions against his kinsmen were motivated primarily by greed, as were his attempts to raise taxes.[11] The ruthlessness of James's methods against Murdoch and his family must have raised fears about his future intentions.

In other cases too James I had few scruples. His arrest of several Highland chiefs in 1428 was unlikely to worry his Lowland mag-

[10] *APS*, ii, 8. [11] *Dethe of the Kynge of Scotis*, 51.

nates, but the fact that he tricked the chiefs into meeting him at Inverness shows an unpleasant facet of his character which was also manifested in his dealings with other nobles. He deprived Malise Graham, great-grandson of Robert II by his second marriage, of the earldom of Strathearn on the grounds that it could not be passed through a female line, compensating him with the lesser title of earl of Menteith, and the hapless Malise spent twenty-six years as a hostage in England from 1427. In 1434 the king arrested George Dunbar, earl of March, and parliament forfeited his lands the following January, apparently setting aside his father's restoration by Albany in 1409. Growing disorder in the south-east, occasioned (at least in part) by the king's promotion of the interests of the earl of Angus, threatened border security, and in this context the example of March's father's treason in 1400 was pertinent, but the arrest was hardly likely to make March a more reliable subject and certain to send shock-waves through the rest of the nobility. When the earl of Mar died in 1435 James ignored the strategic importance of having a powerful supporter in the north-east to act as a counterweight to the lord of the Isles, and kept the revenues of the earldom for himself. The fifth earl of Douglas also found few favours from James. He probably expected to benefit in the wake of Murdoch's fall, in which he had acquiesced, especially in view of his family's support for James's return in 1424, but instead the king forced him to resign certain rights in Selkirk and Ettrick Forest, and confirmed the position of the fourth earl's widow, Margaret, as lady of Galloway, rather than allowing the new earl to take control there. In 1431 Douglas was briefly imprisoned.

The crown's relations with the nobility are analysed more fully in the following chapter, and the incidents outlined here must not be blown out of proportion. Faced with a realm in which royal power had withered after over fifty years of ineffective kingship, James doubtless felt fully justified in taking strong measures against those he considered to be opponents, and this included arresting them at court or council. It is in such actions, however, that any justification for the notion that he was a tyrant must lie.

Thus far, James had been successful in reasserting royal authority and imposing his will on fractious nobles. But in 1436 he was involved in a fiasco which undermined his reputation and gave encouragement to his internal enemies. He launched an attack on the great border fortress of Roxburgh, which was still in English hands; so confident was he of victory that he invested significant political capital in the inevitable triumph. In the event, he was repulsed, and his precious ordnance was lost. It was probably at the ensuing general council meeting in October, at which the king asked for money, that Robert Graham made manifest his opposition to James's methods and apparently laid hands upon his person.[12] On the night of 20 February 1437 Graham stabbed the king in a drain below the Dominican friary in Perth.[13]

The murder shocked contemporaries. While Graham and his fellow-conspirators who burst into the Perth Blackfriars all had personal grievances against the king, and many of them had had links with the Albany Stewarts, it is unlikely that they would have engaged in so desperate an enterprise without some guarantee of support and protection from a leading magnate. Blame was laid at the door of Walter, earl of Atholl, the sole surviving legitimate son of Robert II, and he was duly executed along with the other conspirators. Atholl could have expected to rule the country after the king's death as the closest adult male relative and heir presumptive of the young James II, and he was an obvious beneficiary of James I's removal, but we must examine whether he had particular reasons for involvement in the plot. After all, Atholl had built up his power in Perthshire partly at the expense of the Graham family and in opposition to the Albany Stewarts, and although Robert Graham can be shown to have had links with Earl Walter after 1425, it would be somewhat paradoxical if a band of Albany partisans were to execute a plot on behalf of Atholl.

Brown has argued cogently that contemporaries were correct to blame the earl of Atholl, even though some observers outside Scotland, such as John Shirley, were less convinced of his direct participation in the conspiracy. Atholl had reaped material benefits from his previously good relations with James I, and had been given the earldom of Strathearn by the king in July 1427. The grant was, however, only for his own lifetime, and could not automatically be passed on to his grandson and heir Robert, who was at the Blackfriars on the fateful night and was almost certainly involved in

[12] Ibid., 52.

[13] For what follows see M. H. Brown, '"That Old Serpent and Ancient of Evil Days": Walter, earl of Atholl and the death of James I', *SHR*, 71 (1992), 23–45.

preparing the way for the assassination. Given the king's previous record and his desire to enhance his revenues, it must have seemed likely to Atholl that the crown would recover Strathearn after his death, and that his heir would not then have an especially valuable inheritance. The king had already cast acquisitive eyes on lands controlled by Atholl, and Queen Joan was seeking dower lands in his area of influence. Royal backing for the candidacy of James Kennedy, the king's nephew, for the bishopric of Dunkeld in early 1437 was a further blow to Atholl's interests in Perthshire. Brown argues that it was these personal issues, rather than the repulse at Roxburgh and the demand for taxation, which persuaded Atholl to back the conspiracy to kill James.

However, if Atholl was indeed involved in the plot, he was gambling for high stakes and must have believed that the conspiracy had a realistic chance of succeeding. Because of his place in the royal succession, blame for the murder would inevitably be directed towards him, and to ensure his ultimate triumph he needed to have James's six-year-old heir physically under his control. Successive royal minorities were clearly to demonstrate this essential feature of Scottish politics, and Atholl no doubt hoped to utilise his close connection with Prince James's custodian, John Spens. The failure of the conspirators to despatch Queen Joan was a serious blunder, because she was able to rally opposition to Atholl, but even then it was not inevitable that Earl Walter would not prevail. The queen was English, her character and her sex were further disadvantages in the male-dominated world of fifteenth-century Scotland, and there were doubtless many who believed that Atholl was the natural leader of the realm during the minority of James II. In the light of events it suited Bower and other Scottish chroniclers to allege that Atholl had long harboured ambitions to be king, had been involved in the conspiracy and so deserved to die, but firm proof that he inspired it is more elusive.

The execution of Atholl and his grandson meant that only three adult earls remained in Scotland: Archibald, earl of Douglas; William Douglas, earl of Angus; and Alexander Lindsay, earl of Crawford. Two other earls, Menteith and Sutherland, were hostages in England for James I's debts. Angus died in October 1437, leaving a minor as his heir. There was thus an unprecedented vacuum in the upper echelons of the Scottish political community, which both encouraged the ambitions of lesser men and gave the earls of Douglas a position of dominance which even they had not previously enjoyed. The Black Douglases were in fact notable beneficiaries of the murder of James I and its bloody aftermath, and their own involvement in the conspiracy cannot be totally discounted, although the evidence for it is even more circumstantial than that against Atholl. Earl Archibald had not received the rewards from James I to which he no doubt felt himself entitled, and had witnessed royal intervention in his power base of Ettrick Forest, while his arrest in 1431 may be connected with his involvement in covert negotiations to attempt to secure the release from English custody of Malise Graham, who was also the nephew of James I's assassin.[14] One source states that during the Roxburgh campaign Robert Stewart, Atholl's grandson, was made constable of the host, a mark of his own high standing with the king and a blow to the prestige of Douglas and Angus, whose role as march wardens might have led them to expect such preferment for themselves. There were, therefore, several reasons why the Douglases might have had cause for hostility towards the king, and although suggestions that they supported the murder plot remain mere speculation, the family was nonetheless able to become the dominant power in the new reign. As well as their extensive landed endowment, especially in southern Scotland, they also had several links with the royal line through marriage.

Although the earl of Douglas became lieutenant, at least after the death of Angus, political ascendancy was disputed between the rival families of Crichton and Livingston. William Crichton, who held Edinburgh castle, had been favoured by James I. The Livingstons may have relied initially on backing from Queen Joan, but in 1439 Sir Alexander Livingston, who had custody of Stirling castle, imprisoned the queen and her new husband, James Stewart of Lorn. Crichton subsequently abducted James II and took him back to Edinburgh. While these events in the royal court have naturally attracted the most attention, old scores were being settled throughout Scotland during the minority, with disturbances in Lennox, further disputes over the earldom of Mar, and open warfare between the Lindsays and the Gordons, a dispute which was to take

[14] R. Nicholson, *Scotland: The Later Middle Ages* (Edinburgh, 1974), 320.

on arguably broader significance at the battle of Brechin in 1452. The events of James I's reign had left a legacy of bitterness which encouraged many to take advantage of the sudden diminution of central authority.

The instability of Scottish politics was intensified when Douglas died in 1439, like his cousin Angus leaving a son who was under age. The new earl and his brother were put to death in 1440 at the infamous 'Black Dinner', leaving James Douglas of Balvenie and Abercorn, who had been created earl of Avandale after the death of James I, as heir to most of the Douglas estates. Avandale was a much greater threat to Crichton and Livingston than the young Earl William had been, and it is likely that he was involved in the move to eliminate the two brothers; certainly he raised no objection to their judicial murders, and indeed probably authorised them in his capacity as justiciar south of the Forth. It is significant that the sixth earl was not forfeited, thus enabling many of his lands and his title to pass to James Douglas. James himself died in March 1443, and it was his son William, the eighth earl, who was to be the principal beneficiary of his father's complicity in the Black Dinner. The declaration of the king's majority in the parliament of Perth in June 1445 was a cynical move to give members of the Douglas faction opportunities to enhance their already considerable power, since actions performed in James's name now had increased authority. For example, although the lordship of Annandale had fallen to the crown on the death of the sixth earl in 1440, the eighth earl was certainly hoping to acquire it, and with it perhaps the lordship of Man, with which Annandale had been associated in the past. At the same time Earl William was striving to prevail upon his wife's grandmother Margaret, duchess of Touraine, the elderly widow of the fourth earl, to resign her rights in Galloway, a process which was apparently complete by August 1447, when the earl was at Threave making grants of Galwegian lands without reference to his wife or Margaret.[15] Such ambitions were clear manifestations of empire-building on the part of the Douglases, and doubtless contributed to the king's bitterness towards them.

After his marriage in July 1449 to Mary of Gueldres, James II took personal control of the government. The Livingstons were

[15] M. Brown, *The Black Douglases: War and Lordship in Late Medieval Scotland, 1300–1455* (East Linton, 1998), 275.

forfeited in the parliament of January 1450, a move which was connected at least as much with the need to provide the new queen with a suitable tocher (marriage portion) as with their misdemeanours during the minority. The earl of Douglas also benefited materially from the fall of the Livingstons and their adherents,[16] and received a fresh royal grant of the whole of Galloway and Ettrick and Selkirk Forest; the king abandoned rights which his father had established in the Forest and recognised the resignation of Galloway by the duchess of Touraine.[17] It appeared that close relations between the crown and the Black Douglases had been renewed on terms which benefited the latter, but the issue of the queen's tocher soon brought their interests into direct conflict with those of the king. The scene was set for the showdown between James II and the Douglases which dominated politics up to 1455.

The year 1450 saw the death of Margaret, duchess of Touraine. Legally, the earldom of Wigtown and the lordship of Galloway now reverted to the crown, and the king wanted to give Wigtown to the queen to increase the value of her tocher, despite his concession to the eighth earl earlier in the year. Douglas was at this time making a pilgrimage to Rome to receive the plenary indulgence which had been offered to all those visiting the city during the year of Jubilee and making appropriate offerings, and from all accounts he made a major impression. James II sought to take advantage of the earl's absence from Scotland, a move which resembled the sharp practices of his father and must have made the nobility uneasy.

On his return to Scotland, Douglas demonstrated his loyalty by resigning his lands and titles to the king in the parliament of July 1451. He received most of them back immediately, but it was not until 26 October that he was reinvested with the earldom of Wigtown.[18] On the surface this seemed to mark a resolution of the recent differences between Earl William and James, but the harmony was illusory, and the king's belated and reluctant concession over Wigtown is a reflection of the crown's weakness in the face of Douglas power. William had sought support within Scotland by making a bond of alliance with the earls of Crawford and Ross. Alexander Lindsay, who had succeeded his father as earl of Crawford in 1446, was a major source of disorder, while Ross was

[16] *RMS*, ii, 73, 82. [17] *APS*, ii, 63–4; *RMS*, ii, 71–2. [18] *APS*, ii, 67–73.

also lord of the Isles and dominated areas in the north and west which were largely outside royal control. Ross was married to Elizabeth Livingston, and the fall of her family had caused the king to rescind his promise of the keepership of Urquhart castle on Loch Ness and other favours, leading to a rebellion by Ross in March 1451. With two brothers of the earl of Douglas now holding the earldoms of Moray and Ormond, and thus controlling extensive lands in northern Scotland, the bond between Douglas, Crawford and Ross posed a major threat to James II's independence of action. They were not natural allies, and their agreement may have been designed to protect their own interests from possible encroachment by the crown rather than being openly treacherous, but from the king's standpoint the alliance must have appeared alarming. Such bonds normally included clauses reserving the participants' allegiance to the crown, but there is some reason to suppose that this one did not: the lord of the Isles frequently acted as though he was a sovereign prince, even in Ross. The original document is lost, but if it was unconventionally worded this might explain the king's violent reaction to it.[19]

In late February 1452 James II entertained the earl of Douglas at Stirling. Douglas had demanded, and received, a royal safe-conduct, which was in itself a clear indication of the poor relations between the king and his leading magnate. It also suggests a rapid deterioration in those relations, for the earl had been at court only a month previously. After dinner on 22 February James ordered Douglas to break his bond with Crawford and Ross. The earl refused, whereupon James personally stabbed him with a knife.

The murder of Douglas was surely an unpremeditated act. The breach of the terms of the safe-conduct and the conventions of hospitality made it especially shocking to contemporaries, and it is inconceivable that James would deliberately have risked such opprobrium in order to destroy Douglas, however afraid he was of his alliance with Crawford and Ross. There were surely ways of bringing about Earl William's death without the king needing to implicate himself directly in the deed, and it is likely that two days of fruitless negotiations had so exasperated James that he lost control of himself.

[19] A. Grant, 'Scotland's "Celtic Fringe" in the late Middle Ages: the MacDonald lords of the Isles and the kingdom of Scotland', in R. R. Davies, ed., *The British Isles, 1100–1500: Comparisons, Contrasts and Connections* (Edinburgh, 1988), 131, 140 n.86.

In any event, the murder was bound to inspire the other Douglases to seek vengeance. In March William's brother James, who had now become the ninth earl, went to Stirling, denounced the king with the blast of twenty-four horns, dragged the useless safe-conduct through the streets at the tail of a horse, and plundered and burned the town. These ceremonies marked the Douglases' formal defiance of James II. He had not demonstrated the 'good lordship' requisite in a king, and so they renounced their fealty to him.

Nicholson criticises the Douglases for responding to the murder of Earl William in a conservative and unenlightened manner. He suggests that they could have declared the king deposed as a perjured tyrant, and set up an alternative government to legitimise their actions, instead of indulging in the sack of Stirling and giving the impression that they were interested only in revenge.[20] This argument, however, presupposes both that the Douglases had the requisite support to set up a viable regime, and that they had a realistic alternative to James as king of Scots. In fact they could boast neither. In March 1452 James still had no son to succeed him. The future James III was born only at the end of May, at Bishop Kennedy's castle at St Andrews. It was, therefore, far from clear who would have the best claim to the throne in the event of James II's deposition. Malise Graham was a possible candidate, but he was still languishing in England and, moreover, had few political ambitions; the Douglases may have tried to procure his release in 1451,[21] but if so nothing had come of this initiative. Anyone contemplating a change of ruler had, therefore, to reckon with the likelihood that the Douglases would dominate the new reign and the very real possibility that their ranks would supply the monarch; after all, the family had close marital links with the royal house. Any attempt by the Douglases to remove James, however heinous his crime, was thus likely to be interpreted as a bid further to increase their power in Scotland, and it is doubtful whether a broad cross-section of the political community would have welcomed such an eventuality. The view of the community was most fully expressed in parliament, which could only be summoned by the king or his lawful representative, and the Douglases could have offered no coherent or widely acceptable political settlement in any case.

[20] Nicholson, *Scotland*, 360.

[21] C. McGladdery, *James II* (Edinburgh, 1990), 60.

James II's position was, therefore, less vulnerable than it would have been if he had had a clear heir. As well as benefiting from suspicion of the Douglases and their intentions, he could count on the widespread predisposition of loyalty to an anointed king. When Crawford was confronted by the earl of Huntly at Brechin in May 1452 a contemporary chronicler tells us that more were with Huntly because he displayed the royal banner and was the king's lieutenant, although the battle itself was also an incident in a personal feud and must not be blown out of proportion. Support for the Douglas cause was less firm in south-west Scotland than might have been expected, perhaps because the branch of the family which had come to prominence after the Black Dinner lacked the close connections with Galloway which had been such a source of power to earlier earls, and indeed some Douglas adherents sought charters from the king as though they anticipated that he would prevail in the coming conflict. James, however, overplayed his hand. After parliament exonerated him for the murder of Earl William, he tried to press home his advantage by raiding southern Scotland, but this expedition led to the destruction of crops and was resented. On 28 August the king and the ninth earl came to a formal agreement, called the 'Appoyntement', and in the following January the two men entered into a bond of manrent, in which the king promised to restore the earldom of Wigtown to Douglas. He also undertook to promote the latter's marriage to his brother's widow, Margaret of Galloway, a dispensation for which was granted by the pope in late February 1453.[22] This marriage was critically important for Douglas, since Margaret had inherited some of the lands of the executed sixth earl, her brother, and a continued bond of wedlock was essential if the ninth earl was to retain control of them. The king must have resented these terms, and these conciliatory actions can only be regarded as tactical devices to gain time.

By 1455 James II was ready to launch another assault. His tactics were to attack Douglas strongholds and accuse the family of treason if they took steps to defend them. The ninth earl was, therefore, in an impossible position, forced either meekly to accept the loss of his estates or to become involved in a war with the king that he could hardly hope to win. His ally, the earl of Crawford, had died in

[22] *CPL*, x, 130–1.

September 1453, leaving a minor to succeed him. Douglas himself lacked charisma and probably also the will to depose James, for the competition between the Douglases and James II had primarily been over the *extent* of royal authority rather than over who should exercise it, and although Malise Graham had now returned to Scotland he was not interested in making a bid for the crown. James had broader support than Douglas, and much superior weaponry, including a number of pieces of artillery. Ordnance was certainly used against Abercorn castle, the chief stronghold of the earl's branch of the family, and against the forbidding tower-house of Threave in Galloway, which stood on an island in the river Dee and may have recently been strengthened by new artillery defences, and it is possible that the king also used his new weapons against the castles of Douglas and Strathaven. The advent of an age of gunpowder ordnance did not suddenly make traditional castles redundant, and it was negotiation rather than firepower which gave James possession of Threave, but artillery was so expensive that only the crown was able to afford it, and that gave rulers a considerable advantage in dealing with their rebellious subjects.

It is easy to criticise the earl for his apparent lack of enthusiasm to defend even Abercorn, which precipitated the desertion of his former ally Lord Hamilton. It is more difficult to suggest a coherent strategy that he might have followed. The king started the war, and by 24 April, when he summoned the Douglases to answer charges of treason, he had already ensured that they had condemned themselves by resisting his assaults. In June parliament duly forfeited the family's possessions; the earl had fled to England, and his brothers had been defeated at Arkinholm on 1 May by an army composed largely of southern lairds, the very group which previously had served the family but now took advantage of its fall. In an act of desperate defiance, Douglas granted Threave to the king of England, but there was no prospect of English intervention. Henry VI's reign had seen a steady breakdown of royal authority, and his recent bout of insanity, followed by his unexpected recovery, led to the violent conflicts which became known as the Wars of the Roses. Douglas could expect no assistance. The king's triumph was complete.

Any analysis of James II's reign is bound to be dominated by the story of his relationship with the Black Douglases, although the family was less of a threat to royal power than James sometimes feared and the seemingly life-and-death struggle might suggest. His relations with other magnates display a similar desire for control without necessarily offering appropriate rewards for support. Despite the valuable assistance given to him by Huntly, he dashed his hopes for the earldom of Moray, perhaps fearful that his family, the Gordons, would become dominant in the north-east, while his creation of the earldoms of Rothes, Marischal and Erroll was presumably also intended to check the power of Huntly. The king ignored the long-standing Erskine claims to the earldom of Mar, which was annexed to the crown in 1457 on the grounds that James was the heir of the childless Alexander Stewart, who had died in 1435; the rights of the heirs of Countess Isabella, who had predeceased her husband, were set aside. The king clearly intended to impose his authority on the north-east, and the grant of the earldoms of Moray and Mar to his young sons is proof of this. James displayed a more conciliatory attitude towards the lord of the Isles, condoning his seizure of the castle of Urquhart in the rebellion of 1451, but in this case he probably had little alternative.

Perhaps the most significant legislative enactment of the reign was the Act of Annexation of August 1455. This laid down that certain lands, lordships and castles were to belong to the crown inalienably, so as to give royal revenues a stable foundation. Grants of heritable offices made since the death of James I were revoked, and hereditary wardenships were forbidden. All regalities in crown hands were to be merged with sheriffdoms, and new regalities were to be created only with consent of parliament. This measure was no doubt inspired by the forfeiture of the Douglases and the consequent acquisition by the crown of vast territories and hereditary offices, but its very enactment implied some criticism of James II. At least in part, financial difficulties had been behind the king's attack on the Livingstons in 1449–50 and his assaults on the Douglases, and the Act of Annexation was an attempt by parliament (albeit a vain one) to ensure that crown revenues would henceforth have a solid base.

In 1460 James II was killed by an exploding cannon during an ultimately successful assault on Roxburgh castle. His reign is difficult to assess because of the paucity of sources. The destruction of the Black Douglases appealed to most later historians, who regarded the strengthening of royal power over magnates as both necessary and meritorious. The circumstances of the king's death, assaulting the English-held stronghold which had been the scene of his father's greatest humiliation, did not raise tricky questions about tyranny as in the cases of James I and James III. Much of our knowledge of James II's reign concerns his involvement in military activity, and there is no means of assessing how competent a ruler he would have proved in times of peace. In March 1458 parliament suggested that he should attend to domestic justice and observe newly made statutes,[23] although such implied criticism is commonplace and there is evidence that James was personally involved in judicial ayres. His relations with the nobility appear to have been generally cordial, and his creation of new earldoms and lordships of parliament at minimal cost to himself bound the nobles to the crown more intimately than had previously been customary. But there is also evidence that he had inherited the high-handed attitude of his father. James II murdered one earl of Douglas and attacked the possessions of his successor in order to drive him to treason; the stormy saga over the earldom of Wigtown had earlier demonstrated that the king was both an opportunist and lacking in scruple. While the earl of Crawford was a law unto himself, James's treatment of the Erskine claim to Mar was of very dubious legality, and he failed to reward Huntly as amply as he might. He condoned the violence of the lord of the Isles and rehabilitated the Livingstons in August 1452 because he felt it was politically advantageous to do so. That this capriciousness did not lead to widespread domestic difficulties such as those which brought down his father and son may be attributed primarily to his early death at Roxburgh.

James III's minority was less turbulent than his father's had been and was not marked by dramatic changes among the ranks of officers of state. Its early years were dominated by his mother, Mary of Gueldres, and the bishop of St Andrews, James Kennedy. Later chroniclers chose to denigrate Mary, accusing her of moral lapses, but her regime was neither chaotic nor dominated by factions. In relations with England, she continued her late husband's policy of playing the warring Lancastrians and Yorkists off against one

[23] *APS*, ii, 52.

another, and succeeded in negotiating the return of Berwick. This pragmatic policy was arguably more beneficial to Scotland than Bishop Kennedy's more resolute, but less realistic, defence of Lancastrian interests in the desultory war which was fought in the northernmost counties of England in the years after Edward IV supplanted Henry VI in 1461. Kennedy, whose promotion to the see of Dunkeld in 1437 may have contributed to the earl of Atholl's desire to see the removal of James I, had been translated to St Andrews in 1440 and was responsible for the foundation of St Salvator's College at the university there. His political importance must not, however, be overstated. Bishop Turnbull of Glasgow was a more significant figure during James II's reign, and there is every reason to think that Kennedy, who was abroad in 1460, was eclipsed by Mary of Gueldres until the latter's death on 1 December 1463. Nor did his death in May 1465 mark the onset of a period of unusual instability in Scotland, although it removed a senior figure from the faction-fighting at court between the Kennedy and Boyd families, in which struggle the seizure of the king by the Boyds in July 1466 should be seen as merely an incident. The mistake of Robert, Lord Boyd, was not this coup, but the fact that he subsequently sought the aggrandisement of himself and his family, including the marriage of his son Thomas to the king's sister Mary. Such presumption helps to explain the fall of the Boyd regime in 1469.

By this time James III had entered into wedlock. His bride was Margaret, daughter of Christian I of Denmark. At this time, the crowns of Denmark and Norway were united, and the marriage treaty of 1468 proved to be critically important to Scotland. It included a military alliance, and Christian remitted all sums due to Norway since 1426 in connection with the annual payment under the treaty of Perth, but its principal significance lay in the acquisition by the Scottish crown of the Northern Isles, which were still part of the kingdom of Norway. Margaret's dowry was fixed at 60,000 Rhenish florins, a sum which the impecunious king could not raise, so in lieu of most of it he pledged Orkney and later Shetland as well. This pledge had no time-limit, and in theory could subsequently have been redeemed; furthermore, the marriage treaty gave Margaret the option of leaving Scotland in the event of her husband's death, whereupon she would receive financial compensation in return for her dower lands and the pledge of at least

Orkney would be cancelled. From the standpoint of Christian, therefore, the surrender of the Northern Isles was a temporary financial expedient, but James III had a different view of the transaction. He immediately treated the islands as de facto part of Scotland, and sought to increase the crown's direct interests there by coming to an agreement whereby William Sinclair, earl of Orkney, surrendered his earldom in return for compensation elsewhere. This arrangement must have been anticipated by Sinclair for some years, as he had taken action to obtain lands in the Northern Isles which were not directly connected with the earldom, and it meant that the king was now unlikely to be persuaded to part with his recent acquisitions.

Aside from presiding over this extension of Scotland's boundaries, James III has received little praise from historians. His unfavourable reputation has been heavily influenced by highly coloured accounts of his reign composed in the sixteenth century which portrayed James III as the archetypal bad ruler, although in contemporary literature he is criticised only for presiding over a corrupt and ineffectual judicial system and choosing young counsellors, both conventional complaints. Even so, his biographer cannot resist calling him 'an exceedingly unpleasant man'.[24] A Scottish monarch who had disastrously poor relations with his two brothers, was imprisoned by some of his own nobles while he was leading an army against an English invasion, and died in a battle against forces which included his own son, must surely have made some mistakes, but it is arguable that he was the victim of circumstance rather than the architect of his own downfall.

The criticism that James III failed to execute justice has contemporary authority. For instance, the parliament of July 1473 expressed concern that the king was giving remissions and respites for serious crimes too readily, and in October 1487 he had to promise that for the next seven years he would grant no pardons for criminal actions. Although kings were expected to exercise the prerogative of mercy when appropriate, there was a widespread belief that James's primary motivation was greed, and that he preferred to raise money by fining criminals rather than let justice take its course, unless his own interests were at stake. There is no doubt that the policy was

[24] N. Macdougall, *James III: A Political Study* (Edinburgh, 1982), 4.

financially profitable: in the period from August 1473 to December 1474 the king obtained almost £550 from pardons granted to over sixty people.[25] It is also true that James's criminal legislation was much weaker in execution than in expressed intent, because, like his predecessors, James III lacked the effective means to deal with local judges who often lapsed into venality, idleness or corruption. But he was by no means alone among late fifteenth-century monarchs in making extensive use of fining: in England Henry VII had a very similar approach. There is undoubtedly something in the charge that he was not seen to execute justice by participating in the judicial ayres, but it would be misleading to view James III as substantially different from the other Stewart kings in his perception of the crown's role in law enforcement, and the ayres continued to be held by the justiciars on a regular basis, except perhaps for a time in the aftermath of the political crisis of 1482.[26] His reputation in this regard has suffered from the general impression that his was an unsuccessful reign.

Connected with James's predisposition towards selling pardons is criticism of his debasement of the coinage. The reduction in the silver content of coins was a common expedient among medieval monarchs in an age of bullion shortages, but it created economic instability because traders were reluctant to accept coins at face value if that face value did not reflect the weight of precious metal. James III certainly presided over the issue of 'black money', but this, like the sale of remissions, was arguably a short-term measure by an intelligent but frustrated ruler struggling to meet the rising costs of government.[27] It is no coincidence that the most debased coins, probably mainly of copper, were in circulation during the war years of 1480–2, and the economic dislocation they caused was a factor in the crisis which saw the king arrested at Lauder. James was perhaps not in fact avaricious, but the important factor is that he was perceived as being so. This is seen in the rumours of his vast treasure in Edinburgh, the dispersal of some of his wealth to loyal supporters throughout the kingdom in the spring of 1488

[25] Nicholson, *Scotland*, 499.

[26] H. L. MacQueen, *Common Law and Feudal Society in Medieval Scotland* (Edinburgh, 1993), 61.

[27] L. J. Macfarlane, *William Elphinstone and the Kingdom of Scotland, 1431–1514: The Struggle for Order* (revised edn, Aberdeen, 1995), 170–1.

(presumably to be used to raise and pay troops), and the fact that he had £4,000 with him on the final battlefield of Sauchieburn. It is unsurprising that parliament resisted most of his requests for extraordinary taxation, but this merely increased the pressure on the king to raise money by other means.

James's foreign policy also came under attack from contemporaries, although he was faced with a rather different international scene from that encountered by his predecessors. In 1453 the English had finally been driven from their territories in Gascony, leaving Calais as the only continental possession of the English crown, and the end of the Hundred Years War disturbed the basis of the 'Auld Alliance' of Scotland and France against England, as the French turned their attentions elsewhere. In England, Edward IV had become firmly established on the throne after a crisis in 1470–1 had seen him temporarily deposed in favour of Henry VI. The combination of these two factors meant that there was arguably a much greater potential threat from England than at any time since the end of the fourteenth century.

It is in this context that James III's foreign policy must be viewed. At one level, especially early in the reign, it was devious and over-ambitious, although in this it did not differ substantially from that of his father in the last few years of his life. The king's intervention in French politics, for example his proposed invasion of Brittany in 1472 at the instigation of Louis XI, created risks which were disproportionate to the potential gains of successful involvement: Louis XI's promises of lands in France might not have materialised, and parliament was surely wise to counsel the king to stay at home. At another level, James must be given credit for realising the value of peace with Edward IV of England. The English alliance of 1474 marked a radical change in Scottish foreign policy, and it was to be cemented by a marriage, never in fact fulfilled, between the king's one-year-old heir and Edward's five-year-old daughter Cecilia. To seek an accommodation with England was not without its dangers, for it could be portrayed as both treacherous and unwise, and it angered some of the border magnates whose life revolved around the often poorly observed truces with the English, but it did mark a recognition by the king of the changed international situation. The collapse of the alliance with Edward IV in 1480, however, left James vulnerable both to external invasion and internal revolt.

James III has also been accused of having imperial pretensions. He claimed full jurisdiction in his realm, including in 1469 the capacity to create notaries public, a right traditionally restricted to the so-called universal powers of pope and emperor; notaries appointed by the emperor were no longer to have authority in Scotland. In 1472 it was decreed that the royal arms should cease to include the fleurs de lys emblem, which might suggest subordination to France, and the coinage of 1485 shows the king wearing an imperial crown rather than a coronet. From a modern standpoint, these changes appear more symbolic than sinister, but they were seen by his opponents as indicative of a dangerously pretentious perception of kingship, even as a mark of tyranny. It was by no means unusual for late medieval kings to assert the independence of their realms in these ways, and again James has suffered from his reputation. Like Richard II of England, who also appeared to be manipulating the judicial system for his own ends, and pursued a foreign policy which some of his magnates disliked, James III seemed intent on exalting himself at the expense of traditional relationships within the political community.

The crises of 1479, 1482 and 1488 all cast light on the relations between James and his leading subjects. That of 1479 was primarily a problem within the royal house itself, involving both the king's brothers. The causes are obscure, and the record evidence gives few indications about the victims' careers or the reasons for their fall. The younger brother, John earl of Mar, died in mysterious circumstances. He had been imprisoned, and was subsequently forfeited, which suggests that he was executed for treason; although contemporary rumours and later chronicle accounts allege his involvement in witchcraft, such stories may be based on those surrounding the English duke of Clarence, who had been executed in 1478. Alexander, duke of Albany, had earlier fled to France, but the estates refused to forfeit him in 1479. It seems that they were less inclined than the king to view Albany's breaches of the truce with England as treason, while the allegation that he had held Dunbar castle against the king could be dismissed on the grounds of self-defence.

James III may have had good reasons for his actions in 1479, to which the unfavourable later accounts of his reign were unlikely to give publicity. However, parliament's refusal to condemn Albany suggests that neither the attack on the royal brothers nor the king's pro-English policy commanded wide support. James may have already appeared arbitrary and unpredictable. In 1471 he had granted Lord Avandale a liferent of the earldom of Lennox, while two years later he gave the title of earl to Lord Darnley, only to revoke this later for no apparent reason; John Haldane, one of several claimants to the earldom, was also granted some of the lands. The king treated Lennox as a forfeited possession, which it was not, and his cavalier treatment of property rights was bound to cause alarm. A similar threat to landed power could be perceived in the king's proposal to suppress the priory of Coldingham and reallocate its revenues to the chapel royal of St Mary on the Rock in St Andrews, a move which the pope approved but which was detrimental to the interests of the Home family, which effectively controlled the priory's revenues and disliked the king's policy of accommodation with England and the increasing involvement of royal officials in the marches. A long, if intermittent, struggle ensued between James and the Homes, and was to play a part in the king's eventual downfall. Acts which appeared arbitrary were bound to inspire uncertainty and fear not only among the king's opponents but also among those inclined to support him. It was not so much that James overstepped the bounds of the law – his two predecessors had done that – as that he failed to realise that he needed local backing if he was to assail a magnate family. By his inconsistency, James III forfeited much of the respect which was naturally accorded to a king.

The crisis of 1482 was marked by an English invasion under the duke of Gloucester, during which Berwick was finally lost to the Scots, and the arrest of James III at Lauder by some of his leading subjects. The events of that summer are paradoxical, especially in the received version handed down since the sixteenth century. A king who had been criticised for his pro-English policy was now prevented from opposing the invasion, and Berwick, for so long a symbol of the state of Anglo-Scottish relations, was thus surrendered without a fight; the estates were apparently indifferent to its fate, and the king had to pay for its defence himself. One of the leaders of the English force was James's brother Albany, who was later portrayed as something of a hero, even though under the Treaty of Fotheringhay which he had made with Edward IV he had been promised Scotland as a gift from the English king and would clearly hold it as Edward's subordinate. The seizure of James III was ostensibly on the grounds that he had governed unwisely and had spurned the counsel of his natural advisers, yet in the final analysis he continued to reign without making any promises to change his policies, despite the penetration to Edinburgh of a very large English force. What are we to make of the events of 1482?

A contemporary chronicler gives the reasons for the crisis as war and dearth caused by the debasement of the coinage. He also says that the lords who seized James at Lauder on 22 July were opposed to the king's household, some members of which were killed and others banished.[28] He thus highlights economic problems and suggests that a number of magnates (whom he does not name) sought to replace existing royal counsellors. Later writers strove to identify the 'low-born' companions on whom the king relied, and suggested that a number of them were hanged from Lauder bridge at the instigation of a group of nobles led by Archibald, earl of Angus. They exaggerated the number of executions, overstressed the humble origins of the king's advisers, and unduly emphasised the role of Angus. In fact the coup was probably led by the king's half-uncles, the earls of Atholl and Buchan, sons of Joan Beaufort by her second marriage. Despite the continuing dispute over Coldingham, there is no evidence of Home involvement either in the events at Lauder or in Albany's schemes to seize the crown in late 1482 and early 1483, and indeed Alexander, Master of Home, may have betrayed Albany's plans to the king.

The events of 1482 show the unpopularity of James III, but arguably only among a small group of magnates whose advice he rarely sought. Although James was held against his will and may have feared for his life, we should not necessarily regard his arrest at Lauder as a manifestation of widespread resistance to his regime, nor even as a sign that his opponents were irreconcilable. The negotiations over the next few months were complex and are difficult to interpret because it is impossible to gauge the private ambitions or secret fears of the participants. In the short term there was a major upheaval of administrative personnel, but the king could afford to play for time; the English army could be kept in the field for only a few weeks, and his various opponents were not united and had no clear plan, even though the events at Lauder had been a political coup and its

[28] Macdougall, *James III*, 312.

target (however it had been dressed up) the king himself. James was liberated at the end of the September in circumstances which remain obscure, and by December he was strong enough to ignore parliament's main provision that he should make an accommodation with his brother. Albany's renewed attempt to seize the king in early January 1483 must have emphasised his untrustworthiness, but an agreement concluded with the rebels in March would still have left him as warden of the march and with a role in Scottish politics. That this did not satisfy him is perhaps not surprising in the light of his previous conduct, and his renewed negotiations with the English (which included admitting an English garrison to Dunbar which it took around three years to dislodge) finally led to his forfeiture on 8 July. It is significant, however, that the Lauder coup was not followed by large-scale retribution. The king's half-uncles, including his gaoler Atholl, were soon back in favour, and supported the king in 1488. Although some close advisers were casualties of the crisis, the majority of the king's administrators remained fundamentally loyal to him even when his authority was called into question. And the fact that James continued to reign indicates the inherent strength of the Stewart monarchy. It became apparent that there was no alternative to him, especially now that Albany was seen to have thrown in his lot with England.

Albany's alliance with Edward IV must be seen as treasonable. In 1482 he had not yet been forfeited in Scotland, but may have believed that he had to act quickly if his cause was to win much support there. Whatever his grievances against his brother, however, to seek English help on the basis of the treaty of Fotheringhay was surely the action of a desperate man, especially when the support he had received from parliament in 1479 had been based largely on the estates' opposition to the king's pro-English policy. The degree of his miscalculation can be seen not only in 1482–3 but also in the ignominious defeat that he experienced when he invaded Scotland along with the long-exiled earl of Douglas in 1484. At Lochmaben on 22 July, these two formerly powerful magnates were defeated by a small group of local lairds; Douglas was captured and Albany forced to flee again to France. If Albany had felt in 1482 that he would win support for his bid to depose James III, he had surely discovered by 1484 that his cause had not been best served by appearing with an English army.

The crisis of 1488 saw James III and his eldest son James, duke of Rothesay, on opposing sides in a civil war. Rothesay was not the leader of the rebels, more a figurehead, but the fact that he was prepared to stand against his father in battle demonstrates a serious breakdown of relations between them. The elevation of the king's second son, also called James, to the dignity of duke of Ross on 29 January 1488, and the fact that he seemed to be more significant than his elder brother in Anglo-Scottish negotiations for a complex marriage alliance, may have caused Rothesay to fear disinheritance. There are indications that relations between the king and his eldest son had been cool since 1486, although neither the international diplomacy nor the grant of the dukedom of Ross is clear evidence that James III sought to change the succession; he may, for instance, have wanted to wait until Henry VII had a daughter of his own to marry to Rothesay, and have elevated Ross to a dukedom in order to enhance the younger James's status in the marriage market. Having said that, however, Rothesay would not have joined the rebels had he not had some fear of his father's intentions. The fact that James had alienated his own son surely allows us to appreciate the disaffection of others.

The Homes were in the forefront of the rebellion of 1488, and the cause was the continuing dispute over Coldingham and the king's attempts at coercion, although other border magnates also feared that an Anglo-Scottish accord would increase the level of royal interference in their affairs. Some of the rebels were desperate men, and the king had many advantages. For all his arbitrary acts, he could still rely on a widespread inherent loyalty to the crown, he had papal blessing, and his friendship with Henry VII meant that he was safe from English invasion. His withdrawal to Aberdeen should have taken him into an area where his support was strong and enabled him to raise forces which would crush the rebels.

James III, however, contrived to alienate some of his potential supporters. He had angered the earl of Argyll, until recently royal chancellor, because the creation of his second son as duke of Ross meant that the king was now able to exploit casualties belonging to the earldom during his minority, which impaired Argyll's interests and those of his kinsmen in the west and north. In the parliament of January 1488 the earls of Huntly and Crawford had been appointed justiciars north of the Forth, again threatening interference in areas where Argyll had given years of faithful service to the crown. He may well have seen these moves as actions of an insensitive and ungrateful ruler.[29] The attitude of the northern earls such as Huntly is more difficult to assess. They were certainly inclined to support James III, although they were not present at his final battle at Sauchieburn on 11 June. This may have been because they had not had time to muster their forces and march southwards, but the king was suspected of intending to break agreements which he had made with his opponents at Aberdeen and Blackness, and this lack of good faith may have inclined Huntly and his colleagues to await developments; although it was by no means a foregone conclusion, or even likely, that James would be supplanted as king, the rebels' strength was nonetheless considerable.

The fact that James III died at Sauchieburn has given the events of 1488 undue constitutional significance. The battle itself was a confused series of skirmishes, and the story of the king's death was later greatly embellished in an attempt to prove his cowardice and inadequacy. He was in fact the unfortunate victim of the unpredictability of war, and his unexpected removal from the scene meant that many Scottish magnates were not called upon to declare a specific allegiance to one side or the other. Most had contrived to remain neutral, which may demonstrate a lack of enthusiasm for the cause of the anointed king, but also cautions us against the notion that James III was faced by widespread noble opposition brought about by his arbitrary rule.

Macfarlane sees the reign of James III as a struggle for order in the kingdom, and regards the crises of 1482 and 1488 as inspired by two small and largely unrepresentative minorities taking drastic measures to force the king to accord with their old-fashioned view of the governance of Scotland.[30] But James was unable to bring his subjects to a peaceful acceptance of his style of kingship, and a number of reasons can be suggested for this. Firstly, the king appeared aloof. The increasing use of Edinburgh as a capital meant that his subjects regarded him as a more remote figure than either his father or his son, and this doubtless increased the impression that he had a different concept of the royal office. His disinclination to participate personally in ayres gave the impression that he cared little

[29] *APS*, ii, 182; Macfarlane, *William Elphinstone*, 179–80.

[30] Macfarlane, *William Elphinstone*, 155.

for the processes of justice or the interests of his people. He never strove to make himself popular, and his lack of flamboyance and his reputation for miserliness meant that he did not meet the established standards of kingly behaviour. Secondly, the king could boast no military successes, and was not particularly interested in war tactics or strategy. Those who arrested James at Lauder may have felt that he had surrounded himself with companions who were more concerned with the arts of peace; certainly his pro-English policy was not universally popular and was perhaps ahead of its time, and the large-scale invasion of 1482 was an alarming manifestation of what was likely to happen if the policy broke down. Thirdly, James appeared unpredictable in dealing with his subjects. He was capable of both vindictiveness and generosity, and some such as Huntly and Argyll doubtless believed in 1488 that he had shown insufficient gratitude to his supporters. Huntly had received scant reward for his service against the lord of the Isles in 1476, receiving a paltry 100 merks, while the keepership of Dingwall castle, which Huntly had captured for the king, was given to John, Lord Darnley, in recompense for his loss of the title of earl of Lennox. Seizures of lands could be seen as manifestations of greed, just as in James I's reign, and grants of offices would inevitably disappoint those who lost out. Given the restricted amount of political patronage available, however, it was impossible for a ruler to please everyone, and James III's failures in this regard were not unique. All the Stewart kings were guilty of inconsistency, acquisitiveness and arbitrary actions.

The political crises of James III's reign have many parallels, but the unfavourable historiographical tradition still influences our assessment of the king. By contrast, the reign of his son has often been regarded as a golden age. Yet James IV followed very similar policies to James III. He too died in battle, albeit against the 'auld enemy' rather than at the hands of his own people, and sixteenth-century commentators criticised him for ignoring 'wise counsel' and allowing himself to become involved in an unnecessary military engagement.

The new government was understandably reluctant to launch a detailed investigation into the circumstances of the former king's death, and let it be known that he 'happened to be slain'. The death of James III relieved the new regime of some potential difficulties, but created others. James IV was still young and inexperienced, and remained largely the prisoner of others' policies until at least 1494. Those who had supported the rebellion demanded rewards, one of the first beneficiaries being Patrick Hepburn, Lord Hailes, who became earl of Bothwell, but the replacement of one governing clique by another simply exacerbated existing feuds and created new ones. Royal justice in early 1489 was closely related to the needs of the faction in power, as the ayre of the south-west made clear, and a revolt soon erupted in Renfrewshire and Lennox, where Dumbarton and other strongholds were held against the king, and in the north-east. It was more than a minor disturbance. A poorly documented battle, at which the king was present, was fought at Gartloaning near Aberfoyle on 11 October, and although the royal party appears to have emerged victorious the Hepburn regime realised the narrow base of its support and had to compromise by admitting former enemies to high office. However, the alliance of Bothwell, the earl of Angus and Bishop Elphinstone of Aberdeen, which effectively governed Scotland in the early 1490s, was an uneasy one: Bothwell and Angus were great rivals on the marches, and the skill and experience of Elphinstone, the founder of the university of Aberdeen, was invaluable in preserving a semblance of stability.

After he came to power in his own right, James IV displayed a great interest in foreign affairs. His involvement in continental alliances and vain hopes for a crusade were ambitious, and it can be argued that the internal affairs of Scotland were correspondingly neglected. James, however, has been credited both with the pacification of the Western Isles and with a major reform, the Education Act of 1496. He was also much more visible to his subjects than his father had been, regularly participating in ayres and journeying to distant regions of his realm. He was ostentatious with his wealth and, despite his financial exploitation of his leading subjects, appears to have been generally popular.

The forfeiture of the lordship of the Isles to the crown in 1493 ostensibly ended the MacDonalds' lengthy dominance of the western seaboard as de facto independent potentates, but the parliamentary declaration did not in itself change the attitude of the Islesmen towards their king. By suppressing the lordship, the Scottish government encountered the problem of finding an agency through which it could make its presence felt in a region with no tradition of close control by the crown, and although by 1495 James IV had secured a temporary peace in the Isles, based on trustworthy agents such as the new earl of Argyll and John MacIan of Ardnamurchan, the west of Scotland remained difficult to control. James could achieve military and naval victories, but had neither the time nor the inclination to spend long periods in that part of his realm. He had little option, therefore, but to allow Argyll and, further north, the earl of Huntly to enjoy extensive power in the Highlands and Hebrides, with the danger that they would carve out for themselves just the sort of power base that the forfeiture of the lord of the Isles had been designed to eradicate.

The importance of the Education Act has also been greatly overstressed. It laid down that all barons and substantial freeholders were to send their eldest sons to grammar schools and then, when they had mastered Latin, to university for three years. The intention was to equip members of the landed class with the educational skills required for the effective exercise of their widespread judicial role, and thereby relieve committees at the royal court of the growing pressure of appeals from the localities.[31] In the absence of the financial machinery necessary to fund central institutions, the Act had a strictly practical purpose, but it had only a limited application and even then was largely ineffective; the burden on royal courts continued to increase. Most of James's other legislation was traditional, for instance repeating earlier measures concerning petitions for benefices at Rome. James IV was no great innovator.

James's expenditure was considerable. Not only did he spend lavishly on diplomatic missions, but he also indulged in extensive building programmes and expanded his navy; annual expenditure on the navy rose over sixtyfold during his reign. The king's financial requirements were not, however, matched by parliamentary enthusiasm to permit new taxes. Although between 1488 and 1497 taxation became an almost annual event, mainly to support diplomacy, the yield was uncertain. During this period there were ten parliaments, but thereafter the king called only three, in 1504, 1506 and 1509, on each occasion primarily to pronounce forfeitures resulting from problems in the Isles. At other times, James preferred to rely

[31] *APS*, ii, 238.

on his administrators and on general councils, which were broadly similar to parliaments but could be summoned at shorter notice to deal with specific business. Such a trend can be seen elsewhere at this period, and in James's case it must have seemed especially attractive to dispense with parliament since it was often a forum for dissent, as in the 1480s and during his minority, but the demise of frequent representative assemblies meant that there was no taxation in the decade before 1512, and then it was imposed only on the clergy.[32] How did the king finance his ambitious schemes without seeking grants from the estates?

James made full use of financial windfalls, including those deriving from his exploitation of the church. When Archbishop Scheves of St Andrews died in January 1497 the king nominated his brother James, duke of Ross, to replace him. James was not yet old enough to be consecrated, and in the meantime the crown was able to dispose of the revenues of the see, while the lands of the duchy of Ross were resumed by the king. In due course Archbishop James received the abbeys of Holyrood, Dunfermline and Arbroath, and when he died in 1504, still not consecrated, the see went to Alexander, the king's illegitimate son, who in 1509 additionally received the monasteries of Dunfermline and Coldingham. Many rich ecclesiastical revenues had thus fallen into the coffers of the crown. In March 1498, when the king was twenty-five, he followed the example of his two predecessors and made a formal act of revocation of all the grants made during his minority, giving him the opportunity to raise money through compositions with those who felt threatened in their lands or offices. The dowry of his wife, Margaret Tudor, was a further useful source of income. The king, however, still needed other revenue, and raised money by granting crown lands at feu-ferm (which brought in an immediate downpayment and annual feu duties which were higher than the old rents) and by ruthless exploitation of feudal casualties. Although his predecessors had seen the possibilities in utilising ancient feudal rights, James IV was the first monarch to apply systematically his right of recognition (the repossession of lands when a tenant-in-chief had alienated more than half his estate without royal consent) and his entitlement to seize lands on the grounds of non-entry

[32] For examples of taxes raised without parliamentary authority see N. Macdougall, *James IV* (East Linton, 1997), 172.

(where a landholder had failed to obtain formal infeftment as the king's vassal as required by law). Even if he did not press for the full sum due to the crown in these cases, he was nonetheless able to tap baronial resources on a considerable scale and use negotiations over the ensuing compositions to demonstrate his control over individual nobles. James also sold pardons, although this elicited less criticism than his father had experienced, perhaps because James IV personally participated in the ayres. As a result of these fiscal expedients, crown income increased by a factor of around two and a half times during the reign, and it was this which enabled James to play a role on the wider European stage.

James IV's relations with England involved both peace and war. An opportunity for intervention in English affairs was presented by the arrival in Scotland of the pretender Perkin Warbeck, who claimed to be Richard of York, the younger of the two royal princes whose claims to the throne had been set aside by Richard III. James realised that Warbeck was a fraud, but his presence gave him an excuse for an invasion of northern England in 1496, significantly on the East March rather than further west where Warbeck might have attracted some support. The principal aim of the expedition was to enhance James's reputation at home and abroad by displaying his martial prowess and trying out his artillery, but James may also have wanted to bring Henry VII into a firm peace by demonstrating that he was unable to defend his northern border. He was, however, very fortunate in that Henry's projected major expedition of revenge was prevented by a rebellion in south-west England in 1497, in which the high taxation for the Scottish expedition was a factor. James wanted another campaign, had another brief excursion into England and again escaped unscathed.

The king's marriage to Margaret Tudor in August 1503 was intended to mark the perpetual peace between the two realms concluded the previous year, yet just over ten years later James IV was lying dead on the field of Flodden. A full discussion of the intervening events would be out of place here, but James's basic problem was that his involvement in continental alliances eventually drove him into a position in which he had to choose between the traditional link with France and the new one with England, and in 1512 he elected to support the French king, Louis XII, who was facing an invasion by Henry VIII. By renewing the Franco-Scottish alliance James may have hoped to deter Henry's planned continental campaign; if not, he planned to use his beloved navy, particularly the great ship *Michael*, to interrupt Henry's communications with the Continent in the summer of 1513, but in the event the *Michael* saw little action and was sold to the French the following year.

The magnitude of James IV's defeat at Flodden was largely due to his ineptitude as a commander and a misplaced confidence in his own abilities stemming from the successful raids of 1496 and 1497. But the fact that he had come to be in such a dilemma in 1513 also requires critical analysis. From 1494 onwards the French had been involved in a series of wars in Italy, which spawned several leagues between the powers of Europe. James's problem was that Scotland's principal value to major European states was its potential to threaten England's northern border, and beyond that its diplomatic influence was limited. In involving himself in international diplomacy, therefore, James faced becoming embroiled in events over which he had no control. He was easily flattered by representatives of overseas states, and was led on by promises of a crusade and the wild hope that he would be asked to command it. James was a conventionally religious man, who made regular pilgrimages to the shrine of St Ninian at Whithorn, including in 1507 one on foot from Edinburgh, and to that of St Duthac at Tain, and frequently expressed an interest in a pilgrimage to the Holy Land; it is not, therefore, surprising that he was excited by talk of a crusade. We should not be too readily dismissive of the prospects for an expedition against the Turks in the early sixteenth century, but the king of Scots' role in such a campaign would surely have been relatively minor; however grand James IV's navy might become, especially if the pope authorised clerical taxes to fund it, a crusade would still be much more heavily influenced by the attitude of Italian maritime powers such as Genoa and Venice.

It is important, however, not to overemphasise James IV's crusading ambitions, nor to dismiss his diplomacy as the actions of a 'moonstruck romantic', as Mackie memorably described him.[33] The disaster of Flodden has tended to cast a long shadow across the reign, as though the whole of James IV's personal rule had been a precursor to an inevitable calamity. But there is no reason to think

[33] R. L. Mackie, *King James IV of Scotland: A Brief Survey of His Life and Times* (Edinburgh, 1958), 201.

that James's adoption of a French alliance in 1512 was not carefully considered. The 'perpetual peace' with England had not brought stability to the Borders, nor ended naval incidents. Henry VIII's aggressive posturing was a threat to Scottish as well as French interests, while the English parliament which assembled in February 1512 resurrected the old idea of overlordship.[34] The French alliance was backed by the promise of money and supplies, and the invasion of Northumberland in 1513 was, to judge from the size of the host, popular with James's subjects. The king incurred excommunication for his breach of the 1502 treaty with England, but this must have seemed a price worth paying in return for the benefits of a renewed alliance with France. The expedition was surely more than a simple matter of honour on the part of a diplomatically outmanoeuvred king. He need not, and with hindsight should not, have invaded England in response to Henry VIII's attack on France, but that does not prove that he had not weighed the options carefully.

James IV's reign undoubtedly saw a flowering of Scottish culture, and marked the introduction into Scotland of some of the ideas of the Renaissance. The first Scottish printing press was set up in 1507–8 by the Edinburgh burgesses Walter Chepman and Andrew Millar, thus bringing to Scotland the medium of communication of news and propaganda which was to play such a major part in the dissemination of ideas in the sixteenth century and beyond. Politically, however, James's achievements were limited. His base of support was certainly wider than that of James III, and (at least after the first few years of his reign) he avoided the sort of crisis which had bedevilled his father. Unlike James III he could point to military successes, in England in the later 1490s and on several occasions in the Isles, but the Highlands and Hebrides were not pacified by his expeditions, and the suppression of the MacDonald lordship made it more, rather than less, difficult to deal with the region's centrifugal tendencies except through enhancing the power of the earls of Argyll and Huntly. Domestically James followed similar policies to those of his predecessors, and was equally (if not more) adept at exploiting his legal and fiscal rights to the full. In the field of foreign affairs, James endeavoured to make Scotland a power to be reckoned with, but finished up playing the traditional role of trying to distract

[34] *Statutes of the Realm* (11 vols., London, 1810–28), iii, 43–4.

the English king from his ambitions in France. In doing so, he and a considerable part of his nobility perished at Flodden, and his infant son was left to succeed as James V.

Politically, the minority of James V was more turbulent than those of James II and James III, although a degree of administrative continuity was nonetheless achieved. The new king's nearest adult male relations were John, duke of Albany, and James Hamilton, earl of Arran. Both were grandsons of James II, but Albany had been brought up in France after the flight of his father, and Arran proved unable to rise above the rivalries between his own family and the Douglas earls of Angus. Albany arrived in Scotland in May 1515 and, despite the defection of Arran, was reasonably successful in his attempts to make his regime acceptable. However, his absence in France between 1517 and 1521, prolonged by pressure from Henry VIII on the French to detain him overseas, meant that there was no one to stand above the faction-fighting within Scotland. In June 1520 the pope placed Scotland and its king under his protection and affirmed Albany's authority as Governor,[35] but this international recognition was of limited use when Albany was at that time unable to return to the realm. In a famous incident in 1520, known as 'Cleanse the Causeway', the Douglases drove the Hamiltons out of Edinburgh, and the next few years were dominated by the feud between the two families. The events of these years foreshadowed the confused factionalism of subsequent minorities.

After Albany's final departure in 1524, Arran and Queen Margaret caused the king to be 'erected', meaning that he was given the symbols of sovereignty. This marked the formal end of Albany's governorship, although this was not universally accepted and did not provide for stability. A plan for control of the king to alternate between different factions was scuppered when in 1526 Archibald, sixth earl of Angus, refused to relinquish his custody of the young monarch, had parliament declare the king to be of age, and utilised his position of power to advance his kinsfolk. He had married the queen in August 1514, and although the relationship had proved tempestuous and had soon broken down, the Red Douglases appeared to be the ultimate beneficiaries of the turbulence of the

[35] *The Letters of James V*, ed. R. K. Hannay and D. Hay (Edinburgh, 1954), 79.

minority. In reality, however, their power was insecurely based. Angus's actions in 1526 had largely been forced upon him, because the alternative was to sacrifice his family's political influence and risk being overwhelmed by his enemies.

In 1528 the king escaped from the custody of Angus, and the Douglases were subsequently forfeited by parliament. However, it took James V and his supporters a year to achieve the removal of Angus to England, and then it was only through negotiation. A royal attack on his stronghold of Tantallon in East Lothian failed to achieve its objective, and it proved difficult to co-ordinate the Scottish magnates in an assault on one of their number, especially when Angus could exploit rivalries on the border and seek English assistance. It is possible to see James V's personal rule as being dominated by the threat of a Douglas return, although this is to stress personalities at the expense of broader issues of policy.

The conventional picture of James V is of a monarch who was unscrupulous, slippery and vindictive, a fitting opponent of his uncle Henry VIII of England. His persecution of the Douglases and their connections has been seen as suggesting a sadistic streak, while his success in levying taxation and fines did little to endear him to his prominent subjects. This view is, however, open to challenge. It is true that there is virtually no trace of enthusiastic endorsement of James V in the admittedly exiguous contemporary sources, which suggests that he did not inherit his father's capacity to inspire popularity, but the circumstances in which he assumed power were not conducive to a smooth start to his personal rule. He had chafed under the control of Angus before 1528 when he must have felt himself to be old enough to have at least some say in the realm's affairs, and he urgently required money in order to pursue his father's policy of increasing Scotland's standing in Europe. The king's subsequent reputation suffered from his allegiance to Rome, which aroused the implacable ire of Protestant commentators. In fact, his methods were not strikingly different from those of James IV, and there is little contemporary evidence of tension between him and broad sections of his nobility, although, unlike his father, he was ungenerous in the distribution of royal patronage. He undoubtedly antagonised individuals and was guilty of sharp practice towards them, but in this he was following in the footsteps of his four immediate predecessors.

The foreign policy of James V's reign, and to some extent his domestic policy too, was dominated by the unfolding events of the Reformation. The political and doctrinal upheavals of the sixteenth century were to continue to influence Scottish politics through the reign of Mary and much of that of James VI, but James V was able to keep Scotland at least nominally loyal to Rome. As a result of that loyalty the king received papal appointment of his nominees to major benefices as well as permission to tax the church. For instance, the crown obtained the revenues of the great monastic houses of Melrose, Kelso, Holyrood, St Andrews and Coldingham because the pope granted them to the king's illegitimate infant children. But James's adherence to Roman Catholicism was not universally welcomed. Protestant ideas entered Scotland from the Continent and England, and there was some disquiet at the king's pro-French and anti-English approach. The tensions which emerged in James's reign were to be seen more clearly during the long minority which followed his death.

James V's reign saw the exploitation of several sources of revenue: the wealth of the church; forfeitures and compositions resulting from the king's relations with his nobles; the dowry from the king's marriage; and miscellaneous profits, for instance from the gold mines on Crawfordmuir. Seeking to uphold the crown's feudal rights was not a new policy, although James V pursued it with great vigour, and his taxation of the clergy was on a much larger scale than during his predecessors' reigns. Much of the money raised was used towards the king's building schemes, for instance at Falkland and Stirling, and on the traditional Stewart interest in artillery and the navy. James V was certainly rich by the standard of Scottish kings, but there is little reason to suppose that he hoarded money rather than spending it on the glorification of the Stewart monarchy.

In 1531 the pope permitted the king to collect a perpetual tax of £10,000 per annum from Scottish churchmen, along with a tenth of all Scottish ecclesiastical revenues for three years. Although initially this grant was said to be for 'the protection and defence of the realm', the pretext offered for the unprecedented demand was the establishment of a College of Justice to hear civil cases. However, the College was little more than an enhanced endowment of the pre-existing Court of Session; the papacy did not formally confirm it until 1535, and it was not ratified by parliament until 1541. Its establishment was little more than an excuse to tax the clergy, who collectively enjoyed an annual income perhaps ten times that of the crown. Faced with the prospect of a permanent contribution of about a sixth of their assessed revenue, the prelates compounded for around £72,000 over four years, assigning a further £1,400 per annum in perpetuity for the salaries of the judges, with the intention that the crown would also make a contribution towards their remuneration. But the College was less well endowed than this might suggest. The annual payment of £1,400 was to come, not directly from the prelates, but from the fruits of certain benefices in their patronage to be earmarked for this purpose, the deduction to be postponed during the lifetime of the current incumbents; if not an empty gesture, it was one which cost the leading clerics very little. The king, moreover, used the tenths and the £72,000 on his building programmes. The judges' salaries were paid only irregularly. The tax was clearly for the king's personal convenience, and the complaisance of the pope in permitting its levy must have encouraged James to retain Scotland's links with Rome, proving his Catholic credentials by having a few heretics executed. While it is hard to assess exactly how successful the king was in inducing the church to pay taxation on so unprecedented a scale, there can be little doubt that he raised substantial sums by playing on the fears of the pope and the Scottish clergy that he would emulate his uncle's example.

Relations between the crown and the magnates are often the best indicator of the success or otherwise of medieval Scottish monarchs. Like his predecessors, James V sought to curb the nobility's capacity for independent action while at the same time accepting that Scotland could be effectively governed only if the relationship between the king and his leading subjects was a constructive one. The traditional view of James V was that he alienated his magnates through arbitrary actions and cruel executions, so much so that his later years constituted 'something of a reign of terror',[36] but in fact he was not mindlessly vindictive, even against the Red Douglases.

However, the king knew that Angus might one day be allowed to return to Scotland. In the negotiations of 1529 the earl had

[36] G. Donaldson, *Scotland: James V to James VII* (Edinburgh, 1965), 62.

obtained a promise that his estates would not simply be broken up and redistributed in perpetuity, and he continued to be a factor in Anglo-Scottish diplomacy. James was, however, determined to weaken his potential influence, as is seen in the legal proceedings against the earl of Crawford for non-entry, which were concluded in the crown's favour in May 1532. As a result the king was able to install new tenants on lands in the sheriffdom of Forfar and confirm existing tenancies, thereby binding individuals more closely in loyalty to the crown and weakening their connection with local lords, most immediately Crawford but also Angus, some of whose own lands in the area had already passed into the hands of royal supporters. The earldom of Crawford was an inviting target because of dissensions within the Lindsay family and financial problems, but the legal action must be seen also as a means of destabilising Douglas power north of the Tay, and so the king was persecuting Crawford in pursuit of greater security against Angus.[37]

Only one magnate committed blatant treason during the period of James V's personal rule, namely Patrick Hepburn, earl of Bothwell, who in 1531 promised substantial military aid to Henry VIII if the English king chose to invade Scotland. Bothwell received no support from other magnates, and was treated surprisingly leniently by the king, perhaps because James felt that he was a victim of circumstance who had been exploited by the earl of Northumberland rather than willingly setting himself up as a rebel. Otherwise, relations between James and his leading subjects appear to have been good. This is clearly demonstrated by the fact that in 1536–7 the king was able to spend nearly nine months on a journey to France, during which he married Madeleine, daughter of Francis I. James V must have had confidence in his nobility to absent himself voluntarily from his realm for such an extended period, especially when latterly he had none of his magnates with him. He had appointed a committee of six nobles to rule Scotland in his absence, rather than granting the governorship to a single individual, but this policy does not imply that he mistrusted his magnates, merely that he did not wish one to be promoted at the expense of others who might then feel jealous. It must be concluded that in 1536 crown–magnate relations were stable, and there was every reason for

[37] J. Cameron, *James V: The Personal Rule, 1528–1542*, ed. N. Macdougall (East Linton, 1998), 106–13.

them to be so: there was no war or focus for discontent; the king was an adult, in full control of the realm after the faction-fighting of the minority, and presiding over an efficient legal system which promised redress to the aggrieved.

James V's reputation has suffered as a result of three executions, of the Master of Forbes and Lady Glamis in July 1537, and of James Hamilton of Finnart in August 1540. All were convicted of treason, but in each case the charges were probably spurious. Janet, Lady Glamis, was the sister of the earl of Angus, and the fact that she was burned has been regarded as an instance of the king's vindictiveness towards the Douglases. Hamilton of Finnart had also been involved in the events towards the end of James V's minority, and the long delay before his trial and execution begs questions, especially when in the meantime he had been closely involved with the king's cherished building projects and may have been a royal favourite. Too much emphasis must not be placed on the fate of these three individuals, for their executions do not amount to an all-out assault on Douglas adherents. In the case of John, Master of Forbes, the instigator of the charge was his enemy, the earl of Huntly, and the king was probably not involved in the trial, especially since the young Queen Madeleine was dying, thereby jeopardising years of careful diplomacy; John was, moreover, a notorious criminal and nuisance to his neighbours in north-east Scotland, most of whom were probably glad to be rid of him.

The king's hand can be seen more clearly in the proceedings against Lady Glamis and Hamilton of Finnart. Earlier attempts had been made to bring Janet Douglas to trial, perhaps because she was the most vulnerable of Angus's sisters through her lack of interests on the border, where the constraints of Anglo-Scottish diplomacy might have complicated actions against her. Her execution emphasised that there would be no reconciliation with Earl Archibald, and the ensuing forfeiture of her son brought into crown hands further estates north of the Tay which could be used to neutralise Angus's influence if he should ever return to Scotland. At around the same time action was taken against a small number of others with Douglas connections, but it did not constitute an indiscriminate reign of terror. Hamilton of Finnart, although an illegitimate son of the first earl of Arran, was a political maverick who had succeeded in detaching some territory from his younger, legitimate half-brother. His execution was not a sudden, irrational move against the followers of the Douglases, still less an attempt by the king to terrify the magnates into submission. Rather, it was a carefully chosen targeting of a single individual which was unlikely to have serious political repercussions other than further to emphasise that the king was still prepared to proceed against those whom he perceived to have been his enemies during the minority. In that sense, it was an attack on the Douglases, and it paved the way for the Act of Annexation in the parliament of December 1540, which formally declared most of the Angus estates, among others, to be inalienable crown property. The fact that James saw no need to use the annexed estates to buy support emphasises the strength of the crown and the inherent stability of Scottish politics; the king was so secure that he preferred not to risk arousing jealousy by selectively bestowing favours.

In the summer of 1540 the king and many of his magnates engaged on a naval expedition to Orkney and the Hebrides. Considerable numbers of soldiers accompanied the royal party, as did most of the king's ordnance, so the purpose of the expedition was clearly military rather than recreational. It was beneficial to James V's image for him to appear in the furthermost parts of his realm as a dispenser of law and order, and it might also lead to an improved financial return from the areas in question. The king's journey to the far north and west emphasised his determination to execute justice personally, the importance of which James III had failed to appreciate, and the same policy was used throughout James V's personal rule in the lawless regions on the English border. He came to be criticised in ballads for his severe treatment of criminals, but this reflects the Borderers' reluctance to accept royal intervention in their affairs rather than tyranny on the part of the king. The execution of notorious reivers such as Johnnie Armstrong and George Scott of the Bog must be regarded as a mark of strong and assertive kingship, and it is paradoxical that James V, who participated regularly on justice ayres and frequently visited the Borders, has been condemned for his attention to his obligation to enforce the law and protect his subjects.

James V died at Falkland on 14 December 1542, just days after the birth of his daughter and only surviving child, Mary. The last few weeks of his reign had seen the disbanding of a Scottish army called to resist the incursion of an English force under the duke of Norfolk, and then a humiliating defeat at Solway Moss, where several nobles were captured. Later commentators portray a king who was driven to war by his bishops and could not count on the support of his magnates, many of whom were Protestant sympathisers opposed to the French alliance and desirous of an accommodation with England. There are serious problems with this interpretation, which rests too heavily on the notion that religion underpinned the crisis and that leading prelates, such as Cardinal Beaton, were determined to wage a holy war against the heretic English in the knowledge that Protestantism threatened their own position in the state. In fact, the aggressor was not James, but his uncle Henry VIII, whose ambitions on the Continent required the neutrality of his northern neighbour; the war arose because Henry could not receive assurances that James V would not support Francis I in the event of an English invasion of France. Henry probably wanted merely to secure his border, but his belligerence, coupled with the Privy Council's enquiry into evidence of the archbishop of York's ancient claim to primacy over the Scottish bishops, forced James to muster an army.

There was a degree of dissension among the Scottish magnates, especially between the earls of Moray and Huntly, who were neighbours and rivals in north-east Scotland. In addition, the earl of Atholl was seriously ill. There is, however, no contemporary proof that James appointed a favourite, Oliver Sinclair of Pitcairn, to command the force which was worsted at Solway Moss, although such an appointment might explain why so many Scottish lords surrendered to the English rather than fighting to the death as at Flodden. What appears to have happened is that the force gathered at Lauder in October to meet the threat from Norfolk was disbanded because it was too large and cumbersome to invade Northumberland in poor weather and with food in very short supply. Norfolk had returned to England, so the army was no longer needed for its primary purpose, and its disbandment was doubtless a relief to the local populace, which had already suffered from the passage of Norfolk's force and objected to James V's requisition of food for his troops. There is no need to see the withdrawal from Lauder as a mark of magnate rebellion, however symbolic it may have seemed to hostile writers to place the scene of James V's supposed humiliation in the same location as his grandfather's in 1482; the nobles had been fully prepared to support the king in defending the realm, although some may have counselled against a full-scale invasion of England. A fresh muster was then called for a raid on the West March, and it was during this that the army was defeated at Solway Moss. It is likely that a number of incursions were planned, and that the unsuccessful raid was not a major invasion with a strategic objective such as Carlisle, for it was too late in the season for such an expedition, although the Scots may have hoped to proclaim the papal interdict which had been laid on England. The simplest explanation is that the force was outmanoeuvred and its leaders chose to surrender rather than sacrifice themselves to no purpose. There is no reason to think that they were hostile to the king, nor that James suffered a mental breakdown in the face of a magnate rebellion. He probably died of natural causes, perhaps from cholera.

The death of James V at the age of thirty once again plunged Scotland into the crisis of a minority, this time with the added complication of the Reformation. The struggle between England and France for the hand of the infant queen, and the problems of her turbulent reign, belong to the history of the Scottish Reformation rather than the medieval kingdom. At this point, therefore, it is appropriate to take stock and attempt an analysis of the achievement of the Stewart dynasty up to 1542.

The Stewarts had survived in the direct line, even though five of the seven kings had died prematurely and the other two had been sidelined by other members of their family. Lengthy minorities had alternated with periods of assertive kingship. In striving to re-establish royal authority, James I set the tone for his successors, who all worked to maximise the influence of the crown within the context of a realm with strong local particularisms. Their efforts were made against the backdrop of an evolving international situation in which the 'Auld Alliance' with France against England was no longer an inevitable foundation of Scottish foreign policy, as James III realised and James IV discovered to his cost. Opportunities now existed for Scotland to be involved in the wider European world, both diplomatically and culturally, and James IV's reign epitomises the new outlook, although his father and son both appreciated the importance of international links. The cost of diplomacy and the need to be ostentatious with one's wealth meant that the Scottish kings had to increase their income, but the potential for conflict with their subjects was offset by their ability to tap the wealth of the church, both through the crown's exploitation of major monasteries by having them provided to the king's sons, and through James V's direct taxation of the clergy. Two major issues run through the entire period: the question of relations between the crown and the magnates; and the connected problem of imposing royal authority in the Highlands. These themes will be explored in the next chapter.

7

CROWN AND NOBILITY IN LATER MEDIEVAL SCOTLAND

Any narrative of the reigns of the medieval Stewart monarchs demonstrates the fundamental importance of the relationship between the king and his leading nobles. In a country like Scotland, where central institutions were relatively undeveloped, the co-operation of the magnates was essential for the smooth governance of the realm. Especially in areas which were remote from the heartland of the Scottish kingdom, those who could command strong local support and successfully impose their authority over their tenants and dependants could act as effective agents of the crown, but also had the capacity to defy the king with a degree of impunity, or even to foment rebellion. The troubles faced by the twelfth-century kings in Moray and Ross and on the western seaboard are ample testimony to the potential threat posed by great magnates. It was, therefore, essential for the crown to harness the influence of the nobility in the interests of stable government throughout the realm.

Traditionally, late medieval Scotland was regarded as a land riven by feuds among bloodthirsty magnates whose excesses the kings were powerless to curb. Such an image was an inevitable consequence of our reliance on narrative sources, and our knowledge of affairs in Scotland is still coloured by the relative paucity of documentary records until the very end of the fifteenth century. Chroniclers were inevitably more interested in noteworthy events than in routine matters of government. They report murders, plots, battles, the deaths of kings. They might condemn violence, or even place it within the broader context of Christian morality, but they nonetheless concentrate on dramatic incidents. James II's murder of the eighth earl of Douglas, for instance, was more newsworthy than a lengthy period of constructive relations with another magnate. When we consider also the embellishment of medieval Scottish history by sixteenth-century writers, it is not surprising that the more gory aspects have been emphasised.

Recent scholarship has tended to stress the essential stability of Scottish politics. Considerable emphasis has been placed on the fact that fifteenth-century Scotland was much less disturbed than England, where the weak rule of Henry VI eventually led to political degeneration and the series of military hostilities which became known as the Wars of the Roses; political executions were common in England, but much rarer in Scotland. Such revisionism is welcome, but there is always the risk that it will be taken too far. To use for comparison England in a period of particular turmoil is not necessarily helpful, because in itself it tells us relatively little about Scottish politics, while the view that Scotland was essentially peaceful and stable involves arguments from silence against clear evidence of albeit unusual incidents. It is, therefore, necessary to assess the extent to which the dramatic events of the chronicles were typical of late medieval Scotland.

The king was clearly not in continuous confrontation with his leading magnates. Indeed, such a scenario would have required a degree of unity which the nobility never enjoyed. Even in 1488, many magnates such as Huntly remained at worst neutral in the conflict between James III and the rebels. The Douglases were unable to attract sufficiently wide support to depose the king in 1452, even though James II had murdered the eighth earl against the terms of a safe-conduct, and they had even fewer followers in 1455. None of the Stewart kings alienated even the majority of the magnates; had any done so, he would have been constrained by a baronial council or might even have lost his throne. James III came closest to provoking widespread opposition by offending his friends as well as his enemies, but even after his death there continued to be resistance to the new regime. Other monarchs certainly caused offence to individuals, and both James I and James II were ruthless in crushing opponents. Although it would be inappropriate to see their reigns as straightforward clashes between the authority of the crown and the violent ambitions of a hostile nobility, equally it would be misleading to see them as peaceful. Both kings had to face magnates with major territorial power and broad personal connections, and although James I put down the Albany Stewarts and James II the Douglases, and received support from their subjects while doing so, their approach threatened the interests of other nobles and made them nervous about the king's ultimate intentions. Although after 1455 no magnate (except the lord of the Isles) enjoyed a position of dominance comparable with that of Albany and Douglas, the kings' demands for money through the exploitation of feudal incidents and compositions created the potential for conflict with individuals and, under James III, with a broader swathe of the nobility.

It is difficult to define 'nobility' in late medieval Scotland. Until the 1440s, when 'lords of parliament' began to emerge, there was nothing in Scotland to compare with the English notion of a parliamentary peerage comprising those who could expect a personal summons, and so the lower edge of the magnate class is hard to determine, and any line purporting to divide 'nobles' from 'lairds' cannot but be arbitrarily drawn. At the upper end of the social scale, however, were the earls, occasionally supplemented after 1398 by those on whom the title of duke was bestowed.

On the eve of the Wars of Independence, earls still had considerable control over the provinces from which they took their title, a legacy of the historical development of Scotland and a reflection of the strength of local patriotism and particularism which from the crown's standpoint could be a force for good or ill depending on how it was harnessed. The coherence of the ancient provinces meant that they could function as a unit even when there was no individual with the title of earl to act as a focus of loyalty. There was a distinct difference here between Scotland and England, for in England the title of earl was already a mark of personal status rather than an office with judicial, administrative and military responsibilities in a particular area. The lands of English earls were widely scattered, and they could not draw on the undivided loyalty of the people of individual regions in the way their Scottish counterparts did.

By the middle of the fifteenth century, however, the close link between earls and earldoms in Scotland had broken down, although this development did not necessarily increase royal authority in remote parts of the realm. From 1358 new earldoms were created to honour great magnates, the first being bestowed on Sir William Douglas. The Douglases were certainly very wealthy and became very powerful, especially in southern Scotland; the third earl, Archibald, who died in 1400, possessed the great lordships of Galloway, Lauderdale and Selkirk, twenty-four baronies and many other smaller estates. However, the earldom of Douglas itself did not consist of a piece of territory and the rights which went with it. It was a personal honour, just as the earldom of Crawford was when it was created in 1398. Of the many fifteenth-century creations, only that of Argyll in 1458 was comparable to early medieval earldoms, and that was partly because the Campbell estates were all located in the same area, although the importance of Argyll as a buttress against possible incursions from the Isles meant that a traditional provincial earldom was not inappropriate in that region, provided it was held by a loyal servant of the crown. Even where an ancient title was bestowed, it ceased to have the territorial significance of an earlier period, and the earldoms which were given to the king's children reverted to the crown on their death without heirs. The power of the higher nobility in late medieval Scotland, as in England, therefore rested less on functions carried out by virtue of the title of earl than on an ability to achieve local or national supremacy through building up a personal following.

The problems of fifteenth-century England can be attributed, at least in part, to changes in the nature of lordship as older types of feudal relationship became less relevant to society's demands. The question of 'bastard feudalism' is a complex one into which it would be unprofitable to enter here, but it is likely that inflationary pressures had made the English nobility increasingly reliant on royal favour, and so loss of status at court became relatively more damaging; moreover, crown control of appointments to local offices meant that exclusion from royal favour could lead to a diminution in a magnate's authority in the places where he expected to have influence. The contrast with the earlier period should not, however, be drawn too starkly. The barons who opposed Henry III in 1258 were complaining at their exclusion from patronage just as much as the duke of York and his followers two centuries later. Access to the king and to the lands, wardships and offices in his gift enriched magnates who could then use their additional income to offer rewards in land, office, money, food or livery to potential adherents. If the lord was unable to meet the requirements of these men, they might seek a rival who could.

The situation in Scotland was essentially similar. Because the crown was relatively impoverished, 'money fiefs' on the late medieval English model appear only fleetingly at the end of the fourteenth century, when Robert III tried to reconstruct his old affinity around his son David; with a restricted income, the king could not afford to pay large heritable pensions to his nobles, however much such a practice might bind them to his service. Instead, they had to be endowed with land or given permission to appropriate royal revenues such as the customs, a common feature especially during Albany's governorship. Lands could in certain circumstances be forfeited, and the royal demesne was greatly extended in the fifteenth century as a result of the forfeiture of, among others, the Albany Stewarts, the Douglases and the lord of the Isles, but magnates who relied on assignments of royal revenues were in a much more vulnerable position, which is why the earl of Mar's power in the north-east was so threatened by James I's return in 1424. For Mar and others in a similar situation, good relations with the crown were essential, unless the noble was powerful enough to ignore the king altogether. The creation of new titles of nobility perhaps strengthened the interdependence of king and magnates, but in turn heightened the stakes should the equilibrium be destroyed either by a king who was too rigorous or by a noble family which had ideas above its station.

This does not mean that all members of the nobility were involved in a scramble for political influence at the royal court, and even fewer were interested in the minutiae of administrative practice, although there are exceptions such as Colin Campbell, first earl of Argyll. Most operated at a much more local level, building up circles of friends and adherents who usually had interests in the same region. Unlike the situation in England, changes of power at the centre rarely affected office-holding in the localities, where sheriffs and other royal agents were often appointed on an hereditary basis, and so magnates could, if they wished, remain aloof from national politics without facing serious loss of influence in their own area. As in England, we see a diminution of the importance of land as the basis of a relationship and more emphasis on a broader range of contractual arrangements, a phenomenon marked in Scotland by the issue of bonds of manrent, whereby men promised allegiance to a particular lord in return for some favour. The background to the bond is often unspecified, but it could involve protection, maintenance, land, payments in money, or forgiveness by the lord for some past misdeed. On some occasions the bond of manrent formalised a long-standing relationship between lord and dependant, perhaps stretching back generations; in other cases it marked the conclusion of a dispute or even a bloodfeud. The bond could have the effect of making the parties as kinsmen to each other, or even of strengthening connections between existing kinsfolk, while persons of equal status could enter into bonds of friendship, such as that between Albany and Douglas in 1409. Most bonds were entered into for life, or even hereditarily, although in the fifteenth century some were for a limited period, and they nearly always specifically reserved obligations of loyalty to the king. These bonds acted as social cement by creating formal relationships which were more flexible and less closely linked to the tenure of land than the 'feudal' arrangements of the twelfth and thirteenth centuries.

Although bonds of manrent were a late medieval phenomenon, their purpose was essentially similar to the tenurial relationships which remained important in the fifteenth and sixteenth centuries. They may have developed partly as a result of the creation of new earldoms which did not bestow on their recipients the territorial dominance which earls had previously enjoyed, but this cannot be the whole explanation because changes in social structure had been much less fundamental than this might imply. It is noteworthy that many of the surviving bonds of manrent from the fifteenth and sixteenth centuries derive from Highland areas, where feudalism had made little headway. Greater dependence on pastoral farming, a virtual absence of nucleated villages, and the greater emphasis on kinship ties meant that Highland society was somewhat different from its Lowland counterpart, and the greater flexibility – and often the inherent vagueness – of bonds of manrent enabled lords to bind to their service and allegiance individuals and kin-groups over whom previously they had enjoyed little formal control. Bonds of manrent were by no means an exclusively Highland phenomenon, but in Lowland Scotland they constituted merely one of a number of ways of determining relationships between a lord and his dependants.

Compared with their English counterparts, the Scottish kings were relatively undemanding of their subjects. In the fifteenth century direct taxation was rarely sought, and James I's difficulties in raising it demonstrate the problems which the Stewart monarchs would have faced if they had made a concerted effort to establish central institutions on the English model. In the field of justice, much reliance was still placed on sheriffs, on justiciars on their ayres, and on local notables who had the right to hold burgh, baronial or (at a more exalted level) regality courts, the last of which gave their holder powers equivalent to those of the justiciar, including full criminal jurisdiction, with appeals in civil cases being made only to parliament. The central Court of Session developed only slowly from James I's reign onwards, initially to relieve the royal council of some of its burden of judicial business. Parliament too was a court of justice, which alone could decree forfeitures for treason, and the judicial function of parliament was more prominent in Scotland than in England, where the king's regular requests for extraordinary taxation to finance expensive wars had given the House of Commons a greatly enhanced sense of corporate purpose. Requests for annual parliaments in Scotland, for instance in 1399 and 1404, show that there was perceived to be a need for centralised royal justice; but kings, doubtless concerned by a lack of resources, were reluctant to encourage petitions and excluded from parliament cases where a remedy could be obtained through ordinary common-law procedure. In James III's reign it is possible to detect an increase in the number of appeals in civil actions from local courts to the royal council, but this placed a very heavy burden on the king's officials. An attempt was made in 1487 to restrict the number of cases, although this was reversed the following January. Ordinary judges possibly resented the increasing involvement of the crown, and this may have influenced their view of James III himself, but the popularity of appeals to the council was in fact a reflection of low standards of justice in the localities rather than of aggression on the part of the crown. However, despite this trend towards centralisation, the Stewart monarchs were content to have most legal business, civil and criminal, executed at a local level.

Local jurisdiction was commonplace in medieval Europe, and was an essential prop for the smooth functioning of society. If the intentions expressed in James I's legislation and the 1496 Education

Act are anything to go by, those who presided over courts were almost always amateurs, often lacking in formal education but surely broadly familiar with legal procedure, whose position in local society made them the most appropriate, if not the only, agents capable of executing a sentence. Royal justice exercised by sheriffs and justiciars was, of course, not absent from the countryside. Ayres were supposed to take place twice a year, although complaints and legislation suggest that the ideal was not always realised. James III was criticised for his personal lack of participation and his propensity to grant pardons, but the very existence of this criticism may demonstrate that his lack of zeal was unusual. Ayres did not penetrate to the extreme north and west of the realm, but evidence for the justiciars' activities elsewhere does not support the conclusion that their work was ineffective. Moreover, their courts were made up of the suitors of the sheriffdom, and it was these local men who were responsible for making judgement. Unlike England, the link between royal justice and the leaders of local communities remained strong.

However, the office of sheriff was often held on an hereditary basis and justiciars were frequently great nobles who were not necessarily interested in legal matters, and it would be surprising if some litigants did not feel that personal animosity or inadequacy on the part of the judge had redounded to their disadvantage. The holder of a barony or regality court was unlikely to administer justice impartially in cases where he had a personal interest, and more generally he could use his jurisdiction, for good or ill, to maintain his authority over his dependants. Even the king himself, fount of justice though he theoretically was, need not scrupulously adhere to the law or eschew partiality. Although parliament was never so subservient to the crown that it acted merely as a rubber stamp, the king was frequently able to persuade it to condemn his foes, including the Albany Stewarts in 1425 and the Black Douglases in 1455. In such circumstances it is unsurprising that some sought to pursue their aims extra-judicially, though such a phenomenon is not peculiar to Scotland or to the Middle Ages and cannot be ascribed solely to perceived miscarriages of justice. Companies of armed adherents owing allegiance under bonds of manrent and the existence of powerful kin-groups might contribute to violence but cannot be held solely responsible for it. Nor can the magnates, individually or collectively. An incident such as that at Monzievaird in 1490, when some Murrays were burned in the church by their Drummond enemies, may appear shocking, as indeed it did to contemporaries, but must be neither seen as symptomatic of endemic bloodshed nor dismissed as totally exceptional, for comparable events can be found in the history of almost any society, especially where the pursuit of criminals was the responsibility of the victim and his kin rather than a duty of the state, and where reparation was made to those who had been wronged, not to the crown. Many disputes, especially over property, were settled by arbitration rather than litigation, a method which promised a speedier resolution and a greater chance of permanence. The feud between the Murrays and Drummonds, which had been intensified by James III's unpredictability and inconsistency, was long-lasting and by no means unique, but the overall level of violence cannot be quantified, nor can the role of magnates in it be calculated; it is fruitless to speculate whether fifteenth-century Scotland was more or less violent than any other state.

Since it is impossible to generalise about the Scottish magnate class as a whole, relations between the crown and the nobility will be analysed by examining the specific issue of the Douglases and the question of how, and to what extent, royal authority was exercised in the north and west during the reigns of the medieval Stewart kings. Such an approach runs the risk of emphasising the unusual at the expense of the normal, but the particular problems and opportunities of the Highlands and border areas can shed considerable light on the nature of royal and magnate power in late medieval Scotland.

The rise of the house of Douglas was dramatic. A family of Flemish origin, related to the Murrays but of relatively little significance in the thirteenth century, its members came to dominate Scottish politics before the ninth earl and his brothers fell victim to James II's aggression in 1455. The seeds of the family's greatness were sown by Sir James Douglas, one of Robert I's most effective military commanders. He organised his raids into northern England from Ettrick and Selkirk Forest, a huge area of upland country which was to prove invaluable in enabling his successors to secure their predominance in southern Scotland. In an age of war with England, the militaristic ambitions of the Douglases were the essential foundation of their ability to bind lesser men to them in loyalty and service.

The family's power in southern Scotland led to the creation of the earldom of Douglas in 1358. The first earl was William, the nephew of James, but David II relied more heavily on James's illegitimate son Archibald the Grim. Aware of the strength of Balliol influence in Galloway, manifested after David's capture at Neville's Cross, the king gave him lands and judicial authority over large parts of south-west Scotland, and in the early 1370s Archibald used his dominant position to obtain for himself the earldom of Wigtown, thereby uniting the whole of Galloway under his control. Galloway proved crucial for the continued rise of Douglas power, for after 1388 Archibald was able to inherit the earldom and most of the family lands on the basis of a tailzie from 1342 which restricted their descent to the male line. He overcame his rival, Malcolm Drummond, because of his military power and lack of scruple. Archibald had thus used a combination of royal support and brute force to construct for himself an almost unassailable position in the south-west.

In the south-east, the Douglases had more potent rivals, particularly the earls of Dunbar or March, and the crown too exercised considerable patronage in Lothian when it was strong enough to win supporters from other lords, for instance towards the end of David II's reign or after James I's return from England. When the crown was weak, however, it was unable to compete with great regional magnates such as the Douglases, especially in time of war, since the Douglases could offer their adherents a level of protection which the king could not match. In the early years of the fifteenth century the fourth earl of Douglas, Archibald, built up his power in the south-east so effectively that the earl of March was confirmed in his English alliance and successive royal lieutenants were forced to acquiesce in Douglas aggression towards England. The earl's capture at Humbleton Hill in 1402 and his subsequent imprisonment impaired but did not break the hold of his family on the region, as is seen in the disastrous campaign which precipitated Prince James's exile, and when he returned the lordship of Dunbar to the restored earl of March in 1409, many of March's former vassals still regarded Douglas as their natural lord. The other leading border magnate, the earl of Angus, was also captured at Humbleton and died in English custody, leaving a minor as his heir. With royal power in eclipse, Archibald could enjoy personal hegemony in Lothian.

The fourth earl of Douglas had a reputation which gave him international standing. His participation on the French side in the Hundred Years War was rewarded by a grant of the duchy of Touraine, an unprecedented honour for a foreigner in late medieval France. Charles VII was prepared to be so generous because Douglas could promise an army capable of checking the English advance, a remarkable testimony to the numbers of men in Scotland upon whose military service he could rely. The crushing of his army at Verneuil in 1424 was a blow both to Charles and to Douglas interests in both France and Scotland, for the title of the late earl's heir to Touraine was not recognised by the French and many leading Douglas supporters had fallen with their master. In fact, Earl Archibald had been strikingly unsuccessful in the military sphere. At all his major engagements – Humbleton Hill, Shrewsbury in 1403, and Verneuil – he had finished on the losing side, yet his political and diplomatic skill had combined with the extent of his lordship in Scotland to make him a figure of European significance.

The death of the fourth earl and the return of James I to Scotland altered the relationship between the Douglases and the crown. James was less willing than Albany to acquiesce in Douglas dominance of the south, and he was able to use his royal prestige to attract to his service some men whose previous connections had been with the Douglases. Among these were the Crichtons, who were to play so prominent a role during the minority of James II. The king's following also included James Douglas of Abercorn and Balvenie, the younger son of Archibald the Grim, who was used as a counterweight to the fifth earl, just as David II had enhanced the standing of Archibald the Grim at the expense of the first earl; and like Archibald, James Douglas was ultimately to succeed to the earldom. James I also interfered in the Douglas lands in the West and Middle Marches, even in the Forest, and confirmed the fourth earl's widow, Margaret, in control of Galloway. For the first time for over half a century, there was competition for local adherents between the king and the earl of Douglas, and more peaceful relations with England weakened the earl's power by making his tenants and neighbours less dependent on him for protection and the king less anxious about antagonising him.

The relative ease with which James II crushed the Douglases in 1455 points to the strength of the crown even in areas which were heartlands of Douglas power. The indecision of the ninth earl may have contributed to his failure, but the fact that the king eventually overcame the crisis occasioned by his murder of Earl William in 1452 suggests that royal authority was now strong enough to deal with a powerful Lowland magnate so long as the latter did not enjoy active support from other nobles, although it remains significant that the king was unable to win support for decisive action against Douglas in 1452 and was forced to acquiesce in a tense, if temporary, stalemate. A much more potent threat to the Stewart kings, however, came from the remote regions of northern and western Scotland, and it was not until well into the sixteenth century that this danger was reduced.

As we have seen, royal authority had advanced slowly but inexorably northwards and westwards for much of the thirteenth century, but this progress was halted by the difficult years which followed Alexander III's death. Robert I, building on his reputation as a victor and endowed with an understanding of the nature of Celtic lordship from his years as earl of Carrick, re-established the crown's authority throughout the kingdom, but the subsequent civil war between David Bruce and Edward Balliol, coupled with David's lengthy absences, gave the chieftains of the Highlands and Hebrides the opportunity to reassert their traditional independence. The history of fifteenth-century Scotland is punctuated by conflicts between the crown and the MacDonald lords of the Isles, with the most obvious remedy to the problem of security being to delegate almost viceregal powers to individual magnates in the north-east and Argyll. The aim was to attempt to control the two ends of the Great Glen and other routes through the Highlands, and thus prevent incursions by Highlanders into the heartland of the Scottish realm, but the wide-ranging powers granted to royal lieutenants could themselves pose a threat to the crown.

In March 1371 Robert II granted to his son Alexander the Highland lordship of Badenoch, clearly with the intention of using him as an agent of royal authority in the north. This explains why

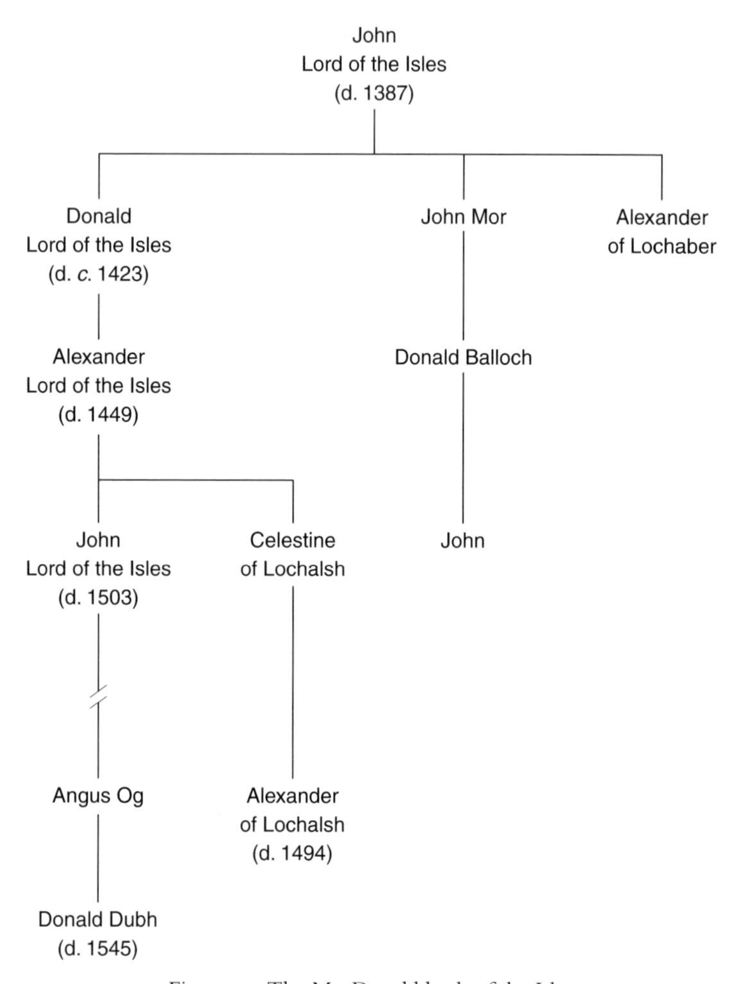

Figure 4 The MacDonald lords of the Isles

Alexander continued to hold Badenoch even when the earldom of Moray was granted to John Dunbar in 1372, but the division of the earldom seriously compromised Dunbar's position, since the security of the lowlands of Moray depended on control of its mountainous hinterland. Alexander Stewart thus had the opportunity to enhance his own position by threatening force, if necessary, against both the earl and the bishop of Moray. Despite the fact that Dunbar was a descendant – albeit through a female line – of Thomas Randolph, for whom the earldom had been revived in 1312,

Alexander must have resented his promotion to a dignity which he probably coveted for himself, especially when it was made as part of a deal to enable his elder brother Robert to obtain possession of the earldom of Fife. His interests were being sacrificed in favour of Robert II's long-standing ambition to ensure Stewart control of Scotland's premier earldom, and the antagonism between the two royal brothers was to be critically important in the late 1380s.

Assessments of the career of Alexander Stewart have been coloured by his attack on Forres and Elgin in 1390 and his unsavoury reputation as the 'Wolf of Badenoch'. He has often been regarded as the archetypal 'over-mighty subject', ready to use violence for his own ends, drawing on the resources of the 'wild, wicked Highland men' of his lordship to wreak terror on the civilised inhabitants of the north-east Lowlands, a cultural distinction which was now being drawn for the first time in Scottish history. His establishment in Badenoch, seemingly free from royal supervision, can be seen as an indictment of Robert II's weak government, and the fact that his actions were used to justify the coups of 1384 and 1388 lends credence to this view.

The reality is more complex. The great magnate families which had earlier exercised power over Badenoch had disappeared. The Comyns had been destroyed by Robert Bruce, the male line of the Randolph earls of Moray had ended with the death of John Randolph at Neville's Cross, and David de Strathbogie, earl of Atholl, who also claimed authority in Badenoch, had been killed at the battle of Culblean in 1335. This, combined with the waning of royal authority, had permitted the expansion eastwards of the MacDonalds, descendants of Somerled, and the development of the political power of semi-independent Gaelic kindreds, whose leaders relied on extensive militarised followings.

From the standpoint of the royal government, therefore, the situation in the north was similar to that of the early thirteenth century, when the Comyns had been used to consolidate the crown's authority in a rebellious area. This was why Alexander Stewart was granted such wide powers by his father. In addition to his lands of Badenoch and Lochaber, he became royal lieutenant in the north and sheriff of Inverness. His marriage in 1382 to Euphemia, widow of the earl of Ross, led to him being granted the earldom of Ross for life, with control over the sheriffdom of Nairn, and he also took the title of earl of Buchan on the strength of some of his wife's lands. In October 1384 a royal charter removed the barony of Abernethy from the earldom of Moray and bestowed it on Alexander, and two years later the earl of Moray granted him the barony of Bona at the northern end of Loch Ness. By this time Alexander was in a very powerful position, controlling the major castles of Ruthven, Lochindorb, Urquhart, Inverness and Dingwall and exercising lordship over a considerable area. He had built up his influence partly by his own efforts, but also by royal favour. The importance of that royal favour became apparent when it came to be withdrawn.

Despite the criticism of Alexander in 1384, and complaints in April 1385 that he was wrongfully detaining his brother David's barony of Urquhart by Loch Ness, which had merely been temporarily leased to him, the lieutenant's position remained largely unaffected by the earl of Carrick's seizure of power; by February 1387 Alexander's authority had even been increased by his appointment as justiciar north of the Forth. His predominance came under threat only when Robert, earl of Fife, replaced his brother as Guardian in 1388. However, his employment of forces of caterans (lightly armed Highland warriors) to uphold his power had involved him in damaging clashes with local prelates and secular lords, especially when the caterans, as was customary, were billeted in areas subject to his authority.

Fife's assault on Alexander's position, discussed above, allowed Alexander of Lochaber, brother of the lord of the Isles, to increase his own authority in the Great Glen. Fife's policy thus had the effect of building up the power of a Hebridean chieftain in a crucial strategic area. More immediately significantly, it had the effect of driving his brother Alexander to violence. As he strove to re-establish his position, he was now forced to rely on his Highland followers, knowing that they would seek alternative lordship if he failed to demonstrate that he could still protect them and offer them prosperity.

It is, therefore, scarcely surprising that Alexander Stewart took advantage of his father's death to assert himself. His principal target was the bishop of Moray, with whom he had a lengthy and largely inconclusive dispute over jurisdiction. He also had more immediate grievances against the bishop, for in 1389 he had been one of the prelates who had ordered Alexander to return to his wife rather than continue to live with the probable mother of his children, Mairead daughter of Eachann. The earl of Buchan was surely also concerned by the indenture made by the bishop and Thomas Dunbar, eldest son of the earl of Moray and now sheriff of Inverness, whereby Thomas promised to defend the men and possessions of the bishopric in return for an annual fee. This indication that he was no longer the recognised source of protection probably encouraged Alexander to demonstrate that he was still a force to be reckoned with. The burning of Elgin cathedral was, therefore, perhaps intended as a manifestation of Alexander Stewart's strength.

If so, then the attack on Forres and Elgin failed dismally. It blackened Buchan's reputation, and strengthened the increasingly prevalent opinion among Lowland communities that the Highlands were a source of disorder and a lair for criminals. The destruction of 1390 certainly shows Alexander's vulnerability, but whether it demonstrates the failure of his lordship is much more questionable. Forced on to the back foot by Fife's attack on his formal jurisdiction, from 1389 he was driven to rely increasingly on Gaelic kindreds and compelled to act in accordance with their rules. This also sheds light on the raid into the lowlands of Angus in 1392, which was led by two of Alexander's bastard sons and which occasioned the death of Walter de Ogilvy, the hereditary sheriff of Angus. This raid can be regarded as an act of naked aggression by an unprincipled cadet line of the royal house, or as an indication that Alexander had lost control of the men of Badenoch, but it could also show that Alexander had become, in effect, a Highland chieftain, whose reputation depended on his success as a warlord. In this context, it is perhaps no surprise that he was unable to deal judicially with the dispute between Clan Kay and Clan Qwhele, which reached its climax in a bloody duel, organised partly for the entertainment of the royal court, on the North Inch of Perth in September 1396.

Much of the landed power which Alexander Stewart had built up in the north in the 1370s and 1380s also slipped from his grasp. The grant of the barony of Bona was cancelled, and Urquhart was in crown hands by 1391. More seriously, Alexander lost control of Ross when in December 1392 his wife Euphemia was granted papal permission to separate from her adulterous husband. The marriage had clearly been one of convenience, although such arrangements were not unusual among the aristocracy of the Middle Ages, nor was it unduly scandalous for the husband to have relationships with other women. Alexander must, therefore, have been either unlucky or more than usually incompetent to allow the benefits of his marriage to Euphemia to slither through his fingers. But his discomfiture, however satisfying it may have seemed to his brother Fife, was not necessarily in the long-term interests of the Scottish crown. The growing power of Alexander of Lochaber in the Great Glen is seen in an agreement in September 1394 whereby Thomas Dunbar tried to persuade him not to attack the earldom of Moray,[1] while the death of Alexander Leslie, earl of Ross, in May 1402 led to the lord of the Isles staking a claim to the earldom by right of his wife Mary, the late earl's sister, at the expense of Alexander Leslie's young daughter. The MacDonald claim to Ross was to play a major part in the history of northern Scotland for much of the fifteenth century.

The year 1402 also saw the deaths of David, duke of Rothesay and earl of Atholl, and of Malcolm Drummond, lord of Mar, while the Scottish defeat at Humbleton Hill led to the imprisonment of Murdoch Stewart, justiciar north of the Forth, and Thomas Dunbar, earl of Moray. The sudden void in effective lordship in the north forced the duke of Albany, de facto ruler of the kingdom, into a grudging reconciliation with the earl of Buchan, and in due course he was forced to accept Buchan's illegitimate son Alexander as earl of Mar.

The unexpected appearance of Alexander Stewart at Kildrummy castle in the summer of 1404, and his marriage to the aged Isabella, countess of Mar and daughter of the first earl of Douglas, came as a shock to Albany. On 12 August Isabella granted Alexander the earldom of Mar, the lordship of Garioch and other possessions, stipulating that, except in the unlikely event of the marriage producing children, the lands and titles would henceforth pass to her husband's heirs. This arrangement bypassed the rival Erskine claim to Mar, which Albany supported, and Isabella's charter did not receive royal confirmation. However, by the end of the year a compromise had been reached, granting Alexander a life interest in Mar and Garioch but specifying that the lands would then pass to his wife's heirs rather than his own.

[1] *Acts of the Lords of the Isles, 1336–1493*, ed. J. Munro and R. W. Munro (Scottish History Society, 1986), 18–19.

Unlike his father, whose northern lieutenancy in the 1370s and 1380s had been viewed by Lowland communities and churchmen as alien and oppressive, fomenting disorder rather than settling it, Mar came to be viewed as a hero, the last effective defence against the inexorable advance of the lord of the Isles. Mar's battle with Donald of the Isles at Harlaw in 1411 was seen not only as a deliverance for the threatened burgh of Aberdeen, but as the triumph of Lowland values over Highland savagery. It mattered little that militarily the battle was indecisive, and that it failed to determine the fate of Ross or the question of who controlled the central Highlands. Mar had proved that he could defend civilisation as Lowlanders knew it. The contrast between him and his father could not have been more starkly drawn.

The contrast is, however, misleading. Mar's strength was based fundamentally on the control that his father had established in the upland areas to the west of the earldom. Alexander's decisive appearance at Kildrummy in 1404 was not unwelcome to the lairds of the north-east. For, unlike the Erskines, who had few interests in the region, Alexander promised attractive lordship, because he could offer protection against Highland caterans through his ability to command them, an ability which stemmed from his father's success in Badenoch. His exploits at Harlaw convinced them still further that Earl Alexander could provide the same sort of security that the Douglases offered their connections on the English border, but the presence in that battle of men from Angus and Mearns as well as from Mar and Garioch shows that he was already the leading magnate in north-east Scotland. Just as Albany had to acquiesce in the domination of Douglas in the south, so he had to accept that the security of the north depended on the continuing influence of Mar, and the financial concessions obtained by Alexander were a mark of the Governor's support.

Royal interests in the north-east were compromised by James I's single-minded assault on the Albany Stewarts after his return to Scotland in 1424. It is unlikely that, after eighteen years in England, James understood the complexities of Highland politics or appreciated the value of the earl of Mar. The king's understandable desire to end annuities from the customs was a severe threat to Mar's capacity to uphold his lordship, and the king initially also supported the claims to Ross of Alexander, lord of the Isles, whom he saw as an ally in his attack on Duke Murdoch and his connections. Mar could have found himself in a position similar to that experienced by his father after Fife's coup in 1388, but extricated himself by moving away from the Albany Stewarts and sitting on the assize which condemned them; it is possible that he received some limited concessions from the king as a price for his support, although simple self-interest and a shrewd appreciation of the way the wind was blowing must have discouraged him from continuing in a doomed alliance with Murdoch and his sons. Once the Albany Stewarts had been destroyed, there was less justification for the alliance between the king and Alexander of the Isles, and so, despite his continuing distrust of him, James I began to consolidate Mar's position again, and the earl played a major part in the king's activities against the MacDonalds right up until his death in 1435.

James I's policy towards the Highlands was broadly in line with his general aims of reasserting royal power and ensuring that the magnates appreciated the fact that they were subordinate to the crown. We have seen how this approach led to nervousness and suspicion on the part of great nobles and how the king's concept of his royal office may have contributed towards his murder. Lowland magnates were unlikely to object to punitive measures being taken against Highland chiefs, but we must still ask whether James I's aggressive approach was in the best interests of long-term security, and whether he really appreciated that different social structures and patterns of lordship were to be found in the north and west of his realm. It has been claimed that James identified himself with the Lowlands to a greater extent than any previous Scottish king.[2] Is this true, and if so what consequences did it have?

In 1428 James arrested Alexander, lord of the Isles, and a number of other Highland chiefs whom he had summoned to Inverness. A few of the latter were subsequently executed, although the king realised that he could not kill or forfeit the more powerful leaders without fomenting serious and widespread disturbances. Throughout this period, however, James displayed a lack of principle which augured ill for the acceptance of his rule in the Highlands. The chiefs arrested in 1428 appear to have believed that they had been summoned to a form of parliament, and doubtless

[2] Nicholson, *Scotland*, 314.

did not expect to be seized. The king also tried to gain control of Ross for himself by means of a highly dubious claim, and he probably attempted to replace Alexander as lord of the Isles by his uncle John Mor. After John was killed in circumstances which added to Highland suspicion of the king's good faith, he then released Alexander and tried to induce him to work as his agent, but succeeded only in driving him to rebellion at the instigation of John's son Donald Balloch.[3] The revolt of 1429 would potentially have been serious if the Hebrideans had obtained help from England and if Murdoch Stewart's son James had not died around this time. As it was, Inverness was burned, but Alexander subsequently capitulated after a heavy defeat by royal forces in Lochaber.

Despite the king's victory, nothing of substance had been achieved. James was forced, just as Albany had been, to turn to the earl of Mar and appoint him as royal lieutenant in the north. The Highlands had not been pacified. In 1431 Donald Balloch again rose in rebellion, and two royal expeditions were defeated, an army under Mar at Inverlochy and another force in Strathnaver.[4] The king now demanded taxation to deal with the Highland threat, but the estates did not trust James and made elaborate precautions for the security of the proceeds, probably feeling that further northern campaigns were less vital than the defence of the English border. The king was, therefore, compelled again to come to terms with Alexander of the Isles and release him from custody. On the death of Mar without an heir in 1435 the earldom was taken into the king's hands. James saw it merely as a source of revenue, not as the focus for the defence of the Lowlands against the MacDonald threat. He accepted Alexander's position in Ross and allowed him control of Inverness.

James I's belligerence towards the Highlands had proved counterproductive. Despite the fear of incursions by caterans and the increasing cultural divide between Lowlanders and Highlanders, parliament had demonstrated a marked lack of enthusiasm when asked to provide funding in the wake of the disastrous expeditions

[3] This interpretation is based on the reconstruction in M. Brown, *James I* (Edinburgh, 1994), 97–101; however, John Mor is traditionally thought to have been dead by 1427.

[4] Bower sees the battle in Strathnaver as one between caterans, but it was probably part of a wider campaign against the king's opponents: *Chron. Bower*, viii, 265–7; Brown, *James I*, 137, 138.

of 1431. Such expeditions, in any case, were of limited long-term significance, even if they were militarily successful at the time as in 1429. There were two fundamental problems faced by the crown in any attempts to increase royal authority in the north and west. Firstly, defeat in battle did not destroy the strong kin-based relationships of Highland society, and life returned to normal when the royal forces withdrew. Secondly, the king had to find a leader with whom he could deal and who could be prevailed upon to accept royal authority. Even if he captured that leader and forced terms on him, there was no guarantee that those terms would be upheld after he was released, nor that the arrest of their chief would subdue the Highlanders. Alexander of the Isles rebelled in 1429 despite the king's attempt to assert his power the previous year, his cousin Donald Balloch was active in 1431, and Alexander ended the reign in a more powerful position than he had been at the outset. He had probably been recognised as earl of Ross by January 1437, and during the minority of James II he was appointed justiciar north of the Forth, a clear reflection of his pre-eminence, since it was unlikely that he would prove an unquestioning agent of the crown. The only workable policy was one of containment, and in the context of James I's reign this meant supporting the earl of Mar, but the king had temporarily weakened Mar's position in order to engineer the fall of the Albany Stewarts, and he provided no replacement when Mar died. This suggests that James had a limited grasp of both the Highland problem and the potential solutions, although we might recall that Robert earl of Fife, whose experience of Scottish politics was extensive, had similarly failed to appreciate his brother Alexander's value as a bulwark against the ambitions of Alexander of Lochaber in the late 1380s.

There were few fundamental changes in the half-century following James I's murder. The period saw the rise of the Gordon earls of Huntly in the north-east and of the Campbell earls of Argyll at the southern end of the Great Glen, but the policy remained largely one of containment interspersed with inconclusive military activity. The affairs of the north and west were not always uppermost in the minds of the Scottish government, nor the priority for parliament unless Highland raids threatened the interests of Lowland magnates and lairds. Even when John, lord of the Isles, made his bond with Crawford and Douglas, James II could do little. He murdered Douglas, but could only acquiesce in John's gains during the rebellion of 1451 and his appropriation of royal rents in the Inverness area in the wake of the Douglases' forfeiture. James had more pressing concerns in southern Scotland and no guarantee of parliamentary support for a risky Highland expedition. In February 1462 John, along with Donald Balloch and the latter's son and heir John, entered into an agreement with Edward IV of England, the so-called treaty of Westminster–Ardtornish, whereby the lord of the Isles and his kinsmen agreed to take over Scotland and divide it between themselves and the exiled earl of Douglas under Edward's suzerainty.[5] These plans came to nothing, and too much emphasis should not be accorded to a fundamentally impracticable scheme, but the very fact that the indenture was made demonstrates the independence of action that John could enjoy. As so often, the Scottish government was powerless to resist.

In December 1475 parliament declared the forfeiture of John MacDonald, probably because the treaty of Westminster–Ardtornish had come to light after James III made peace with Edward IV in 1474, and an expedition was launched against him. He submitted the following year and lost the earldom of Ross and lands in Knapdale and Kintyre, although he was created a lord of parliament as Lord of the Isles. However, this attempt to integrate the great Hebridean chieftain into the mainstream of Scottish political society failed, just as earlier similar attempts had. John's submission did not mean that his far-flung western lordship was brought within the sphere of royal authority, even though he was much more prepared to act as an agent for the king than Alexander had been in the 1430s. By giving the impression that he was identifying himself more closely with the interests of the crown, John weakened his own authority and could not control members of his own family such as his illegitimate son Angus Og and his nephew Alexander of Lochalsh. It was almost impossible for him to be a royal agent and a local leader at the same time.

The forfeiture of the lordship of the Isles in 1493 has often been seen as a notable feature of the successful reign of James IV, marking an appropriate end to medieval anarchy at the dawn of a new age. The reality was less clear-cut, for the destruction of the lordship did

[5] *Acts of the Lords of the Isles*, 111–15.

not reflect a total eclipse of MacDonald power, and it made it even more difficult for the king to find an agent in the west who was both reliable and widely respected. There were several serious rebellions in the fifty years following the forfeiture, all aiming to restore the illegitimate descendants of John MacDonald and well supported by west-coast chieftains. Neither James IV's expeditions to the Isles, successful in the short run though they were, nor James V's royal progress through the Hebrides and subsequent formal annexation of the lordship succeeded in bringing the western seaboard fully within the political and administrative structures of the Scottish kingdom.

Just as Robert II had aimed to control the north through his son Alexander, and the dukes of Albany and James I had relied on the earl of Mar, so royal policy towards the west in James IV's reign was based on enhancing the position of loyal servants. The situation in 1493 provided a good opportunity to forfeit the lord of the Isles, because of internal divisions within the MacDonald kin and because the lord's grandson and heir, Donald Dubh, was in the custody of the Campbells. Even if this decision was not made at their prompting, it was the Campbells who remained the principal agents of royal authority on the western seaboard, while in 1501 Alexander, earl of Huntly, was given sweeping powers in the north, although the crown relied also on others willing to do its bidding, such as John MacIan of Ardnamurchan, who killed Alexander of Lochalsh in 1494 and may have been responsible for the notably thorough destruction of the lord of the Isles' chief castle and hall at Finlaggan on Islay.[6] An act of October 1496 decreeing that clan chiefs were to be personally responsible for the execution of any royal summons against their dependents was clearly an attempt to undermine their authority in the interests of increased crown control, although it would be effective only in proportion to the degree of royal influence in the Isles, which in practice was wielded by the earls of Argyll. The Campbells doubtless saw the new enactment as an opportunity to build up their power at the expense of other kindreds, but it did nothing to pacify the region. James's Act of Revocation in 1498 further fuelled the fires of discontent, because loyal chieftains found that recent grants of lands and offices to them by the king were

[6] D. H. Caldwell and G. Ewart, 'Finlaggan and the lordship of the Isles: an archaeological approach', *SHR*, 72 (1993), 164–6.

insecure and would have to be renewed at considerable expense. Huntly's aggrandisement provoked widespread resistance and alarmed the Campbells, while the mysterious escape of Donald Dubh in 1501 led to several disturbed years in the west, the threat posed by Donald being intensified after the death of his grandfather John in January 1503. The rebels did not imperil James IV's throne, but they nonetheless demonstrated how tenuous the crown's control was over the former lordship of the Isles; even the earl of Argyll, alienated by Huntly's increased influence, may have contemplated support for Donald Dubh. The recapture of Donald in 1506 did little to relieve the underlying tensions in the west.

It is, therefore, hard to sustain the argument that the crown had greater influence in northern and western Scotland in the early sixteenth century than it had enjoyed in the thirteenth. Military expeditions had little permanent impact. Royal pressure on individual leaders was a blunt instrument because any chieftain who appeared too subservient to the king would lose the local authority that he required if he was to act as an effective agent of the crown. Containment was possible if trusted lieutenants could control both ends of the Great Glen and other routes through the central Highlands, but this meant bestowing wide jurisdictional and territorial powers on individual magnates and allowing them considerable latitude in entering into arrangements with their neighbours. Direct royal involvement in the north-west Highlands and the northern Hebrides was rarely attempted and the crown's influence there was ephemeral at best; when in December 1505 the rebel Torquil MacLeod of Lewis was summoned to appear to answer charges of treason, the proclamation was made at Inverness, over a hundred miles from Torquil's castle at Stornoway. The MacDonald lords of the Isles have a much stronger claim even than the Douglases to be late medieval Scotland's 'over-mighty subjects'.

MacDonald power can be explained partly by geographical factors and partly by the accidents of succession. The MacDonalds and their numerous kinsfolk and followers were the king's subjects, and they inhabited lands which were indubitably part of the Scottish realm, but the lordship of the Isles was physically set apart from the heartland of the kingdom by the great barrier of the Highland massif, and the culture and social customs of the western seaboard were difficult to integrate into a Scotland which was increasingly dominated by Lowland values and spoke a language derived from English rather than Gaelic. This physical and cultural isolation encouraged the concept of a great, semi-independent maritime lordship, harking back (consciously or otherwise) to the old kingdom of the Isles and with lords who were still inaugurated on a hallowed stone in the traditional manner of Celtic rulers. It was from the great Somerled that the MacDonalds claimed descent. They were able to dominate the entire west coast because of the eclipse of their MacDougall cousins during the Wars of Independence and because they inherited the lands of Clan Ruairi by marriage when the male line failed in the fourteenth century, while the claim to Ross articulated by Donald of the Isles enabled the family to unite under a single lord those parts of the realm that the kings of Scots had always found most difficult to control. In the middle of the fifteenth century Alexander of the Isles and his son John arguably regarded Ross as the most important part of their dominions, a shift of emphasis eastwards which served to reinforce the MacDonalds' role as major magnates in mainland Scotland as well as in the Hebrides. It is no wonder that the lords of the Isles felt strong enough, and remote enough, to negotiate with foreign rulers such as the kings of England and to issue charters which did not even pay lip-service to the superior authority of the king of Scots.

The contrast between the MacDonalds and the Douglases must not be too firmly drawn, because both families rose to prominence by a combination of dynastic success, brute force and possession of the means to reward and protect followers. The Douglases controlled Selkirk and Ettrick Forest for generations without appreciable crown interference, just as the MacDonalds were largely autonomous in the west. The royal government accepted the territorial acquisitions of both families, bestowed offices on them, and helplessly acknowledged their role on the wider political and diplomatic stage. But the scale of the MacDonalds' activities sets them apart even from the Douglases: they captured castles, such as Ruthven and Urquhart in 1451; they led a sizeable army almost to Aberdeen in 1411 and fought a major battle at Harlaw which ended as a draw; and they defeated royal forces at Inverlochy in 1431 and at 'Lagebraad' in Ross around

1480. The lords of the Isles were by no means unique in using force to achieve their ends, but their capacity to defy the crown was unparalleled.

Neither the Douglases nor the MacDonalds were typical even of the higher nobility of later medieval Scotland. The history of both families, however, illustrates how the crown needed great magnates to protect the realm against both external and internal threats, and how those magnates could themselves undermine royal authority. The foundation of Douglas power, as we have seen, rested on a requirement for defence against the English. The crown built up the territorial and jurisdictional authority of the family to meet a long-term need for firm rule on the border, and in doing so successive kings and Governors were forced to accede to Douglas ambitions, both within Scotland and in the context of cross-border raiding. The reduction in the English threat under the inept rule of Henry VI enabled assertive kings such as James I and James II to weaken Douglas lordship by detaching some local lairds from their previous allegiance, a policy which was feasible only because the crown could offer richer rewards than the Douglases and because the lairds were no longer so heavily dependent on the Douglases' ability to protect them. The same period saw the intensification of the threat from the lord of the Isles, who proved much more intractable than the Douglases because his power base was more remote and less dependent on royal favour. Attempts to control the Highlands and Hebrides through the lord of the Isles proved abortive, because the MacDonalds acceded to royal demands only when it suited their interests; even the appointment of Alexander as justiciar in the north was little more than a recognition that he was the major figure in the region. In order to combat the lord of the Isles, the crown bestowed wide powers on individual magnates: Alexander Stewart and his son; the Campbells; the earls of Huntly. They performed the same function with regard to the lords of the Isles as the Douglases did towards the English, a parallel which demonstrates both the virtual independence of the MacDonalds and the threat they posed to the king of Scots' authority within his realm.

This use of great magnates to defend the realm and exercise a vestige of royal authority in distant provinces was not a sign of weakness on the part of the crown, merely a recognition that medieval Scotland could be ruled in no other way. The policy was not peculiar to the Stewart monarchs. We need only look at the wide-ranging Comyn influence in the north in the thirteenth century to appreciate the essential point that royal government in Scotland was heavily devolved to the localities. The danger was that magnates would abuse their position to threaten the interests of the crown, and so kings had to be assertive while at the same time not alienating those on whom their authority ultimately rested. It was a difficult balancing act, especially when late medieval Scotland saw so many royal minorities, but it was one with which David I would have been broadly familiar.

As discussed above, aristocratic power in the fifteenth century was essentially based on establishing and extending a retinue of followers, though not necessarily by grants of land such as had marked the 'feudal' period. Such followers might be attracted to a particular lord because he could offer them protection, or because his wealth and influence gave them the prospect of office, lands or other material gain. Any diminution in the territories or jurisdictional power of a particular magnate would, therefore, make him less attractive as a lord, and if the magnate owed his position partly to royal favour, any reduction in that favour would prove detrimental to his local influence. Kings could use their patronage to support their friends and harm those who were lukewarm in their allegiance, but the exercise of that patronage had to be skilfully managed if the king were not to be surrounded by disgruntled magnates. James III did not have that skill, which explains why he faced so many political crises.

In England, the Wars of the Roses came about largely because Henry VI was unable to use his patronage to control his nobles. Fifteenth-century Scotland experienced no similar breakdown of royal authority, nor the dynastic upheavals that followed. This was partly because Scotland had already been through a comparable catharsis during the Wars of Independence, and, notwithstanding their popular reputation, medieval nobles were usually disinclined to indulge in violent feuds, rebellions or civil war. Such events were destructive of property, and might well lead to forfeiture, exile or even death. Self-interest therefore predisposed magnates towards peaceful settlements of their disputes.

So how much political violence was there in late medieval Scotland? Few magnates succumbed to the executioner's axe, but several perished prematurely as a result of political upheavals. The first duke of Rothesay, the sixth and eighth earls of Douglas, and James III's brother John, earl of Mar, all fall into this category, and significantly all four died through the initiative of the king or his representative. Albany's rough treatment of the Drummonds, his elimination of Rothesay, and the threat to Prince James which drove him into exile demonstrate the lack of scruple which so frequently characterised Scottish politics at this period. And even if Albany is dismissed as a special case, even kings could be arbitrary. James I executed Highland chiefs, imprisoned Douglas, and overturned Albany's judgement in favour of the earl of March. James II's conduct towards the Douglases can hardly be described as gentle, or indeed legal. James V pursued Lady Glamis and Hamilton of Finnart. These instances of violence do not amount to the blood-soaked centuries of traditional Scottish historiography, but they do show that kings as well as magnates were sometimes prepared to achieve their ends by violence.

The survival of the direct line of the Stewart monarchs has been seen as a mark of the stability of late medieval Scottish politics, particularly when contrasted with England. This is partly a reflection of an inherent loyalty to a legitimate king, which is seen, for instance, in the way the dynasty survived so many minorities, in the vengeance meted out to the murderers of James I, by the fact that James II faced no long-term consequences from breaking a safe-conduct, and by the albeit reluctant consensus which marked the early years of James IV's reign. As so often, James III's reign provides something of a contrast, but even he managed to survive until Sauchieburn, and would still have enjoyed significant support after the battle had he not been killed. The durability of the dynasty rested also, however, on the lack of a realistic alternative. In 1452 the Douglases could offer no rival candidate to James II, while in 1482 Alexander, duke of Albany, required English help in his bid to topple his brother James III. James IV succeeded in 1488 as the late king's eldest son. The royal line started with an enormous inherent advantage, and its removal would require a broad political consensus. It was, after all, a long time before anyone was prepared to relieve even Henry VI of his crown.

Any serious threat to the ruling king would most probably come from a close relative, and indeed the thesis of crown–magnate harmony depends in part on excluding many political crises on the grounds that they were events in a Stewart family feud. This distinction is unhelpful; indeed, the Wars of the Roses could be interpreted similarly. The fecundity of Robert II led to the Stewartisation of the higher nobility in the later fourteenth century, and the years up to 1437 were marked by often violent events which owed their origin to this phenomenon: the coups of 1384 and 1388; the attack on Elgin by the Wolf of Badenoch; the death of Rothesay; the exile of James; the elimination of the Albany Stewarts; James I's murder; the execution of Atholl. These incidents were all caused by strife within the ruling family, but the fact that the chief protagonists were closely related surely does not minimise the political importance of blood-letting on such a scale that by 1437 very few earls remained and in the 1450s the Douglases could find no alternative to James II. Many of James III's problems can also be seen as internecine: he had Mar killed; Albany tried to oust the king; James's eldest son opposed him at Sauchieburn. James III's inadequacies as a ruler meant that he had other enemies too, but his father had to fight the Douglases and the earl of Crawford, his grandfather forfeited the earl of March, and all three faced the power of the MacDonalds.

In the end, however, co-operation between crown and magnates was beneficial to all concerned. The civil strife of the period of the Wars of Independence, though exacerbated by external pressures, had clearly illustrated the dangers inherent in a breakdown of relations, just as a similar period of political instability between 1542 and the 1590s was followed by a reaction against internal conflict and a desire to tackle the problem of feuding. The threat of instability was most serious when the nobility was reduced in size, as in James II's reign, and the creation of new earldoms and lordships of parliament helped redress the balance. But powerful nobles could still wield considerable power in their own areas, as the Campbells and Gordons were to demonstrate as clearly as the Black Douglases had earlier done, and the fall of a great lord could create fresh turbulence in particular localities, as is seen in Perthshire after Atholl's execution in 1437 and in Galloway after 1455, while the crown's intervention in areas hitherto outside its sphere of direct influence could also cause tension, as when James I intervened in Ettrick, James IV tried to pacify the Isles, and James V moved against the border reivers. It is unrealistic to envisage the political community of late medieval Scotland invariably resolving its internal differences by reasoned debate and compromise, but equally it would be wrong to return to the now discredited view of interminable feuds and bloodshed throughout the realm. As so often, the reality lies somewhere between the two extremes.

8

THE ROAD TO REFORMATION

The dramatic events of the Protestant Reformation have tended to cast a long shadow over the preceding centuries, and as a result the failings of the late medieval church have often been emphasised at the expense of its virtues. This is perhaps especially true of Scotland, both because of the virulence of many early Protestant commentators such as John Knox, and as a result of the paucity of evidence about religious practice in pre-Reformation Scotland which might be set against the much more abundant material relating to the institutional aspects of the church. It is a straightforward matter to discover examples of scandalous promotions and avaricious clerics holding several benefices, note the decline in the ideals of monasticism, and dismiss as half-hearted the attempts at reform by the hierarchy in the 1550s. This approach, needless to say, presents only part of the picture, and implies that the Scottish church was so debased by the middle of the sixteenth century that it required drastic, not piecemeal, reform. Such reform was hampered, it might be argued, by Scotland's adherence to the corrupt and venal Renaissance papacy.

This chapter examines the late medieval church in Scotland from a number of standpoints, investigating the impact of the papacy on ecclesiastical patronage, relations between the popes and Scottish kings at a diplomatic level, the undoubted abuses of pluralism and non-residence and the breakdown of monastic life, the evidence for continued vibrancy, particularly in the context of popular religious practice and a growing interest in native Scottish saints, and the incidence of heresy in Scotland. Developments are viewed in their historical context rather than simply from the standpoint of the Reformation, for it was not inevitable that Scotland would break with Rome, let alone adopt a more extreme doctrinal position than England.

Relations between Scotland and the papacy continued to be very important. However, instead of the legal business conducted by judges-delegate which constituted the most significant point of contact in the thirteenth century, the main areas of papal involvement in the two centuries before the Reformation were the granting of dispensations and the increasing number of papal appointments or provisions. Many dispensations were issued to meet the spiritual requirements of pious individuals of both sexes and all classes, for example permitting named individuals to choose a confessor and receive from him plenary remission of sins at the point of death. Papal sanction was also required if marriage partners were too closely related to be joined in legitimate wedlock under the complex rules of canon law, and dispensations to marry were frequently sought in the upper echelons of society, partly so that any children of the relationship would not face the moral stain or material disadvantages of illegitimacy. Some dispensations, for instance those allowing clerks to hold several benefices or monks to serve parish churches, were open to abuse, but most were relatively uncontroversial, and the papacy's role as a 'well of grace' was largely undisputed. Provisions were much more contentious.

The practice of papal provision must be understood within the broader context of ecclesiastical patronage. With the exception of bishoprics, monasteries and a few other benefices such as deaneries of cathedrals, which were filled by election, a particular individual or corporation had the legal entitlement to nominate a candidate to a vacant benefice. The bishop would, unless the clerk in question was obviously unsuitable, then write a letter of institution to the nominee, formally appointing him to the living, and order the archdeacon or dean of Christianity to induct the new incumbent, usually in a symbolic ceremony whereby he was formally given corporal possession of the church. Many churches were originally in lay patronage, especially when the local lord had taken the initiative in their foundation, although often the right to present had subsequently been granted to a monastery or other ecclesiastical body. It was an important asset, because it enabled the patron to support his family or friends and reward his clerical servants; and kings, secular lords, bishops, abbeys and academic colleges all used the benefices in their patronage for this purpose. It was much cheaper than granting younger sons land of their own or offering salaries to officials, and the routine administration of the realm and its great lordships could not have operated had the right of patronage to ecclesiastical benefices not existed.

The crown was in a particularly strong position in this regard, because rights of presentation, like other secular property, could fall into the king's hands through forfeiture or wardship. The extinction of the lordship of the Isles in 1493, for example, brought the crown much patronage in the Hebrides and Argyll. In addition, royal privileges could be exercised during the vacancies of bishoprics. In England this regalian right included control over the patronage exercised by the bishop, which meant that any benefice normally under episcopal collation which fell vacant within the period in question could be filled by the king, who stoutly defended his rights in the royal courts and occasionally through legislation. Although the evidence is much less full, a similar situation probably prevailed in Scotland, and in January 1450 the prelates formally conceded royal rights to the temporalities of vacant sees in return for James II's permission for bishops to dispose of their movable property by will, a long-standing ambition of the Scottish hierarchy. It is possible that the crown subsequently sought to extend its rights of presentation during vacancies and obtained permission from Scottish church councils to do so, but the nature and outcome of the inevitable conflicts with rival claimants have never been adequately assessed. What is clear is that the Scottish kings, like their English counterparts, were determined to press to the limit any opportunities to exercise patronage over benefices.

Papal provision was based on the principle that the pope had the right to fill all benefices, and it therefore threatened the patronage of both laymen and local ecclesiastics. While this principle was never pressed to extremes, provisions were numerous in late medieval Scotland, especially in the fifteenth and sixteenth centuries, and created both opportunities and problems for patrons and hopeful clerics alike. It must be noted that nearly all provisions were granted as the result of a petition to the pope by the candidate himself or someone acting on his behalf, and the great registers of these supplications constitute a priceless source for late medieval Scottish history. After the thirteenth century only a very small proportion of recorded provisions were attempts by the pope to promote a favourite, and only a minority of papal grants offered preferment to clerks who were not native to the area where they sought the benefice. One of the most notable features of the fifteenth and sixteenth centuries is the skill with which the king and his leading lords were able to exploit a system which at first sight might seem inimical to their interests.

There were two basic types of papal provision. Some clerks were granted a particular benefice which had fallen vacant in a manner specified as making it liable for provision, for instance because the previous incumbent had died at the papal curia, had been a papal official, or had been promoted from the now vacant benefice by papal authority. In practice, many supplications for provision were made on the basis that the benefice was *legally* vacant (in the eyes of the supplicant) and had long been so, but where to all intents and purposes there was a current incumbent. A direct provision gave a clerk only a claim to seek the benefice by due process of law, not an absolute right to it, and disputes between rival candidates were numerous. The second type of provision was the expectative grace, which promised a benefice which was not yet vacant but would in due course be so. Some such graces were wide-ranging, but most reserved a prebend in a specified cathedral or a benefice in the gift of a named ecclesiastical patron. Long queues of hopeful clerks often formed, with consequent squabbles over precedence, and the position was further complicated by the practice of the papal chancery of backdating some graces to give their recipients advantage over those who were already waiting. Especially in the early years of provision, when direct grants to benefices already vacant were relatively rare, expectative graces posed the greater threat to local patronage, because it could be many years before patrons could clear the backlog of papal provisors and start presenting their own candidates again. This was why bishops and monasteries sometimes petitioned the pope for provisions to be made to their own clerks, or for permission briefly to set aside the queue of men with expectative graces and present their own nominees. Provisions, however, were much more likely to affect benefices in the gift of ecclesiastics than of laymen, and this encouraged lay lords to petition the pope for favour to be shown to their relatives and connections, thereby using the system of provision as a valuable adjunct to their own patronage.

It is helpful to make a distinction between provisions to bishoprics and monasteries on the one hand and those to lesser benefices such as cathedral prebends and parish churches on the other. In strict legal terms the distinction is not especially meaningful, but the greater political and financial importance of bishoprics and abbeys meant that appointments to them were much more likely to involve the king and his magnates than were promotions to humble parochial benefices. Provision was, moreover, the normal means of appointment of Scottish bishops from the middle of the fourteenth century onwards; Michael de Malconhalgh, who was elected to Whithorn in 1355, was probably the last prelate to enjoy possession of his see without papal title until after the Reformation. Provisions to Scottish religious houses, which were rare in the fourteenth century, were much commoner in the fifteenth and sixteenth, so that all the major abbeys came to be filled by provision rather than capitular election. This raises the question of where the initiative for these provisions came from.

It is often assumed that appointments to bishoprics were effectively in the hands of the crown, and those to monasteries under the control of the king or his leading subjects. In other words, the pope was asked to provide a particular individual and was happy to oblige. This system was formalised in 1487, when Innocent VIII granted an indult allowing James III eight months' grace during which the king could suggest a candidate for vacant abbeys and bishoprics, and in 1535 Paul III extended the period to a year. It can be argued that royal control over the higher offices of the church had been secured even before 1487, and that subsequent instances where the pope took the initiative, as after the death of the excommunicate James IV at Flodden or when he could exploit rivalries within Scotland during royal minorities, were exceptions rather than the rule.

For the late fifteenth and sixteenth centuries this may be broadly true, although the years immediately before the indult had been marked by a dispute over the see of Dunkeld and by much confusion over the status of Coldingham priory. It explains how many monasteries passed into the nominal control of young members of the royal house or had a series of abbots from the same noble family. In view of the extensive lands held by bishops and their value as counsellors, administrators and diplomats, the king had every reason to want to promote those who were likely to be loyal servants, while the great wealth of the major abbeys was too tempting to be overlooked by either the crown or the Scottish nobility. If the prelate was below the age at which he could lawfully hold land, his temporal estates could be exploited by the crown or those to whom the right of administration had been granted, while monastic superiors were naturally disposed to favour their own kinsfolk, for instance by feuing land to them or making a member of their family bailie of the abbey's estates. For these reasons, lay lords had every incentive to use papal provision to exploit the wealth of the Scottish church, and in many respects it was easier to prevail on the pope than to intimidate the chapter to elect a suitable candidate. While it must be remembered that Innocent VIII did not undertake in 1487 that he would necessarily approve the king's nominee, and may even have envisaged that the indult would terminate on James III's death, the royal candidate started with a considerable advantage over potential rivals. Not only had the pope promised to consider him, but he could expect support from the crown within Scotland.

However, before the Great Schism irreparably damaged the prestige of the medieval papacy, popes were much more inimical to secular control over the church. The reform movement of the late eleventh and twelfth centuries had sought to curb lay patronage, and this remained a papal priority. This does not mean that popes deliberately antagonised secular rulers by refusing to sanction their requests, and the royal candidate would usually receive provision so long as a petition on his behalf reached the Apostolic See before a rival lodged a claim of his own. In the fourteenth century, however, most Scottish bishops were initially elected by the cathedral chapter and then provided by the pope, who normally quashed the election on the grounds that it was technically illegal because nearly all episcopal sees had been formally reserved to papal collation. Powerful laymen may have exerted pressure on the chapters in some cases, but there is little evidence for it. Some bishops, moreover, owed their promotion to their service to the papacy, examples being Alexander de Kininmund in Aberdeen in 1329 and Thomas de Wedale in Whithorn in 1359. Others were successful because they approached the pope before the local election had been reported to the curia. John de Stramiglot, for instance, obtained the abbey of Dunfermline in 1351 because, as a student at Paris, he was able to demonstrate to Clement VI that it was liable for provision before the convent's candidate, John Black, had had the opportunity to petition for confirmation. These men were not necessarily unacceptable to the crown, but the king was not behind their appointment. Although royal influence undoubtedly increased as the Middle Ages wore on, we must still be cautious before we assume that the crown was directly concerned in promotions to all bishoprics, let alone monasteries; even in the wake of the indult of 1487, opportunities surely remained for magnates, royal counsellors, chapters and even the hopeful individuals themselves to suggest possible names for the king to notify to the pope, and this helps to explain the lengthy and complex disputes which were fought over many monasteries in the sixteenth century.

The papacy had a financial incentive to become involved in appointments to bishoprics and major monasteries, for it levied a series of taxes on the provisor, collectively known as service taxes. Prelates entered into a solemn obligation to pay, usually by instalments at specified dates, although in practice adjournments were frequently granted. Popes sometimes allowed bishops to borrow money, despite the church's objection to the charging of interest on loans, but these licences disappear from the records after the middle of the fourteenth century. During the Great Schism some Scottish bishops, most notably Henry Wardlaw of St Andrews, paid service taxes in tiny instalments,[1] while others such as Gilbert de Grenlaw of Aberdeen managed to pay in full almost immediately.[2] It was doubtless the difficulty of inducing prelates to pay which prompted the papal chamber or Camera to demand that prelates fulfil their obligations for service taxes before their bulls were issued, although this involved them in a considerable financial

[1] Vatican Archives, Registra Avinionensia 319, fol. 70, 70v; 324, fols. 176, 233v; 327, fol. 45; 331, fol. 72v.

[2] H. Hoberg, *Taxae pro Communibus Servitiis* (Vatican City, 1949), 3; Vatican Archives, Introitus et Exitus 366, fol. 17v.

undertaking which normally involved the engagement of Italian banking houses and could leave sees and monasteries legally vacant for lengthy periods.

Leading laymen could also be involved in provisions to less important benefices, especially where the prospective incumbent had close connections with the royal court or was in the service of a great lord, but most bulls were obtained by the hopeful clerks themselves. Although many graces were unopposed, achieving corporal possession of the benefice was often difficult, and much litigation at the papal curia ensued. Problems could arise for several reasons. In the middle of the thirteenth century, when the system was novel in Scotland and operated largely to the benefit of papal servants and other foreigners, some provisions failed in the face of a combination of prejudice, antipathy to the notion that the pope could interfere with local patronage, and fear of setting an evil precedent. When native clerks began to exploit the system the commonest reason for a dispute was that there was more than one candidate for the same benefice. This could come about in a number of ways. Sometimes the provisor encountered a rival who had been presented by the normal patron, although such direct clashes between papal and local jurisdiction were much less frequent than the post-Reformation notion of interfering popes might suggest. It was probably more common for there to be more than one provisor seeking the same benefice, or for individuals with expectative graces to compete among themselves or against men with direct provisions on the grounds of a specific vacancy. What is striking is that, at least in the fourteenth and early fifteenth centuries, relatively few benefices were available for provision at any one time, which tended to lead to disputes over those which were, such as Cavers in Roxburghshire.[3] The rules which governed liability for provision were strictly adhered to, and although the categories were later extended, those who supplicated for papal favour had to select their target in accordance with the criteria which the papacy had laid down. Not all the petitioners' statements were accurate, and possession often proved to be nine-tenths of the law, although we must assume that few laid claim to a benefice which they had little realistic chance of obtaining.

[3] A. D. M. Barrell, *The Papacy, Scotland and Northern England* (Cambridge, 1995), 119–20.

In addition to the practical difficulties of bringing a bull of provision to effect, the candidate faced considerable expenditure. Even if he could avoid the cost of a trip to the curia by having his name included on a list sent by the king, a university or other patron, he still needed to pay charges for the writing and release of the bull itself. Moreover, from 1342 all those who obtained a direct provision to a specific benefice were bound to pay a tax known as annates. Initially, the amount demanded was theoretically equivalent to a year's income, which inevitably meant that payment in the fourteenth century was slow, especially when the tax was levied by local agents of varying degrees of diligence. By the early fifteenth century Scottish clerks usually had to make a personal obligation in the Apostolic Camera to pay annates at specified terms, as with service taxes, before the provisor knew whether in practice the benefice would be available to him. Expectative graces were rather cheaper to obtain, as only occasionally did the Camera attempt to levy annates from benefices obtained as a result, but they were little more than promises of future preferment and did not offer an immediate source of revenue with which to recoup the costs of seeking the provision in the first place.

In view of these problems, it is legitimate to ask why so many Scottish clerks actively sought provision. One reason was that those who had gone abroad to university, which was necessary until St Andrews was founded in 1410, had lost contact with local patrons and so sought papal favour instead. While this was undoubtedly sometimes the case, and Scottish clerks are prominent in the great rolls sent to the Apostolic See by French universities in the fourteenth century, many of those who had the means to read for degrees were already wealthy and well connected, and their links with Scotland had not been totally severed. Graduates may, however, have been inclined to obtain papal provisions in order to give themselves another option beside those available at the hands of Scottish patrons. What graduates did first, non-graduates could emulate, and lay lords in particular could encourage their clerks to seek provisions because it reduced the pressure on their own patronage, which was rarely disrupted by papal graces. As more provisions were made to Scottish benefices, those already in possession became increasingly nervous and sought confirmation of their tenure from the pope even if they had no particular reason to suppose that their incumbency was uncanonical. The process therefore gathered momentum all the time. The added demand for provisions necessitated a broadening of the categories of benefice which were available for papal collation, which in turn drew yet more clerks into the system. Such developments had financial advantages from the standpoint of the Apostolic See, but it would be too cynical to see them totally in fiscal terms. Increased demand had to be met by increased supply, for after all the initiative for particular provisions almost always lay in the locality rather than in Rome.

After the end of the Great Schism, few provisions were made to churches within the dominions of the English king, including those parts of Ireland which he controlled. Only bishops continued to be provided, and their appointment was regulated by the crown. Several European monarchs also entered into agreements, formal or informal, with the papacy, taking advantage of its financial and political difficulties in the wake of the Schism. James I enacted several measures which have a bearing on relations with the papacy, in which he was followed by later kings, but provisions continued seemingly unabated. Before dismissing the measures as ineffective, however, we must examine the legislation more closely.

A statute of 1424 laid down that no clerk was to cross the sea or send a procurator on his behalf without obtaining royal licence, or purchase a pension out of any benefice. The legislation of 1428 additionally forbade the king's subjects to indulge in 'barratry'. The term is somewhat obscure, but a 'barrator' appears to have been a cleric who was considered to have used underhand means to obtain a benefice which properly belonged to another, the root meaning of 'barratry' being 'to deceive'.[4] The stress on pensions and the fact that the issue of deception is raised point to the legislation being directed towards those who made frivolous claims to benefices in the hope of persuading the lawful incumbent to offer financial compensation rather than undergoing the risk and expense of a long lawsuit, and there are in fact strong indications that this practice was on the increase and that some clerks were blackmailing incumbents in the hope of being granted a pension on the fruits of the benefice. Although he was undoubtedly concerned by the

[4] *APS*, ii, 5, 16; D. E. R. Watt, 'The papacy and Scotland in the fifteenth century', in B. Dobson, ed., *The Church, Politics and Patronage in the Fifteenth Century* (Gloucester, 1984), 121.

export of money from the realm to transact business at the papal curia, it was probably never the king's intention to hinder bona fide provisions, particularly when he and his leading subjects could derive such benefits from the system. How effective the legislation was, even in those limited terms, is hard to assess. The practice would be difficult to eliminate when popes granted provisions on the basis of the content of the petitions presented to them without checking the facts, but the legislation could be employed against those who subsequently tried to have the provision executed in Scotland.

It is unclear whether Scottish courts did proceed against barrators. Parliament periodically enacted legislation concerning provisions, but increasingly it was directed at possible infringements of regalian right. Pensions were certainly being paid out of many benefices at the time of the Reformation, and sometimes the amounts were substantial. In the early 1560s, for instance, John Davidson not only held two vicarages, valued collectively at £30, but also a pension of £40 from the church of Kinkell in Aberdeenshire and one of £33 6s 8d from the parsonage of Glasgow. Andrew Galloway had a similar pension from Kinkell, although this drain on the church revenues must be put into the context of the parson's residual income of a little under £435.[5] The origin of some pensions was a device known as *resignatio in favorem*, a resignation of a benefice to another cleric. This was different from 'simple' resignations of churches through old age or infirmity or for the purpose of exchanging benefices, since the *resignatio in favorem* usually involved a compensatory grant by the new incumbent to his predecessor. These devices have been variously interpreted. Because of their similarity to grants of land to heirs in an attempt to evade feudal payments on the death of the original possessor, they have sometimes been seen as a means whereby benefices were kept out of royal hands. They have also been regarded as attempts to retain particular benefices, including monasteries, in the same family, with, say, an uncle resigning in favour of a nephew. Both these theories contain some truth, but such a resignation might also occur in the context of a lawsuit, with one party relinquishing his claim to the other in return for financial compensation. It has been suggested

[5] *The Books of Assumption of the Thirds of Benefices: Scottish Ecclesiastical Rentals at the Reformation*, ed. J. Kirk (Oxford, 1995), 420, 445, 448.

that the resignation was normally made not by the incumbent, but by a litigant who had scant chance of success, who was then bought off by the lawful possessor on the grounds that doing so was cheaper than a lengthy period of litigation.[6] If this is so, then the device of *resignatio in favorem* was used to legitimise the very practice that the statutes against barratry were meant to address.

The Great Schism marked a watershed in the history of the late medieval papacy. Because of the interminable political strife of Italy, the popes had been based north of the Alps for much of the fourteenth century, usually at Avignon, where the papal curia developed a strongly French ethos. Most of the Avignon popes professed a desire to return to Rome, and Urban V and Gregory XI briefly did so, but Gregory died in March 1378 and a disputed election followed. The cardinals initially chose the archbishop of Bari, Bartholomew Prignano, but the new pope, who took the name of Urban VI, proved less pliable than they had hoped, and a number of cardinals proceeded to elect Robert of Geneva on the grounds that their choice of Urban had been influenced by the Roman mob. Robert took the name of Clement VII and subsequently returned to Avignon. Each pope claimed that the other was a usurper, and both attracted support from secular powers. Rulers determined their loyalty through political considerations: the French adhered to Clement VII, for instance, and were joined in that allegiance by the Scots, while the English government backed Urban VI. Both popes were succeeded by fresh claimants, and in 1409 a third pontiff was chosen by the Council of Pisa, which had been called to heal the breach. It was only after more than forty years of schism that Christendom united behind a single pope in the person of Martin V, and in the meantime the Council of Constance had sought to elevate the authority of general councils over that of the pope, laying the foundations for a struggle between the two ecclesiastical powers which lasted through the first half of the fifteenth century. While it was not especially unusual for rival popes to be chosen by disgruntled rulers, usually the Emperor, the length and bitterness of the Great Schism had a serious impact on papal authority. In order to buy and retain secular support, the popes had to make concessions, and they continued to do so during the conciliar period and beyond.

[6] I. B. Cowan, *The Scottish Reformation: Church and Society in Sixteenth Century Scotland* (London, 1982), 67.

The impact of the Great Schism and the conciliar movement was felt most keenly at the level of international diplomacy. Wars against rival powers could frequently be justified as campaigns against schismatics. The duke of Albany risked isolation by persisting in his allegiance to the Avignonese pope Benedict XIII until the summer of 1419, when most of his fellow-rulers had deserted his cause. The Scottish government was able to exploit the fact that Eugenius IV was at loggerheads with the Council of Basle, although kings were generally disposed to support the pope, as a fellow-monarch with whom a working relationship could usually be forged, rather than put total faith in the oligarchic and unpredictable general councils. In the intellectual sphere, the problems occasioned by the Schism led to much debate about the nature and extent of papal authority, and several universities were founded in various parts of Europe, including St Andrews. It must be doubted, however, that the Schism had much bearing on the everyday life of the Scottish church.

Pontiffs occasionally made provisions to bishoprics outside their allegiance in order to oblige secular rulers without formally degrading the prelate in question. In 1388, for instance, Alexander Neville was translated to St Andrews from York because he had fallen foul of Richard II's government. Political developments also explain the provision of Gruffydd Yonge, Owain Glyn Dŵr's bishop of Bangor, to Ross in 1414. In neither case was the new bishop able to exercise any authority in what was essentially a titular see. The three Scottish bishoprics which were not named in *Cum universi* became especially entangled in the events of the Schism because of their continuing links with foreign metropolitans. In Galloway, memory of York's jurisdiction was fresh. The diocese of Sodor came to be split between a line of bishops based on Man, who adhered to the Roman obedience, and a line exercising authority in the Scottish part of the diocese. In Orkney, which ecclesiastically was still part of the province of Trondheim and politically not yet part of the Scottish realm, the bishops appointed by the Avignon popes perhaps had difficulty in gaining a foothold, although the situation is unclear in view of the strong Scottish influence in Orkney by this date. These issues did not necessarily affect the pastoral work of the bishop who was accepted locally, but they emphasised the anomaly of ecclesiastical obediences cutting across political boundaries when Christendom was split into rival camps. After the Schism the diocese of Sodor remained split, with the Scottish portion now detached from the influence of the cathedral at Peel on Man, while York's jurisdiction in Galloway was not revived. In 1430 James I declared that the Galwegian clergy should be treated like their counterparts in other Scottish dioceses,[7] which removed the final vestiges of Whithorn's subordination to York, although the papal provision of its bishops since 1359, by removing the requirement for metropolitan confirmation, had already severed the link. Whithorn had long been taxed with the rest of the Scottish church and its bishop had received mandates along with his Scottish colleagues. In 1422, when Alexander Vaus was translated to Whithorn from Caithness, his new see was said to be immediately subject to the papacy.[8] The Schism consolidated this new relationship, but did not create it.

The politics of the Schism provide the backdrop for an incident which demonstrates the value to the crown of controlling the appointment of bishops while simultaneously showing the importance of papal approval. In 1402 the duke of Albany attempted to remove the maverick Walter Danielston from Dumbarton castle by having him appointed as bishop of St Andrews, an office for which he had few obvious qualifications. Albany hoped thereby to recover the castle for the crown and secure the stronghold for the future advantage of his son Murdoch, who had married the daughter of the earl of Lennox. This interference by a lay magnate in the succession to Scotland's premier see was possible because the pope was virtually a prisoner in his palace at Avignon, which meant that the election in 1401 of Robert III's half-brother, Thomas Stewart, had not been confirmed by Benedict XIII. Albany persuaded Thomas to resign his claim in favour of Danielston, but the latter's death around Christmas 1402 rescued St Andrews from his clutches and neatly solved the problem of Dumbarton.[9] These were, however, unusual circumstances. Normal business was soon resumed.

At a lower level, the Schism impinged little. There were a few complications, such as the pastoral care of the church of Kirkgunzeon, which was normally served by monks of the English

[7] *RMS*, ii, 35. [8] *CPL*, vii, 287.

[9] S. Boardman, 'The man who would be king: the lieutenancy and death of David, duke of Rothesay, 1378–1402', in R. A. Mason and N. Macdougall, eds., *People and Power in Scotland: Essays in Honour of T. C. Smout* (Edinburgh, 1992), 3–4, 11.

abbey of Holm Cultram, but such problems could be circumvented by appointing a Scottish cleric, in this case a monk of Glenluce, to minister there.[10] In 1390 the Roman pope Boniface IX granted the bishop of Durham diocesan powers in Berwick, Roxburgh and other parts of St Andrews diocese which were under English occupation, and attempts were made to exercise this jurisdiction until 1423.[11] It was the end of the Schism which paradoxically caused the greatest difficulties. Clerks who owed their preferment to the Avignon popes were concerned that Scotland's adherence to Martin V might jeopardise their tenure, and many, sensing which way the wind was blowing, sought confirmation by the new pope even before Albany's government had deserted Benedict XIII. There was even some doubt about the status of the new university of St Andrews. In the event, however, Martin V's pragmatic approach enabled most Scottish clerks to retain their benefices and the university continued to function.

Relations between crown and papacy were perhaps strained in 1472, when the see of St Andrews was raised to the status of an archbishopric, well over three centuries after David I had petitioned the pope for this concession. The move would have been logical in the twelfth century, but was less obviously necessary in the fifteenth, when the metropolitan's right to confirm bishops within his province had been set aside by the use of papal provision and the Scottish bishops had become familiar with the notion that they were all legally equal. Over the next twenty years some sought exemption from the jurisdiction of the new archbishop of St Andrews, and in 1492 Glasgow too was raised to metropolitan status. While the exemption in 1474 of Thomas Spens, bishop of Aberdeen, could be justified on the grounds that he was conducting a lawsuit against the archbishop, the elevation of St Andrews clearly had serious and undesirable consequences.

The events of 1472 have often been regarded as reflecting the ambition of the then bishop of St Andrews, Patrick Graham, or even as a hostile move by the pope in a long struggle over ecclesiastical

[10] *Calendar of Papal Letters to Scotland of Clement VII of Avignon, 1378–1394*, ed. C. Burns (Scottish History Society, 1976), 166. For later developments see *Calendar of Papal Letters to Scotland of Benedict XIII of Avignon, 1394–1419*, ed. F. McGurk (Scottish History Society, 1976), 207, 290–1; *Chron. Bower*, vi, 69.

[11] R. L. Storey, *Thomas Langley and the Bishopric of Durham, 1406–1437* (London, 1961), 146.

patronage. However, it has also been argued that the initiative for the elevation came from the royal government in an attempt to achieve co-extensive boundaries for church and state, to lessen the number of appeals to Rome by enabling suits over benefices to be held in Scotland, and to have a single trusted prelate in a position to discipline others; it has even been suggested that the creation of a Scottish archbishopric was a mark of national consciousness. None of these standpoints is entirely convincing. The notion that Sixtus IV deliberately sought a confrontation with the king is hard to justify unless it is believed that relations between Scotland and the papacy in the fifteenth century were punctuated by crises, as the frequent reissue of legislation against barratry might at first glance suggest. There is, however, no clear indication that such crises took place, nor is it apparent how the creation of an archbishopric at St Andrews might resolve clashes over patronage. On the other hand, it is not obvious why James III might want St Andrews to have metropolitan status. He may have felt that it would enhance the prestige of his kingdom and vicariously of himself, but he (or at least his counsellors) should perhaps have realised that the elevation of St Andrews would inevitably cause tension elsewhere. Suits over benefices, moreover, continued to be taken to Rome, as they had been in fourteenth-century England despite there being two archbishops in the English church. Patrick Graham's ambition cannot be ruled out, and his subsequent madness has been attributed to the persecution he received at the hands of a vindictive monarch, but it is unlikely that the pope would have changed the status of a see on the petition of a single individual, and surely more probable that he either desired it himself or, more likely, had been prompted by the king. The king was probably behind Innocent VIII's declaration of the primacy of St Andrews in 1487 and the appointment of the archbishop as papal legate, a move which may also have received backing from a papal nuncio who had visited Scotland the previous year, although it is conceivable that the elevation owed something to a private initiative on the part of Graham's successor, William Scheves. In the event, the pope soon yielded to the inevitable complaints and exempted the bishops of Glasgow and Moray from the jurisdiction of St Andrews, and after Sauchieburn the new regime appears to have backed Glasgow's claim for metropolitan status. The manoeuvres which led to the bull of 1472, however, remain obscure.

Examples of abuses within the pre-Reformation Scottish church are easy to find in record sources and contemporary literature, but are much less straightforward to quantify. We have seen how some clerks derived large pensions from benefices, and how the device of *resignatio in favorem* could sometimes be used to ensure that churches passed to another member of the same family. Clerical concubinage appears to have been widespread, with senior ecclesiastics such as David Beaton, latterly archbishop of St Andrews and cardinal, paying little attention to canonical teaching on chastity. According to the critics, pluralism was common, and non-residence among clerics meant that the faithful were deprived of the sacraments, while the regular life was in disarray as nobles plundered the revenues of monasteries for their own profit.

This wholly negative view must be challenged. The belated attempts at reform by the hierarchy from 1549 show that abuses existed, but in many cases they always had. Concerns over the levels of clerical learning and competence were intensified by the increasing degree of lay literacy and the threat from heresy, but there is no evidence that sixteenth-century parish priests were appreciably more ignorant than their predecessors. Non-residence had long been prevalent among at least the higher clergy, who could use their position and influence to seek dispensations and, moreover, could justify absenteeism on the grounds that their talents enabled them to perform significant duties for the crown, for which their benefices provided the necessary income. Pluralism too had long been a feature in the lives of the higher clergy. Walter Bower tells us, albeit with a degree of exaggeration, that when William Wishart was postulated as bishop of St Andrews in 1271 he was already bishop-elect of Glasgow, archdeacon of St Andrews and holder of twenty-two rectories and prebends, as well as being royal chancellor,[12] and there were several notorious pluralists in thirteenth-century England. The papal bull *Execrabilis* of 1317 attempted, with some success, to regulate pluralism by emphasising the distinction between benefices which involved the cure of souls, such as parish churches, and those which did not, like cathedral prebends. In practice, it was possible to hold several sinecures simultaneously without

[12] *Chron. Bower*, v, 381, 486.

facing any penalties, but in the period immediately before the Great Schism pluralism appears to have been strictly controlled by the pope, and Urban V gave Thomas Harkars a brusque response when he petitioned for the removal of a clause in an earlier bull whereby he had been ordered to resign a benefice.[13] It is clear that pluralism was sanctioned more readily in the fifteenth century and that it was widely prevalent in Scotland in the sixteenth, although not all pluralists were greedy careerists. The decline in the real value of pensionary vicarages meant that some churches could not be served unless the incumbent had alternative sources of income, which were normally based on a second benefice; the problem was less a reflection on sixteenth-century clergy than on the acquisitiveness of thirteenth-century monasteries. Non-residence is harder to trace than pluralism without records of episcopal visitations, but an absentee rector or vicar did not necessarily mean that parishioners were deprived of the sacraments. In England there was a sizeable clerical proletariat, especially before the fourteenth-century plagues, and much routine pastoral care in the parishes fell to underpaid stipendiary priests with no security of tenure. In Scotland, which was a poorer and more thinly populated country, the clerical underclass was probably smaller, and it must be doubted that many churches were served directly by the 'sublime and literate persons' so beloved of Urban V, but we should be wary of assuming that the sacraments were not being performed.

Although the Scottish monasteries were not dissolved at the Reformation like their English counterparts, recruitment ceased in 1560 and those who chose to remain in their communities gradually died off. Material damage inflicted during English invasions, especially in the 1540s, and by the actions of reformers, for instance at Lindores, Scone and Dunfermline, reduced the viability of some monasteries and encouraged their further dilapidation, although at some houses there is evidence of repair and rebuilding. Over the ensuing half-century most of the former monastic estates were erected into lay baronies for the benefit of the families which controlled them, and it was the fact that many revenues had already been diverted to laymen before the Reformation which explains why there was no need, and no enthusiasm, for formal dissolution.

[13] Barrell, *Papacy*, 241–3.

Because religious houses disappeared, however, they could be identified much more closely than parishes and universities with the discredited pre-Reformation church, and so there has been a tendency among Protestant writers to condemn monasteries as at best lax and at worst dens of vice. Again, examples of decline can be found, and by the later Middle Ages many monks had moved away from a truly communal life and enjoyed private accommodation and generous individual allowances, but some houses were thriving in the sixteenth century, perhaps taking advantage of a probable rise in the population which may have made the security of monastic life more attractive. At Kinloss in Moray two abbots, Thomas Crystal and Robert Reid, increased the number of monks, built up the monastic library, and attracted the services of Giovanni Ferrerio, a Renaissance scholar from Piedmont who settled at Kinloss and taught the young monks. At Cambuskenneth near Stirling Alexander Myln, who became abbot in 1518, improved the academic standing of the monastery and attempted to introduce strict observance of the Augustinian rule,[14] and efforts towards reform and greater emphasis on university attendance are found at several other Scottish houses. A Carthusian monastery was established at Perth as late as James I's reign. Such examples provide a necessary corrective to the image of decadence and decline.

The role of the abbot was crucial. He was a father-figure for the monks, and his attitude to regular observance and discipline set the tone for the whole monastery. Before the development of the system of papal provision, he was elected by the chapter either from within its own number or from another house of the same order, and until 1430 even those Scottish abbots who were provided had invariably already espoused the regular life.[15] In that year, however, Alexander Fraser, vicar of Abertarff and a secular clerk, was granted the priory of Beauly, and thus began the practice whereby monasteries were bestowed on clerks who were not members of the order. Although examples are few before the 1470s, the change turned out to be highly significant, because it enabled careerists to seek regular benefices as well as secular ones. Previously, a clerk with ambitions

[14] M. Dilworth, *Scottish Monasteries in the Late Middle Ages* (Edinburgh, 1995), 36–7, 65; Cowan, *Medieval Church*, 145–6.

[15] On what follows see M. Dilworth, 'The commendator system in Scotland', *IR*, 37 (1986), 51–72.

for abbatial dignity had to enter a monastery, and could expect to be there for many years before his chance of promotion came, if it ever did. Now it was possible to seek parish churches, cathedral prebends, archdeaconries and other secular benefices and then petition for a vacant abbey or priory when the opportunity arose. Even if the pope required that the new monastic superior should take the habit, as he frequently did in the fifteenth century, this was little more than a condition which the provisor could accept or reject; he had not had to make an earlier commitment to the restrictions imposed by membership of a religious order. Not all those appointed in this manner were neglectful of their duties – neither Myln nor Reid had previously belonged to an order – but the way was open for the abuse of papal provisions by the king and his magnates.

Sometimes monasteries were ruled by commendators. A commendator was not a regular abbot, but rather assumed the office and emoluments of abbot without necessarily making a monastic profession. He was basically an administrator, and for centuries commendation had been used to enable someone who was not the legal holder of an ecclesiastical office to exercise the functions attached to it, usually in cases of emergency when the duties might otherwise not have been performed. The arrangements made during the Great Schism to serve the church of Kirkgunzeon, discussed above, are an example. In sixteenth-century Scotland, however, the practice was used to benefit the commendator rather than the institution of which he was head, and appointments were increasingly made for life. Bishops were sometimes made commendators of religious houses in order to increase their income, and in the years between Flodden and the Reformation almost half of the Scottish monasteries were used for this purpose, while the crown took the revenues of houses which had been granted to youthful members of the royal family. The appointment of unsuitable monastic superiors was condemned by, among others, a friar of Jedburgh, Adam Abell, who called upon James V to remedy the evil practices of his two predecessors, but the system was too useful to leading laymen to be abandoned.

The appointment of a commendator did not, however, alter the status of the benefice, and a regular abbot frequently succeeded right up until the 1550s. Excluding Iona and Tongland, which were held by successive bishops of the Isles and Whithorn respectively, only one house, Dunfermline, was ruled continuously by commendators from before 1513 to the Reformation. The Cistercian abbey of Balmerino, by contrast, was never ruled by a commendator or an abbot who had not been a monk, although regular observance there was lax.[16] Nor were commendators in Scotland laymen, as is often suggested. They were frequently secular clerks rather than professed monks or canons, but were expected to be in, or at least to assume, major clerical orders, which implied celibacy. Whether commendators paid more than lip-service to this last requirement or not, they were unable to marry and produce legitimate heirs until after 1560, a clear indication that until then they were considered clerks rather than laymen.

The period which produced commendators also saw the disposal of much church land at feu-ferm.[17] The system, which was encouraged by act of parliament in 1458,[18] was not limited to ecclesiastical holdings, although most of the surviving evidence relates to estates which had been granted to bishoprics and monasteries in earlier centuries. Feuing involved the granting of a charter whereby the recipient was to hold the land heritably in return for an advance payment, an annual feu-duty which was higher than existing rents, and sometimes other less frequent dues. From the standpoint of the grantor, feuing provided an immediate financial windfall and the prospect of increased rents, although in an inflationary age the real value of these rents soon diminished. The feuar obtained security of tenure, although he might have to take on particular problems of estate management, for instance dealing with truculent tenants or making good damage caused by natural disasters, and the initial outlay was considerable. It is hardly surprising that often a generation or two passed before the feuars could afford to obtain the requisite papal or royal confirmation of their charter.

The rapid increase in feuing in the sixteenth century threatened the customary rights of inheritance of those who already occupied the lands in question. There was a danger that landlords, anxious to

[16] M. Dilworth, 'Scottish Cistercian monasteries and the Reformation', *IR*, 48 (1997), 147.

[17] On this topic see M. H. B. Sanderson, *Scottish Rural Society in the Sixteenth Century* (Edinburgh, 1982).

[18] For a rather different interpretation of this statute see A. Grant, *Independence and Nationhood: Scotland 1306–1469* (Edinburgh, 1991), 84.

raise as much capital as possible, might sell the land to the highest bidder and thereby harm their erstwhile tenants. In fact many lands were feued to people of humble stock, and the process therefore created a new class of proprietors originating from below that of the lairds. A considerable proportion of these feuars already occupied the land, so feuing did not necessarily cause much dislocation in the possession patterns of local society. Even if the new proprietor was an outsider, he must often have preferred to collect rents from the existing tenants rather than introduce new settlers or exploit the estates himself by paid agricultural labour. A grant at feu-ferm did not usually cause the removal of the local peasantry from their holdings.

Feuing was a part of the series of processes in the sixteenth century whereby monasteries divested themselves of their former rights and responsibilities. The practice was not new, and indeed can be traced back into the thirteenth century and even earlier, but it became much commoner after James V began to tax the church heavily in the 1530s. The preambles of charters frequently use taxation as the excuse for a grant at feu-ferm, but this may partly be aimed at making the transactions look less like business deals and thereby keeping them within the bounds of canon law, which forbade the alienation of ecclesiastical property in most circumstances. The heads of many corporations doubtless saw advantages in realising some of the value of their landed assets in cash, which could be used by themselves and their families, rather than facing the possibility of expropriation if the Scottish king should choose to follow Henry VIII's example and dissolve the monasteries for his own profit. Even if in the longer term the feuars gained, they initially faced churchmen who were determined to strike a hard bargain.

This stress on material considerations can give the impression that the higher clergy had little interest in, or aptitude for, the propagation of Christian doctrine. Assessments of the quality of prelates as pastors must, however, have due regard to the very different function of leading churchmen in the Middle Ages compared with more recent times. Bishops were expected to be able administrators, and were often employed by the king both internally as royal officials and abroad as diplomats. The pastoral side of their duties is harder to detect, and may often have been delegated to assistants; during the trial of an apostate priest in 1539, Bishop George Crichton of Dunkeld admitted that he had never read the Bible. Some prelates, such as Cardinal David Beaton, have been portrayed as worldly and selfish, pursuing policies at home and abroad in their own interests while paying scant regard to the abuses of the contemporary church. On the other hand, James Kennedy of St Andrews has been the subject of a eulogistic biography, while William Elphinstone, bishop of Aberdeen, has been described as 'remarkably unselfseeking and indifferent to power' and 'a genuine patriot [who] strove constantly to make the community of the realm a workable reality'.[19] It may be no coincidence that both Kennedy and Elphinstone founded educational establishments. In any case, even if we accept the favourable judgements on them, they are not typical of the Scottish episcopate as a whole, any more than Beaton is representative of the sixteenth-century hierarchy.

There is little evidence which sheds light on the religious practices of the Scottish people in the late Middle Ages, although in broad outline they were probably similar to elsewhere. The centralisation of the Western church under the aegis of the twelfth- and thirteenth-century popes had served to clarify issues of doctrine and impose a series of rules which were, in theory at least, universally applicable.

The parish church remained at the centre of local life, both spiritually and physically. Many parish churches in Scotland were small and plain compared with their counterparts in the richer areas of England, but they still dominated the local landscape. The church was often the only stone building in the village, and compared with the sometimes flimsy dwellings of the peasantry it must have seemed a fitting setting for the mystic link between mankind and God. In the burghs, where more ample funds were available to adorn churches, there was greater sophistication in architecture, and some late medieval collegiate churches such as Roslin, south of Edinburgh, contained intricate carving.

The services in a medieval church were conducted in Latin. Because they followed fixed patterns, the congregation must have gained a certain familiarity with them, even if actual comprehension

[19] Macfarlane, *William Elphinstone*, 13.

was limited to a very few. In great churches such as cathedrals and abbeys there was an almost constant succession of services through the day and night; even in lesser churches, the proliferation of private altars in the later Middle Ages meant that divine offices were being celebrated almost continuously. Virtually everyone was baptised and thereby a member of the Christian family, but by modern standards there was relatively little participation in services by the congregation. The music, although often elaborate in larger churches, was largely the property of the clergy. Holy Communion was rarely offered to the laity, and even then only the priest partook of the wine. The sacrament was often celebrated on the other side of a screen, which served to emphasise the difference between cleric and layman. Although parishioners were encouraged to confess their sins, the church demanded this only at Easter, and we cannot tell whether even this rule was effective. Preaching was probably relatively uncommon, especially in rural areas, and was perhaps most effectively offered by the friars, and so there was little formal instruction in the faith within the context of services in the parish church. And while some lay people undoubtedly had a deep vein of piety and reverence even for things they did not fully understand, were struck by the awe-inspiring mystery of the sacraments, and indulged in private contemplation and devotion outside the context of organised religion, others were doubtless very bored and restless during services. Whoever the legal rector or vicar might be, the clerk who officiated was probably usually drawn, if not from the local community, at least from the same social stratum as the majority of the parishioners, a fact which may have made some members of the congregation, familiar with his past and character, sceptical that he really could act as a mediator between them and God.

The medieval church placed considerable emphasis on the idea of judgement, both after death and, ultimately, at the end of the world. By stressing the eternal consequences of misbehaviour on earth, the church hoped to impose some discipline on a society which, even if not senselessly violent and brutish, was often not exactly subtle in sorting out its problems; and by drawing attention to the end of the world, and the impossibility of predicting when it might happen, the church hoped to encourage people to contemplate on their lives and activities. The message was brought home partly through wall paintings, stained-glass windows and other visual aids, because themes such as the end of the world and the pains of hell could be depicted in such media more effectively than could more abstract concepts such as love and redemption. Most medieval windows have long since been broken, and the paintings were whitewashed at the Reformation, and we therefore know little about them in a Scottish context, but where they do survive they illustrate, better even than words, the nature of the Christian doctrine which many medieval people received.

Evidence for the response of the congregation to the practices of the church is very scanty. In England complaints were made during the visitations of bishops to parishes if services were not being held, which suggests that the laity missed them when they were not performed. It is unlikely that the faithful in Scotland were any different, especially when the church placed such emphasis on the importance of attendance at Mass even though the laity rarely took communion. Pilgrimages to local, national and international shrines were also encouraged, either as part of a penance enjoined by a priest or to pursue private devotions or seek a cure for illness or infirmity. James IV was an assiduous pilgrim to the shrines of St Ninian at Whithorn and St Duthac at Tain, thereby following the trend towards greater interest in native Scottish saints which led to the production of the Aberdeen Breviary in the early years of the sixteenth century and the replacement of the English service books known as the Sarum Use, imports of which were prohibited in 1507.[20] Pilgrimages can be regarded as excuses for holidays, the medieval equivalent of a trip to the seaside, and they were sometimes encouraged by offering indulgences as incentives to pilgrims, but it would be too cynical simply to dismiss the spiritual side of the practice on these grounds.

Late medieval popular religion was dominated by prayers for the dead, a consequence of the increased emphasis placed by the church on the doctrine of purgatory. Purgatory was a state between heaven and hell, where the dead were chastised for sins committed on earth and purified prior to entering the blessedness of heaven. The doctrine had developed partly in view of the fact that penances on earth were becoming less severe and so had to be replaced by the

[20] *Registrum Secreti Sigilli Regum Scotorum*, ed. M. Livingstone and others (Edinburgh, 1908–), i, 223–4.

expiation of guilt after death, but the increasing stress on the existence of purgatory was also part of the medieval church's judgemental approach. The length of time spent in purgatory could run to thousands of years, but could be reduced by the prayers of those still alive, by the intercession of saints, particularly the Blessed Virgin Mary, and by obtaining indulgences.

Indulgences first appear in the context of the crusades, participation in which was seen as so meritorious as to deserve direct entry into paradise. At least that appears to have been the impression given by those recruiting for the expeditions. It is unlikely that Pope Urban II intended to be so generous when he launched the First Crusade in 1095, but theologians subsequently developed a theory to meet the popular perception of what an indulgence was. Moreover, the issue of plenary indulgences soon extended outside the context of the crusades. As well as widening the circle of recipients to those who helped crusaders, popes offered similar remissions to those who attended the periodic Jubilees in Rome and made suitable offerings on the altars of the city's churches. These Jubilees began in 1300 and were originally meant to be every hundred years, but in practice they were financially profitable and excuses were found to stage them much more frequently, for example in 1450 when the eighth earl of Douglas made such an impression in Rome. It was a short step from this to the pope offering plenary indulgences on demand, in return of course for a fee; and in the fourteenth century, especially after the arrival of the Black Death, considerable numbers sought plenary remissions from the papacy. People from the British Isles were particularly enthusiastic, but the grace was limited to those who could afford it, and that was a small percentage of the overall population. Greater accessibility to indulgences was provided by itinerant *questores* operating under papal or episcopal licence, whether genuine or otherwise, of whom Chaucer's fictional Pardoner is the most famous example. The abuse of indulgences in Germany was one of the factors which drove Martin Luther to rebel against the established church, but pardoners are rarely mentioned in Scottish sources. This may be because indulgences were rarely hawked in Scotland, or simply because the work of pardoners is hidden by the lack of surviving evidence, but we should note both the enthusiasm of Scots for indulgences issued directly by the pope in the later fourteenth century and the silence on this issue of Knox and other Protestant historians who would surely have castigated the activities of pardoners in Scotland had the opportunity presented itself.

Smaller indulgences were also issued by popes, bishops and occasionally other churchmen, promising remissions of fixed periods of penance if the recipient performed certain specified actions. This usually involved visiting a church on a named feast day and making an appropriate contribution to its repair or refurbishment, or for the use of the poor. It could also extend to other meritorious deeds such as building bridges. Until the end of the fourteenth century at least, the length of time promised in the remission was generally small: in 1363, for instance, the pope offered only a year and forty days for those visiting the allegedly ruined cathedral of Elgin at the feast of the Trinity, even though the bishop had requested seven times as much.[21] Indulgences seem nonetheless to have been quite popular. In part, they offered an excuse for a day out, like a pilgrimage might, but there was a strong obligation to give according to one's means to the good cause in question; it is hard to deny, therefore, that those who participated expected some future benefits, and trusted that the pope or bishop could deliver the promised remission.

As we have seen, the belief in the efficacy of prayers for the dead had underpinned donations to the church and its institutions for centuries. Those who endowed monasteries in the twelfth and thirteenth centuries expected that the monks would pray for their souls and thereby help them after their death. By the fourteenth century, few were sufficiently committed to traditional monasticism to establish houses, and most funding in the two centuries before the Reformation was directed instead towards chaplainries, equivalent to the English chantries. A chaplainry was a foundation dedicated to prayers for the souls of the founder and his or her family, and usually, piously, the souls of 'all the faithful departed'. Sometimes a whole chapel or collegiate church was dedicated for this purpose, more often an altar or a candle on an altar; some chaplainries were supposed to last for ever, others for a limited time. This meant that, as well as being much cheaper to set up than conventional monasteries, they suited a range of income groups. Donors also sometimes

[21] *Calendar of Entries in the Papal Registers Relating to Great Britain and Ireland: Petitions to the Pope*, ed. W. H. Bliss (London, 1896), 401.

used them as a form of advertising, because inscriptions and pictures on windows reminded those who remained of the person who had died and of his or her generosity to the church, but most of the benefits were intended to be in the next world rather than on earth. Chaplainries and colleges were still being founded in the early sixteenth century, which points to a continuing belief in their usefulness in the eyes of a broad spectrum of society. It may be easy today to be sceptical about indulgences and prayers for the dead, and to marvel at the gullibility of people from all walks of life who bought plenary indulgences, and of citizens who reserved a considerable proportion of their estate for the establishment of a chaplainry, but to do so would be to misunderstand the nature of late medieval religion.

How much the central doctrines of Christianity were understood by the common people is almost impossible to evaluate. Although lay literacy was increasing, especially in the burghs, and may have been encouraged by the foundation of three universities in fifteenth-century Scotland and by the Education Act of 1496, and although printing had come to Scotland in the first decade of the sixteenth century, most Scots must have remained illiterate. They could, of course, still listen to preachers, whether from within or outside the institutional church, and it was the charisma of such preachers which ultimately enabled Reformed opinions to take root in Scotland. But even they must have found it difficult to foster a general interest in theological niceties as they were discussed among intellectuals. This does not, of course, mean that ordinary folk were indifferent to religion. In an age of ignorance, with scientific knowledge virtually non-existent, the hand of supernatural powers was visible everywhere. Many of the religious rituals of the farming year can have been little different from the pagan ceremonies of the pre-Christian era, and had the same function. The church had sanctified these rituals, but it had not brought – and could not bring – the people as a whole to a deep and sincere understanding of Christian doctrines. In some respects, the religion of medieval Christians was based on terror of the hereafter, on superstition, on a blind, unquestioning faith in the saints and in churchmen as intercessors, even on a baleful and suffocating ignorance. But the familiar trappings of religion were always there, and in times of trouble the very changelessness of the church's services must have been a comfort to the afflicted. It is in this fundamentally conservative context that we must investigate the development of heterodoxy in Scotland.

The incidence of heresy in late medieval Scotland is hard to assess. There must always have been many who held unorthodox opinions, if only out of ignorance of theological precepts, but these people usually enter the records only when the church was actively hunting down heretics. In Britain an impetus to persecution was provided by the dissemination of the views of the Oxford academic John Wyclif, who died in 1384 after several years of bitter invective against the pope and the friars and the production of learned works denying transubstantiation (the doctrine that the bread and wine consecrated in the Mass are transformed into the body and blood of Christ) and advocating predestination, a doctrine which undermined the church's advocacy of good works in order to obtain salvation. Wyclif's anti-clericalism, especially his calls for the disendowment of the church, struck a chord in the England of the late 1370s and early 1380s, a period of military defeat, political confusion and social unrest. From these beginnings sprang the movement known as Lollardy, although most of its adherents came from the lower echelons of society after it became linked with treason in a rebellion in 1414 and was no longer politically acceptable among the ruling classes. In 1401 the statute *De heretico comburendo* was promulgated in England, allowing for the burning of heretics who had relapsed after previously acknowledging their errors and accepting the forgiveness of the church. At around the same time Jan Hus was the inspiration for a reforming movement in Bohemia, which was savagely repressed by the ecclesiastical authorities. Lollards and Hussites both desired a return to a more primitive church, as the friars had, and they too placed great emphasis on the study of Scripture. The Bible was translated into vernacular languages, which alarmed the church. The official version of the Bible was St Jerome's translation into Latin, known as the Vulgate, and the science of theology was based on the study of this hallowed text. Translations of Scripture can distort – as the Vulgate had done – and the presence of heretical glosses in some Lollard Bibles caused the English ecclesiastical authorities to regard possession of vernacular religious works as tantamount to heresy. They saw private

Bible-reading, and uncontrolled popular preaching, as threats to order in the hierarchical society in which the church played so prominent a role.

Some English bishops were very active in proceeding against Lollards in the fifteenth century, although there were few executions and it must be questioned how many of those who were interrogated held doctrinally unorthodox views rather than being merely anti-clerical or ignorant. Reluctance to pay teinds, which is a common feature of the records of sixteenth-century civil courts in Scotland, does not necessarily imply heterodoxy, although it may hint at dissatisfaction with the church and its activities. The fact that James IV lightly dismissed allegations against some Ayrshire folk in 1494 suggests that he did not see heresy as a threat, but it would be reasonable to suppose that some Lollard ideas had reached Scotland during the fifteenth century. A man called James Resby, described by Bower as 'an English priest of the school of John Wyclif', had been burned at Perth in 1408, and another heretic perished in Glasgow diocese in 1422. At least one Bohemian exile, Paul Crawar, also reached Scotland, for he was executed in July 1433. It is unlikely that these were isolated individuals. Bower makes much of the diligence of the inquisitor, Laurence of Lindores, saying that he gave no peace to heretics anywhere in the kingdom, and suggests that Wyclif still had followers in Scotland in the 1440s, whereas another chronicler, Andrew of Wyntoun, draws attention to the first duke of Albany's hatred of heretics. One of the avowed purposes of the new university of St Andrews was to be a bulwark against heretical views. In 1425 parliament made a statute against heresy, although burnings had already taken place without it. Bower's stress on the advantages of hearing Mass may imply that anti-sacramental views were circulating in Scotland. This all suggests that heresy was perceived to be a problem in the fifteenth century, although it may have appeared a greater threat to the institutional church than it really was.

The church was faced with a much more serious danger when the ideas of Martin Luther began to enter Scotland in the 1520s, probably direct from the Continent rather than via England, especially at the outset. In 1525 parliament promulgated a statute against the import of Lutheran works, threatening with imprisonment and escheat those who brought such literature through Scottish seaports, and prohibiting the discussion of Luther's ideas except for the purpose of refuting them.[22] This measure presupposes that heretical books, probably mainly English vernacular Bibles, were reaching Scotland, and they presumably had a market if merchants were prepared to carry them. The act of 1525 was ratified and extended in 1527, 1535 and 1541, as and when the government felt that a fresh clampdown was warranted. The 1541 parliament reaffirmed traditional Catholic doctrine on the sacraments and the worship of the Blessed Virgin Mary, declared that no one was to impugn papal authority on pain of death and forfeiture of goods, and banned discussion of the Bible except by theologians approved by universities, but also called upon churchmen to reform themselves.[23] We can detect here both James V's determination to remain in the Roman fold, doubtless because of the financial advantages such a policy promised, and a feeling that ecclesiastical reform was needed in order to combat heresy. It is, of course, impossible to ascertain exactly how widely Protestant opinions were held, or the extent to which religious considerations dictated, or were dictated by, individuals' views on relations with England and France. Post-Reformation writers naturally dwelt on instances of martyrdom, such as the burning of Patrick Hamilton in 1528, and castigated James V for failing to follow the example of his uncle, Henry VIII, in breaking with Rome. There is no contemporary evidence for the tale that the king had a blacklist of prominent individuals who could be accused of heresy when he wanted to proceed against them,[24] but James's continued allegiance to the pope necessitated both legislation and direct action against iconoclasts and others who held Protestant sympathies. However, there is no sign of a marked Protestant resurgence after James's death, which may indicate that the level of repression during his reign was lower than some later writers alleged.

The arrival of Lutheran doctrines must, however, have created debates within families, circles of friends, religious houses, universities and the growing number of schools, where there is evidence for sustained intellectual and ideological activity in the late Middle Ages. Orthodox religion was hard to champion because of the undoubted abuses of pluralism, absenteeism and the holding of benefices by minors, and the widespread diversion of ecclesiastical revenues to the crown and leading magnate families. Despite this,

[22] *APS*, ii, 295. [23] Ibid., 370–1. [24] Cameron, *James V*, 294–6.

many Scots were probably reluctant to accept major changes in liturgical practice and religious belief, and it was not until the series of events which culminated in the so-called Reformation Parliament of 1560 that a decisive shift towards Protestantism occurred. The relatively late date of the Scottish Reformation meant that it owed more to the fervent rejection of past practices by John Calvin than to the more moderate views of Luther and his disciples, and was fuelled by the expansion of Bible study after reading it in the vernacular became lawful by act of parliament in 1543. This act, with its safeguard against heresies, has been seen as evidence of the influence of evangelical humanists at the royal court in the latter part of James V's reign,[25] and it may be that at this point the running was still being made by moderates seeking reform from within the existing ecclesiastical establishment. John Knox exemplifies the passion of Scottish Protestantism, but his influence before 1560 was much more limited than his own writings imply. Apart from a brief visit to Scotland in 1555–6, he was abroad from 1547 to 1559, and it was during his period on the Continent that he drank so deeply at the Calvinist well.

The parliamentary measures of 1560 were negative rather than positive. They abolished the Mass and rejected papal jurisdiction, but did not create fresh administrative structures for the church. Bishops remained in office, and lost only those powers which they derived from the pope, while incumbents continued to enjoy the revenues of their benefices, and former monks their portions, irrespective of what doctrines they held. At least superficially, the structure of the old church was still intact, and the reformers faced the thorny problem of how Protestant ministers were to be endowed. There was no enthusiasm among the nobility for the dissolution of the monasteries, because much of their wealth was already in lay hands, and legal difficulties prevented the ejection of clerks from benefices to which they had been canonically instituted. Although the parliament of 1560 had, unusually, been attended by many lairds who were presumably keen to be involved in such significant changes, the greater magnates were lukewarm about any moves which might threaten them financially by depriving them of the lands and revenues they had obtained from the church.

[25] C. Edington, *Court and Culture in Renaissance Scotland: Sir David Lindsay of the Mount* (Amherst, 1994), 58.

The success of the Scottish Reformation was not, therefore, assured. Queen Mary never ratified the legislation of 1560 and remained a Roman Catholic, even though her third marriage, to the earl of Bothwell, so enraged the pope that she forfeited the support she might otherwise have received from that source. Protestant modes of worship spread only slowly and fitfully to the more conservative parts of the realm, and although many incumbents and former monks took up offices in the reformed church, it is uncertain in many cases whether they were motivated by conviction or expediency. There was thus no abrupt break with the past, and this makes the actions of the Reformation Parliament appear all the more sudden and unexpected. Contemporary and later writers in the Protestant tradition were, unsurprisingly, determined to convey the impression that there had been a profound spiritual transformation in sixteenth-century Scotland, and their influential accounts have caused historians to search for religious explanations for the political standpoints of individuals. While it would be rash to deny that some Scots acted in accordance with their conscience, it is surely relevant to seek alternative explanations for events such as the debacle at Solway Moss in 1542, the split after James V's death between those who sought to continue the French alliance and those who advocated a closer relationship with England, and indeed the events of the 1560 parliament itself. Until 1558 at the earliest the Scottish political community had been indecisive, neither wholeheartedly embracing Protestantism nor demonstrating much attachment to an old church widely acknowledged to be in grave need of reform. The sudden focus of the next two years is striking, and probably owes its origin to events outside Scotland rather than internal factors. The accession of Elizabeth to the English throne after the five-year reign of her Catholic sister Mary raised the prospect of a renewed alliance between Scottish Protestants and the English government and ended the period during which the regent Mary of Guise could afford to indulge Protestants in Scotland, while the succession of the Scottish queen's first husband Francis as king of France in July 1559 threatened a closer co-ordination of policy between Scotland and France even than that which had prevailed under Mary of Guise. The reformers must have found this situation especially threatening since the warring powers of France and Spain had recently come to terms in the treaty of Cateau-Cambrésis, and so a clampdown on Protestant activity in Scotland was now more likely. But even those who had little interest in doctrinal change must have felt apprehensive at the prospect of Scotland becoming little more than a satellite of the French kingdom, and this may have fostered a sense of national identity which provided fertile ground for the legislation of the Reformation Parliament. In the event, the unexpected death of Francis in December 1560 once again transformed the situation because it drove Queen Mary to return to her realm, so that, after a long period when government had been conducted in the name of an absentee minor, Scotland had to face the personal rule of a woman who may already have been showing signs of the unpredictability and capriciousness which, more than her adherence to Roman Catholicism, were to lead to her forced abdication in 1567. In the short term, Mary's return may have heightened the stakes, but it also initiated a series of events which were to be crucial to the success of the Scottish Reformation. The queen's behaviour served to discredit the old church, and her replacement by her infant son gave the reformers the opportunity to consolidate their position. Throughout these momentous events, however, political expediency played at least as great a part as religious convictions.

Summarising the essential features of the late medieval Scottish church is a task fraught with difficulty. This is not only because our knowledge is so heavily weighted towards institutional matters which interested the higher clergy and their families but impinged little on the everyday lives of humble parishioners, but more especially because the church, for all its conservatism, was no more static than the world in which it operated. In Scotland there was both an increasing interest in the saints of the distant Celtic past and a close and multi-faceted relationship with a papacy which had been instrumental in standardising ecclesiastical practices throughout western Christendom. In a late medieval context close relations with the popes meant provisions (with their fiscal consequences) and numerous dispensations of various kinds. Both areas of papal activity were capable of being abused, and some of the problems of the Scottish church stemmed from inappropriate relaxations of canon law, for instance to allow the king's illegitimate children to hold bishoprics and abbeys, and provisions which in practice served to strengthen the hold of the crown and leading magnates over ecclesiastical appointments. The Protestant reformers were easily able to break the power of the pope in Scotland, but the removal of lay control over the patronage and revenues of the Scottish church was an altogether different matter. David I may have been 'ane sair sanct for the Croune', but his sixteenth-century successors had to some extent recovered the endowments so generously bestowed on ecclesiastical institutions in a very different age of faith and religious renewal.

CONCLUSION

This book has been primarily concerned with the five centuries between the accession of Malcolm Canmore and the Reformation Parliament. Inevitably, this period saw considerable political, ecclesiastical and social developments within Scotland and changing relations with the outside world. There is no single, unifying factor which explains how the Scottish kingdom evolved as it did or why its history differs from that of other parts of the British Isles. Rather, medieval Scotland must be examined from the standpoint of a number of overlapping and sometimes contradictory themes.

The extent of royal power in Scotland was affected by both geographical realities and strong provincial identities. The twelfth- and thirteenth-century kings were responsible for the introduction of new administrative structures, many imported from Norman England, and they strove to consolidate their authority by using trusted agents to act on their behalf in the peripheral regions of their realm. Freskin and his descendants in and beyond Moray, the Bruces in Annandale, the Stewarts in the Clyde estuary and, somewhat later, the Comyns in Buchan and Badenoch were all employed to control dangerous areas where the crown's influence was reduced by distance or the existence of powerful local lords. These men all belonged to immigrant families, and their role in Scottish history can give a misleading impression of the significance of feudalisation and the introduction of Anglo-Norman institutions. For David I and his successors were neither able nor willing to reject the past: they enjoyed good relations with some native magnates, especially the earls of Fife; and the survival of thanages and the continued use of officials with Gaelic names clearly demonstrate the element of continuity in Scottish government.

The thirteenth century witnessed the absorption into the Scottish state of areas which hitherto had successfully resisted royal authority, including Moray, Ross, Galloway, even Argyll and arguably the southern Hebrides as well. This extension of central power was destined to be of short duration, partly because of the confusion of the Wars of Independence but more especially because its roots were very shallow. The descendants of Somerled who acknowledged the Maid of Norway as Alexander III's heir in 1284 may have issued charters which used feudal terminology, but they had not become fully assimilated in the political community. From the late fourteenth century onwards the MacDonalds, who had benefited from the eclipse or extinction of their MacDougall and MacRuairi cousins, were able to defy successive kings of Scots with virtual impunity, since military expeditions against them had only transitory effect. Royal policy was to allow loyal magnates such as the earls of Argyll and Huntly to enhance their own power in strategically important areas, just as the twelfth-century kings had done. The threat from England meant that similar measures had to be taken on the border, hence the rise of the Douglases and the development of a frontier culture which was inimical to royal intervention. Scotland could not be ruled from the centre; successful governance depended, as it always had done, on the development and maintenance of constructive relations between the crown and leading local magnates. Royal power was sometimes in abeyance because the king was a minor, a captive, an exile or (in the case of Robert III) inadequate, but loyalty to the legitimate monarch was a powerful force for stability. The Stewart kings were often ruthless and sometimes vindictive, but James III's brother Albany still had to rely on English help for his bid for the throne.

The close ties which had bound together the nobility of Scotland, England and France in the twelfth and thirteenth centuries were severed by the Wars of Independence, but Scottish kings and magnates still strove to play a role on the wider European stage. Relations with the papacy remained important and usually cordial well into the sixteenth century, and trade with the Low Countries, northern Germany and Scandinavia contributed to the prosperity of many east-coast ports. James II, James III and James V all sought wives overseas, and similar marriage alliances were made by other members of the ruling family. Diplomatically, however, France was the major continental power from a Scottish perspective. The alliance between Scotland and France against England was a central feature of the Wars of Independence and the Hundred Years War, among other things leading David II to disaster at Neville's Cross and the fourth earl of Douglas to a French duchy and a military reputation that he scarcely deserved. But political contacts with France were not new in 1295. William the Lion was captured at Alnwick during a rebellion against Henry II which involved the French king; Alexander II performed homage to Louis in his war against John; both Alexander II and Alexander III sought their second wives in France; some Scots fought alongside the French at Tunis in 1270. Nor did the alliance end with the English expulsion from France in 1453, although the changed international situation created complications for Scottish diplomacy. James IV met his death on an invasion of northern England which, in broad outline, would have been familiar to many of his predecessors. Expeditions southwards, whether they originated in a quest for territory, a desire for booty, a hope of embarrassing the rulers of England, or (as here) the need to fulfil international obligations, can be found in the reigns of most Scottish kings from Kenneth MacAlpin onwards.

The development of national identity is the most elusive, but perhaps most important, issue in medieval Scottish history. The fusion of the peoples of early Scotland had enabled a recognisable state to be created by the end of the eleventh century, although its borders were as yet imperfectly defined and the relationship between the king and local potentates by no means resolved in favour of the former. Whether there was any perception of a Scottish identity is, however, very doubtful, and links with the Irish Sea and Norse worlds remained strong. Immigration from England and France, the advent of feudalism and the establishment within the realm of international religious orders brought Scotland into a world of chivalry which transcended the boundaries of individual states; although only a privileged few could avail themselves of that world, the outlook of the Scottish government and church had been transformed. With extensive cross-border landholding and generally peaceful relations between Scotland and England in the thirteenth century, we might expect a diminution of the sense of a Scottish identity, at least among the ruling classes, yet the successful resistance to Edward I by the Comyns and their allies demonstrates the pull which the concept of Scotland had on the loyalty of many magnates. Moreover, many leading clerics such as Bishop Wishart were prominent opponents of English rule, even after Robert Bruce had incurred excommunication; the internationalism of the church did not preclude defence of the interests of a particular state.

The Wars of Independence were the catalyst for the articulation of a view of Scottish history which stressed the distinctiveness of the Scots and, for the first time, downplayed their Irish origin. The arguments presented to Boniface VIII and the more famous Declaration of Arbroath increasingly portray the Scots as a nation rather than merely the inhabitants of a state, although it was the existence of a viable and well established Scottish realm which enabled resistance to Edward I to be organised, and it is debatable how far individuals were conscious of a distinctive ethnic identity before Edward's aggression forced them into that awareness. Antipathy towards the English was certainly a marked feature of the late medieval Scottish mentality, as James III was to discover when he made peace with Edward IV. It is manifest in chronicles, and even more clearly in epic works on Scottish heroes like the *Bruce* of John Barbour and the *Wallace* ascribed to Blind Harry. Those who lived near the border were acutely aware of their identity, even though families on both sides had a common interest in warding off the attentions of the governments of their respective countries.

This subsequent perception of the crisis as a national struggle underestimates the element of civil strife in Scotland after 1286. Robert Bruce, who emerged as the victor, had an uneasy relationship with the Comyn-led government and was prepared to enter into Edward I's peace when it looked as though their common enemy John Balliol might return to Scotland in 1302, and after 1306 the Comyns adhered to the English because of what had happened in the Greyfriars of Dumfries. Loyalties were not determined primarily by patriotism, and indeed the concept was unfamiliar to the majority of contemporaries, but later commentators saw the Wars of Independence as a watershed, and in terms of Anglo-Scottish relations that view is justified.

Paradoxically, increasing animosity towards England was matched by a greater consciousness of the distinction between Highlands and Lowlands and antipathy to the Gaelic language. Anglo-Norman immigrants in the twelfth century had assimilated many of the customs of the people over whom they now exercised lordship, while native magnates had entered into relations with the king of a recognisably feudal type. Kings were still inaugurated in ceremonies which had their roots deep in the Celtic past. Continuity had thereby been preserved and provincial loyalties were upheld even in areas which were heavily settled by newcomers. While the Highland economy was more thoroughly pastoral and English speech was becoming predominant in most of eastern and southern Scotland, there is no hint before the later fourteenth century that contemporaries drew a meaningful line between Lowland and Highland. Yet later medieval writers frequently draw attention to the evils perpetrated by caterans, parliament told James I that Highlanders were not to be trusted, and the earl of Mar built a reputation on his opposition to Donald of the Isles at Harlaw.

To some extent this development was an inevitable consequence of historical processes. The Gaelic language had long been in retreat, and the cultural distinction between the peaceful Lowlands and the wild areas to the north and west reflects the limits of royal power in the late Middle Ages. Although the early sixteenth century saw renewed interest in native saints, the Scottish identity so manifest in the late medieval period still owed much less to Celtic traditions than might have been expected. There was no conscious rejection of ideas and institutions which had originated south of the border, although Scots law and administrative practice were sufficiently divergent from their English counterparts to be a recognisable mark of distinctiveness at the end of the thirteenth century. Scottish nationhood was founded partly on anti-English feeling, but more importantly on a sense of pride in the achievements of a small country which had been forged from divergent traditions, had developed a method of governance suitable for its political and geographical peculiarities, and could play a significant part in the community of European states and the international Christian church.

SELECT BIBLIOGRAPHY

This bibliography lists works which have been particularly valuable in the composition of this book and some others to which interested readers may refer for further enlightenment on individual topics. It is by no means exhaustive, and in particular does not include primary sources, even if these are cited in the footnotes. Full details of most of these can be found in D. Stevenson and W. B. Stevenson, *Scottish Texts and Calendars: An Analytical Guide to Serial Publications* (Royal Historical Society and Scottish History Society, 1987); and *List of Abbreviated Titles of the Printed Sources of Scottish History to 1560*, published as a supplement to the *SHR* in 1963.

Anderson, M. O., 'Lothian and the early Scottish kings', *SHR*, 39 (1960), 98–112
Kings and Kingship in Early Scotland (Edinburgh, 1973)

Angus, W., and Dunlop, A. I., 'The date of the birth of James III', *SHR*, 30 (1951), 199–204

Arthurson, I., 'The king's voyage into Scotland: the war that never was', in D. Williams, ed., *England in the Fifteenth Century: Proceedings of the 1986 Harlaxton Symposium* (Woodbridge, 1987), 1–22

Ash, M., 'William Lamberton, bishop of St Andrews, 1297–1328', in G. W. S. Barrow, ed., *The Scottish Tradition* (Edinburgh, 1974), 44–55
'The diocese of St Andrews under its "Norman" bishops', *SHR*, 55 (1976), 127–50

Balfour-Melville, E. W. M., *James I, King of Scots, 1406–1437* (London, 1936)

Bannerman, J., *Studies in the History of Dalriada* (Edinburgh, 1974)
'The Scottish takeover of Pictland and the relics of Columba', *IR*, 48 (1997), 27–44

Barrell, A. D. M., *The Papacy, Scotland and Northern England, 1342–1378* (Cambridge, 1995)

'The background to *Cum universi*: Scoto-papal relations, 1159–1192', *IR*, 46 (1995), 116–38

Barrow, G. W. S., *The Kingdom of the Scots: Government, Church and Society from the Eleventh to the Fourteenth Century* (London, 1973)

The Anglo-Norman Era in Scottish History (Oxford, 1980)

Robert Bruce and the Community of the Realm of Scotland (3rd edn, Edinburgh, 1988)

'Badenoch and Strathspey, 1130–1312. 1: secular and political', *Northern Scotland*, 8 (1988), 1–15

'Badenoch and Strathspey, 1130–1312. 2: the church', *Northern Scotland*, 9 (1989), 1–16

Kingship and Unity: Scotland 1000–1306 (repr., Edinburgh, 1989)

'Frontier and settlement: which influenced which? England and Scotland, 1100–1300', in R. Bartlett and A. MacKay, eds., *Medieval Frontier Societies* (Oxford, 1989), 3–21

'A kingdom in crisis: Scotland and the Maid of Norway', *SHR*, 69 (1990), 120–41

Scotland and Its Neighbours in the Middle Ages (London, 1992)

'The Scots and the north of England', in E. King, ed., *The Anarchy of King Stephen's Reign* (Oxford, 1994), 231–53

'The date of the peace between Malcolm IV and Somerled of Argyll', *SHR*, 73 (1994), 222–3

Boardman, S., *The Early Stewart Kings: Robert II and Robert III, 1371–1406* (East Linton, 1996)

'Lordship in the north-east: the Badenoch Stewarts, I: Alexander Stewart, earl of Buchan, lord of Badenoch', *Northern Scotland*, 16 (1996), 1–29

Bonner, E. A., 'The genesis of Henry VIII's "Rough Wooing" of the Scots', *Northern History*, 33 (1997), 36–53

Brooke, D., *Wild Men and Holy Places: St Ninian, Whithorn and the Medieval Realm of Galloway* (Edinburgh, 1994)

Broun, D., *The Irish Identity of the Kingdom of the Scots in the Twelfth and Thirteenth Centuries* (Woodbridge, 1999)

Broun, D., Finlay, R. J., and Lynch, M., eds., *Image and Identity: The Making and Re-making of Scotland Through the Ages* (Edinburgh, 1998)

Brown, A. L., 'The priory of Coldingham in the late fourteenth century', *IR*, 23 (1972), 91–101

'The Scottish "Establishment" in the later 15th century', *Juridical Review*, new ser. 23 (1978), 89–105

Brown, J. M., ed., *Scottish Society in the Fifteenth Century* (London, 1977)

Brown, K. M., *Bloodfeud in Scotland, 1573–1625: Violence, Justice and Politics in an Early Modern Society* (Edinburgh, 1986)

Brown, M. H., '"That Old Serpent and Ancient of Evil Days": Walter, earl of Atholl and the death of James I', *SHR*, 71 (1992), 23–45

James I (Edinburgh, 1994)

'Scotland tamed? Kings and magnates in late medieval Scotland: a review of recent work', *IR*, 45 (1994), 120–46

'Regional lordship in north-east Scotland: the Badenoch Stewarts, II: Alexander Stewart earl of Mar', *Northern Scotland*, 16 (1996), 31–53

'The development of Scottish border lordship, 1332–58', *Historical Research*, 70 (1997), 1–22

The Black Douglases: War and Lordship in Late Medieval Scotland, 1300–1455 (East Linton, 1998)

Burns, J. H., *Scottish Churchmen and the Council of Basle* (Glasgow, 1962)

'The conciliarist tradition in Scotland', *SHR*, 42 (1963), 89–104

Caldwell, D. H., ed., *Scottish Weapons and Fortifications, 1100–1800* (Edinburgh, 1981)

Caldwell, D. H., and Ewart, G., 'Finlaggan and the lordship of the Isles: an archaeological approach', *SHR*, 72 (1993), 146–66

Cameron, J., *James V: The Personal Rule, 1528–1542*, ed. N. Macdougall (East Linton, 1998)

Campbell, J., 'England, Scotland and the Hundred Years War in the fourteenth century', in J. R. Hale, J. R. L. Highfield and B. Smalley, eds., *Europe in the Late Middle Ages* (London, 1965), 184–216

Cant, R. G., 'Norse influences in the organisation of the medieval church in the Western Isles', *Northern Studies*, 21 (1984), 1–14

Cowan, I. B., *The Scottish Reformation: Church and Society in Sixteenth Century Scotland* (London, 1982)

The Medieval Church in Scotland, ed. J. Kirk (Edinburgh, 1995)

Cowan, I. B., and Shaw, D., eds., *The Renaissance and Reformation in Scotland* (Edinburgh, 1983)

Crawford, B. E., 'The pawning of Orkney and Shetland: a reconsideration of the events of 1460–9', *SHR*, 48 (1969), 35–53

Scandinavian Scotland (Leicester, 1987)

Davies, R. R., *Domination and Conquest: The Experience of Ireland, Scotland and Wales, 1100–1300* (Cambridge, 1990)

ed., *The British Isles, 1100–1500: Comparisons, Contrasts and Connections* (Edinburgh, 1988)

Dickinson, W. C., *Scotland from the Earliest Times to 1603* (3rd edn, rev. A. A. M. Duncan, Oxford, 1977)

Dilworth, M., 'The commendator system in Scotland', *IR*, 37 (1986), 51–72

Scottish Monasteries in the Late Middle Ages (Edinburgh, 1995)

'Scottish Cistercian monasteries and the Reformation', *IR*, 48 (1997), 144–64

Donaldson, G., *The Scottish Reformation* (Cambridge, 1960)

Scotland: James V to James VII (Edinburgh, 1965)

Scottish Kings (London, 1967)

Scottish Church History (Edinburgh, 1985)

Dowden, J., 'The appointment of bishops in Scotland during the medieval period', *SHR*, 7 (1909–10), 1–20

The Medieval Church in Scotland (Glasgow, 1910)

The Bishops of Scotland, ed. J. M. Thomson (Glasgow, 1912)

Driscoll, S. T., 'Church archaeology in Glasgow and the kingdom of Strathclyde', *IR*, 49 (1998), 95–114

Dunbar, J. G., and Duncan, A. A. M., 'Tarbert castle: a contribution to the history of Argyll', *SHR*, 50 (1971), 1–17

Duncan, A. A. M., 'Councils general, 1404–1423', *SHR*, 35 (1956), 132–43

'The early parliaments of Scotland', *SHR*, 45 (1966), 36–58

The Nation of Scots and the Declaration of Arbroath (Historical Association, 1970)

Scotland: The Making of the Kingdom (Edinburgh, 1975)

'The battle of Carham, 1018', *SHR*, 55 (1976), 20–8

'*Honi soit qui mal y pense*: David II and Edward III, 1346–52', *SHR*, 67 (1988), 113–41

'The war of the Scots, 1306–23', *TRHS*, 6th ser. 2 (1992), 125–51

'The process of Norham, 1291', in P. R. Coss and S. D. Lloyd, eds., *Thirteenth Century England V: Proceedings of the Newcastle upon Tyne Conference, 1993* (Woodbridge, 1995), 207–30

'Yes, the earliest Scottish charters', *SHR*, 78 (1999), 1–38

Duncan, A. A. M., and Brown, A. L., 'Argyll and the Isles in the earlier Middle Ages', *Proceedings of the Society of Antiquaries of Scotland*, 90 (1956–7), 192–220

Dunlop, A. I., *The Life and Times of James Kennedy, Bishop of St Andrews* (Edinburgh, 1950)

Durkan, J., *William Turnbull, Bishop of Glasgow* (Glasgow, 1951)

Edington, C., *Court and Culture in Renaissance Scotland: Sir David Lindsay of the Mount* (Amherst, 1994)

Ewan, E., *Townlife in Fourteenth-Century Scotland* (Edinburgh, 1990)

Ferguson, P. C., *Medieval Papal Representatives in Scotland: Legates, Nuncios, and Judges-Delegate, 1125–1286* (Stair Society, 1997)

Ferguson, W., *Scotland's Relations with England: A Survey to 1707* (Edinburgh, 1977)

Fisher, A., *William Wallace* (Edinburgh, 1986)

Frame, R., 'The Bruces in Ireland, 1315–18', *Irish Historical Studies*, 19 (1974), 3–37

The Political Development of the British Isles 1100–1400 (Oxford, 1990)

Gemmill, E., and Mayhew, N., *Changing Values in Medieval Scotland: A Study of Prices, Money, and Weights and Measures* (Cambridge, 1995)

Gilbert, J. M., *Hunting and Hunting Reserves in Medieval Scotland* (Edinburgh, 1979)

Goodman, A., and Tuck, A., eds., *War and Border Societies in the Middle Ages* (London, 1992)

Grant, A., 'Earls and earldoms in late medieval Scotland (c. 1310–1460)', in J. Bossy and P. Jupp, eds., *Essays Presented to Michael Roberts* (Belfast, 1976), 24–40

'The development of the Scottish peerage', *SHR*, 57 (1978), 1–27

'The revolt of the lord of the Isles and the death of the earl of Douglas, 1451–1452', *SHR*, 60 (1981), 169–74

Independence and Nationhood: Scotland 1306–1469 (repr., Edinburgh, 1991)

Grant, A., and Stringer, K. J., eds., *Medieval Scotland: Crown, Lordship and Community. Essays Presented to G. W. S. Barrow* (Edinburgh, 1993)

Green, J., 'Anglo-Scottish relations, 1066–1174', in M. Jones and M. Vale, eds., *England and Her Neighbours, 1066–1453: Essays in Honour of Pierre Chaplais* (London, 1989), 53–72

'David I and Henry I', *SHR*, 75 (1996), 1–19
Griffiths, R. A., 'Edward I, Scotland and the chronicles of English religious houses', *Journal of the Society of Archivists*, 6 (1979), 191–9
Hadley Williams, J., ed., *Stewart Style, 1513–1542: Essays on the Court of James V* (East Linton, 1996)
Head, D. M., 'Henry VIII's Scottish policy: a reassessment', *SHR*, 61 (1982), 1–24
Henderson, I., *The Picts* (London, 1967)
Hill, P., *Whithorn and St Ninian: The Excavation of a Monastic Town, 1984–91* (Stroud, 1997)
Hudson, B. T., 'Kings and church in early Scotland', *SHR*, 73 (1994), 145–70
Johnsen, A. O., 'The payments from the Hebrides and Isle of Man to the crown of Norway, 1153–1263: annual ferme or feudal casualty?', *SHR*, 48 (1969), 18–34
Kirby, D. P., 'Strathclyde and Cumbria: a survey of historical development to 1092', *Transactions of the Cumberland and Westmorland Antiquarian and Archaeological Society*, new ser. 62 (1962), 77–94
Lunt, W. E., *Papal Revenues in the Middle Ages* (2 vols., New York, 1934)
Lustig, R. I., 'The treaty of Perth: a re-examination', *SHR*, 58 (1979), 35–57
Lynch, M., Spearman, M., and Stell, G., eds., *The Scottish Medieval Town* (Edinburgh, 1988)
McDonald, R. A., 'Scoto-Norse kings and the reformed religious orders: patterns of monastic patronage in twelfth-century Galloway and Argyll', *Albion*, 27 (1995), 187–219
'Matrimonial politics and core–periphery interactions in twelfth- and early thirteenth-century Scotland', *Journal of Medieval History*, 21 (1995), 227–47
The Kingdom of the Isles: Scotland's Western Seaboard, c. 1100–c. 1336 (East Linton, 1997)
McDonald, R. A., and McLean, S. A., 'Somerled of Argyll: a new look at old problems', *SHR*, 71 (1992), 3–22
Macdougall, N., *James III: A Political Study* (Edinburgh, 1982)
James IV (repr., East Linton, 1997)
ed., *Church, Politics and Society: Scotland 1408–1929* (Edinburgh, 1983)
ed., *Scotland and War, AD 79–1918* (Edinburgh, 1991)
Macfarlane, L., 'The primacy of the Scottish church, 1472–1521', *IR*, 20 (1969), 111–29
'Precedence and protest at the Roman curia, 1486–1493', *Renaissance Studies*, 2 (1988), 222–30
'The elevation of the diocese of Glasgow into an archbishopric in 1492', *IR*, 43 (1992), 99–118
William Elphinstone and the Kingdom of Scotland, 1431–1514: The Struggle for Order (rev. edn, Aberdeen, 1995)
McGladdery, C., *James II* (Edinburgh, 1990)
Mackie, R. L., *King James IV of Scotland: A Brief Survey of His Life and Times* (Edinburgh, 1958)
Maclean, L., ed., *The Middle Ages in the Highlands* (Inverness, 1981)

McNamee, C. J., 'William Wallace's invasion of northern England in 1297', *Northern History*, 26 (1990), 40–58
The Wars of the Bruces: Scotland, England and Ireland, 1306–1328 (East Linton, 1997)
McNeill, P., and Nicholson, R., eds., *An Historical Atlas of Scotland, c. 400–c. 1600* (St Andrews, 1975)
McNeill, P. G. B., and MacQueen, H. L., eds., *An Atlas of Scottish History to 1707* (Edinburgh, 1996)
Macquarrie, A., *Scotland and the Crusades, 1095–1560* (Edinburgh, 1985)
'Early Christian religious houses in Scotland: foundation and function', in J. Blair and R. Sharpe, eds., *Pastoral Care Before the Parish* (Leicester, 1992), 110–33
'An eleventh-century account of the foundation legend of Laurencekirk, and of Queen Margaret's pilgrimage there', *IR*, 47 (1996), 95–109
The Saints of Scotland: Essays in Scottish Church History, AD 450–1093 (Edinburgh, 1997)
MacQueen, H. L., *Common Law and Feudal Society in Medieval Scotland* (Edinburgh, 1993)
MacQueen, J., *St Nynia* (2nd edn, Edinburgh, 1990)
McRoberts, D., 'The Scottish church and nationalism in the fifteenth century', *IR*, 19 (1968), 3–14
ed., *Essays on the Scottish Reformation, 1513–1625* (Glasgow, 1962)
Madden, C., 'Royal treatment of feudal casualties in late medieval Scotland', *SHR*, 45 (1976), 172–94
'The royal demesne in northern Scotland during the later Middle Ages', *Northern Scotland*, 3 (1977–8), 1–24
Mason, R. A., 'Kingship, tyranny and the right to resist in fifteenth-century Scotland', *SHR*, 66 (1987), 125–51
ed., *Scotland and England, 1286–1815* (Edinburgh, 1987)
Mason, R. A., and Macdougall, N., eds., *People and Power in Scotland: Essays in Honour of T. C. Smout* (Edinburgh, 1992)
Meehan, B., 'The siege of Durham, the battle of Carham and the cession of Lothian', *SHR*, 55 (1976), 1–19
Menzies, G., ed., *Who are the Scots?* (London, 1971)
ed., *The Scottish Nation* (London, 1972)
Moonan, L., 'The Inquisitor's arguments against Resby, in 1408', *IR*, 47 (1996), 127–35
Murray, A., 'The procedure of the Scottish exchequer in the early sixteenth century', *SHR*, 40 (1961), 89–117
'The Comptroller, 1425–1488', *SHR*, 52 (1973), 1–29
Neville, C. J., 'The political allegiance of the earls of Strathearn during the War of Independence', *SHR*, 65 (1986), 133–53
Nicholson, R., 'A sequel to Edward Bruce's invasion of Ireland', *SHR*, 42 (1963), 30–40
Edward III and the Scots: The Formative Years of a Military Career, 1327–1335 (Oxford, 1965)

'David II, the historians and the chroniclers', *SHR*, 45 (1966), 59–78
'Feudal developments in late medieval Scotland', *Juridical Review*, new ser. 18 (1973), 1–21
Scotland: The Later Middle Ages (Edinburgh, 1974)
Oram, R. D., 'In obedience and reverence: Whithorn and York, *c.* 1128–*c.* 1250', *IR*, 42 (1991), 83–100
'A family business? Colonisation and settlement in twelfth- and thirteenth-century Galloway', *SHR*, 72 (1993), 111–45
Oram, R. D., and Stell, G. P., eds., *Galloway: Land and Lordship* (Edinburgh, 1991)
Owen, D. D. R., *William the Lion, 1143–1214: Kingship and Culture* (East Linton, 1997)
Penman, M., '*A fell coniuracioun agayn Robert the douchty king*: the Soules conspiracy of 1318–1320', *IR*, 50 (1999), 25–57
Power, R., 'Magnus Barelegs' expeditions to the west', *SHR*, 65 (1986), 107–32
Prestwich, M., 'The English campaign in Scotland in 1296, and the surrender of John Balliol: some supporting evidence', *BIHR*, 49 (1976), 135–8
Edward I (London, 1988)
'Edward I and the Maid of Norway', *SHR*, 69 (1990), 157–74
Rae, T. I., *The Administration of the Scottish Frontier, 1513–1603* (Edinburgh, 1966)
Reid, N., 'Margaret "Maid of Norway" and Scottish queenship', *Reading Medieval Studies*, 8 (1982), 75–96
'The kingless kingdom: the Scottish guardianships of 1296–1306', *SHR*, 61 (1982), 105–29
ed., *Scotland in the Reign of Alexander III, 1249–1286* (Edinburgh, 1990)
Reid, W. S., 'Clerical taxation: the Scottish alternative to dissolution of the monasteries, 1530–1560', *Catholic Historical Review*, 35 (1948), 129–53
'Trade, traders and Scottish independence', *Speculum*, 29 (1954), 210–22
'Sea-power in the Anglo-Scottish war, 1296–1328', *Mariners' Mirror*, 46 (1960), 7–23
Richardson, H. G., and Sayles, G., 'The Scottish parliaments of Edward I', in their *The English Parliament in the Middle Ages* (London, 1981), no. XIII
Ritchie, R. L. G., *The Normans in Scotland* (Edinburgh, 1954)
Sanderson, M. H. B., *Scottish Rural Society in the Sixteenth Century* (Edinburgh, 1982)
Cardinal of Scotland: David Beaton, c. 1494–1546 (Edinburgh, 1986)
Ayrshire and the Reformation: People and Change, 1490–1600 (East Linton, 1997)
Scammell, J., 'Robert I and the north of England', *EHR*, 73 (1958), 385–403
Sellar, W. D. H., 'The origins and ancestry of Somerled', *SHR*, 45 (1966), 123–42
'Family origins in Cowal and Knapdale', *Scottish Studies*, 15 (1971), 21–37
'The earliest Campbells – Norman, Briton or Gael?', *Scottish Studies*, 17 (1973), 109–25
'Warlords, holy men and matrilineal succession', *IR*, 36 (1985), 29–43
ed., *Moray: Province and People* (Edinburgh, 1993)
Shead, N. F., 'The origins of the medieval diocese of Glasgow', *SHR*, 48 (1969), 220–5

'The administration of the diocese of Glasgow in the twelfth and thirteenth centuries', *SHR*, 55 (1976), 127–50

Simpson, G. G., 'The claim of Florence, count of Holland, to the Scottish throne, 1291–2', *SHR*, 36 (1957), 111–24

'The Declaration of Arbroath revitalised', *SHR*, 56 (1977), 11–33

ed., *Scotland and Scandinavia, 800–1800* (Edinburgh, 1990)

ed., *The Scottish Soldier Abroad, 1247–1967* (Edinburgh, 1992)

ed., *Scotland and the Low Countries, 1124–1994* (East Linton, 1996)

Smyth, A. P., *Warlords and Holy Men: Scotland AD 80–1000* (repr., Edinburgh, 1989)

Stones, E. L. G., 'The English mission to Edinburgh in 1328', *SHR*, 28 (1949), 121–32

'The Anglo-Scottish negotiations of 1327', *SHR*, 30 (1951), 49–54

'The treaty of Northampton, 1328', *History*, 38 (1953), 54–61

'The submission of Robert Bruce to Edward I, *c.* 1301–1302', *SHR*, 34 (1955), 122–34

'The appeal to history in Anglo-Scottish relations between 1291 and 1401', *Archives*, 9 (1969), 11–21, 80–3

'English chroniclers and the affairs of Scotland, 1286–1296', in R. H. C. Davis and J. M. Wallace-Hadrill, eds., *The Writing of History in the Middle Ages: Essays Presented to Richard William Southern* (Oxford, 1981), 323–48

Stones, E. L. G., and Blount, M. N., 'The surrender of King John of Scotland to Edward I in 1296: some new evidence', *BIHR*, 48 (1975), 94–106

Storey, R. L., 'The wardens of the marches of England towards Scotland, 1377–1489', *EHR*, 72 (1957), 593–615

Thomas Langley and the Bishopric of Durham, 1406–1437 (London, 1961)

Stringer, K. J., *Earl David of Huntingdon, 1152–1219: A Study in Anglo-Scottish History* (Edinburgh, 1985)

'State-building in twelfth-century Britain: David I, king of Scots, and northern England', in J. C. Appleby and P. Dalton, eds., *Government, Religion and Society in Northern England, 1000–1700* (Stroud, 1997), 40–62

ed., *Essays on the Nobility of Medieval Scotland* (Edinburgh, 1985)

Swanson, R., 'The university of St Andrews and the Great Schism, 1410–1419', *Journal of Ecclesiastical History*, 26 (1975), 223–45

Thomson, J. A. F., 'Some new light on the elevation of Patrick Graham', *SHR*, 40 (1961), 83–8

The Later Lollards, 1414–1520 (Oxford, 1965)

'Innocent VIII and the Scottish church', *IR*, 19 (1968), 23–31

Thornton, T., 'Scotland and the Isle of Man, *c.* 1400–1625: noble power and royal presumption in the northern Irish Sea province, *SHR*, 77 (1998), 1–30

Topping, P., 'Harald Maddadson, earl of Orkney and Caithness 1139–1206', *SHR*, 62 (1983), 105–20

Watson, F. J., 'Settling the stalemate: Edward I's peace in Scotland, 1303–1305', in M. Prestwich, R. H. Britnell and R. Frame, eds., *Thirteenth Century England VI: Proceedings of the Durham Conference, 1995* (Woodbridge, 1997), 127–43

Under the Hammer: Edward I and Scotland, 1286–1306 (East Linton, 1998)

Watt, D. E. R., 'University clerks and rolls of petitions for benefices', *Speculum*, 34 (1959), 213–29

'The minority of Alexander III of Scotland', *TRHS*, 5th ser. 21 (1971), 1–23

'The papacy and Scotland in the fifteenth century', in B. Dobson, ed., *The Church, Politics and Patronage in the Fifteenth Century* (Gloucester, 1984), 115–32

'Scottish university men of the thirteenth and fourteenth centuries', in T. C. Smout, ed., *Scotland and Europe, 1200–1850* (Edinburgh, 1986), 1–18

Webster, B., 'David II and the government of fourteenth-century Scotland', *TRHS*, 5th ser. 16 (1966), 115–30

Scotland from the Eleventh Century to 1603 (London, 1975)

Medieval Scotland: The Making of an Identity (Basingstoke, 1997)

Weiss, R., 'The earliest account of the murder of James I of Scotland', *EHR*, 52 (1937), 479–91

Whyte, I. D., *Scotland Before the Industrial Revolution: An Economic and Social History, c. 1050–c. 1750* (Harlow, 1995)

Williamson, D. M., 'The legate Otto in Scotland and Ireland, 1237–1240', *SHR*, 28 (1949), 12–30

Woolf, A., 'Pictish matriliny reconsidered', *IR*, 49 (1998), 147–67

Wormald, J., 'Bloodfeud, kindred and government in early modern Scotland', *Past and Present*, 87 (1980), 54–97

Lords and Men in Scotland: Bonds of Manrent 1442–1603 (Edinburgh, 1985)

Court, Kirk and Community: Scotland 1470–1625 (repr., Edinburgh, 1991)

Young, A., *Robert the Bruce's Rivals: The Comyns, 1212–1314* (East Linton, 1997)

INDEX